Hack and HHVM
Programming Productivity
Without Breaking Things

Owen Yamauchi

Beijing · Boston · Farnham · Sebastopol · Tokyo

Hack and HHVM

by Owen Yamauchi

Copyright © 2015 Facebook, Inc. All rights reserved.

Published by O'Reilly Media, Inc., 1005 Gravenstein Highway North, Sebastopol, CA 95472.

O'Reilly books may be purchased for educational, business, or sales promotional use. Online editions are also available for most titles (*http://safaribooksonline.com*). For more information, contact our corporate/institutional sales department: 800-998-9938 or *corporate@oreilly.com*.

Editor: Allyson MacDonald	**Proofreader:** Jasmine Kwityn
Production Editor: Melanie Yarbrough	**Indexer:** Ellen Troutman-Zaig
Copyeditor: Rachel Head	**Interior Designer:** David Futato
	Cover Designer: Ellie Volkhausen
	Illustrator: Rebecca Demarest

September 2015:   First Edition

Revision History for the First Edition
2015-09-02:   First Release
2016-01-15:   Second Release

See *http://oreilly.com/catalog/errata.csp?isbn=9781491920879* for release details.

978-1-491-92087-9

[LSI]

Table of Contents

Foreword

In 2012, I started working on a project called "strict-mode" with Alok Menghrajani. The goal was, in a nutshell, to build a statically typed version of PHP on top of HHVM.

The success of that project (which later became Hack) has amazed me ever since. What began as a basic typechecker has become a full-blown programming language with industrial-strength tools to back it up.

Looking back, we have come a long way. When we first pitched the idea to the HHVM team, I am pretty sure they thought we were crazy. But somehow, we convinced them to join us in the adventure.

At the end of June 2012, Facebook deployed Hack code to production for the first time. Just like that, without any management approval, without any process of any kind, Facebook had a new language in production.

At that time, I was expecting someone to knock on our door to stop us, but somehow that day never came.

Many engineers followed after that, and before we knew it, most new code within Facebook was written in Hack. We then decided to automatically convert the rest of our PHP codebase to Hack. We went from a dynamically typed to a statically typed codebase at a gigantic scale (tens of millions of lines).

That process was especially challenging given the client/server architecture that we adopted for the typechecker. We wanted instantaneous response times from the typechecker, because PHP developers were used to a very fast edit/refresh cycle. That's why we needed the Hack typechecking server: a daemon maintaining the typing information in the background at all times. Of course, the tricky part was to keep the state of the server consistent with the filesystem.

It took many sleepless nights to stabilize the typechecking server, but that approach is really what makes Hack so special today. The typechecker response times are instantaneous (so fast we use it for auto-complete), and it can keep up with a huge volume of updates.

I am very pleased that there's now a definitive reference book on Hack and HHVM. Owen has done a very good job of explaining even the subtlest parts of the language (such as type inference), and everything else you need to know to be productive in Hack/HHVM (debugging, etc.).

Have fun with Hack and HHVM!

—Julien Verlaguet, creator of Hack

Preface

For most of its history, Facebook has held internal hackathons every few months. For hackathons, engineers are encouraged to come up with ideas that aren't related to their day jobs—they form teams and try to make something cool in the span of a day or two.

One hackathon in November 2007 resulted in an interesting experiment: a tool that could convert PHP programs into equivalent C++ programs and then compile them with a C++ compiler. The idea was that the C++ program would run a lot faster than the PHP original, as it could take advantage of all the optimization work that has gone into C++ compilers over the years.

This possibility was of great interest to Facebook. It was gaining a lot of new users, and supporting more users requires more CPU cycles. As you run out of available CPU cycles, unless you buy more CPUs, which gets very expensive, you have to find a way to consume fewer CPU cycles per user. Facebook's entire web frontend was written in PHP, and any way to get that PHP code to consume fewer CPU cycles was welcome.

Over the next seven years, the project grew far beyond its hackathon origins. As a PHP-to-C++ transformer called HPHPc, in 2009 it became the sole execution engine powering Facebook's web servers. In early 2010, it was open sourced under the name HipHop for PHP. And then, starting in 2010, an entirely new approach to execution —just-in-time compilation to machine code, with no C++ involved—grew out of HPHPc's codebase, and eventually superseded it. This just-in-time compiler, called the HipHop Virtual Machine, or HHVM for short, took over Facebook's entire web server fleet in early 2013. The original PHP-to-C++ transformer is gone; it is not deployed anywhere and its code has been deleted.

The origins of Hack are entirely separate. Its roots are in a project that attempted to use static analysis on PHP to automatically detect potential security bugs. Fairly soon, it turned out that the nature of PHP makes it fundamentally difficult to get static analysis that's deep enough to be useful. Thus the idea of "strict mode" was born: a modification of PHP, with some features, such as references, removed and a sophisticated type system added. Authors of PHP code could opt into strict mode, gaining stronger checking of their code while retaining full interoperability.

Hack's direction since then belies its origin as a type system on top of PHP. It has gained new features with significant effects on the way Hack code is structured, like asynchronous (async) functions. It has added new features specifically meant to make the type system more powerful, like collections. Philosophically, it's a different language from PHP, carving out a new position in the space of programming languages.

This is how we got where we are today: Hack, a modern, dynamic programming language with robust static typechecking, executing on HHVM, a just-in-time compilation runtime engine with full PHP compatibility and interoperability.

What Are Hack and HHVM?

Hack and HHVM are closely related, and there has occasionally been some confusion as to what exactly the terms refer to.

Hack is a programming language. It's based on PHP, shares much of PHP's syntax, and is designed to be fully interoperable with PHP. However, it would be severely limiting to think of Hack as nothing more than some decoration on top of PHP. Hack's main feature is robust static typechecking, which is enough of a difference from PHP to qualify Hack as a language in its own right. Hack is useful for developers working on an existing PHP codebase, and has many affordances for that situation, but it's also an excellent choice for ground-up development of a new project.

Beyond static typechecking, Hack has several other features that PHP doesn't have, and most of this book is about those features: async functions, XHP, and many more. It also intentionally lacks a handful of PHP's features, to smooth some rough edges.

HHVM is an execution engine. It supports both PHP and Hack, and it lets the two languages interoperate: code written in PHP can call into Hack code, and vice versa. When executing PHP, it's intended to be usable as a drop-in replacement for the standard PHP interpreter from PHP.net (*http://php.net*). This book has a few chapters that cover HHVM: how to configure and deploy it, and how to use it to debug and profile your code.

Finally, separate from HHVM, there is the Hack typechecker: a program that can analyze Hack code (but not PHP code) for type errors, without running it. The typechecker doesn't really have a name, other than the command you use to run it, hh_client. I'll refer to it as "the Hack typechecker" or just "the typechecker."

As of now, HHVM is the only execution engine that runs Hack, which is why the two may sometimes be conflated.

Who This Book Is For

This book is for readers who are comfortable with programming. It spends no time explaining concepts common to many programming languages, like control flow, data types, functions, and object-oriented programming.

Hack is a descendant of PHP. This book doesn't specifically explain common PHP syntax, except in areas where Hack differs, so basic knowledge of PHP is helpful. If you've never used PHP, you'll still be able to understand much of the code in this book if you have experience with other programming languages. The syntax is generally very straightforward to understand.

For those with PHP experience, there's nothing here that you won't understand if you've never worked on a complex, high-traffic PHP website. Hack is useful for codebases of all sizes—from simple standalone scripts to multimillion-line web apps like Facebook.

There is some material that assumes familiarity with typical web app tasks like querying relational databases and memcached (in Chapter 6) and generating HTML (in Chapter 7). You can skip these parts if they're not relevant to you, but they require no knowledge that you wouldn't get from experience with even a small, basic web app.

I hope to make this book not just an explanation of how things are, but also of how they came to be that way. Programming language design is a hard problem; it's essentially the art of navigating hundreds of trade-offs at once. It's also subject to a surprising range of pragmatic concerns like backward compatibility, and Hack is no exception. If you're at all interested in a case study of how one programming language made its way through an unusual set of constraints, this book should provide what you're looking for.

Philosophy

There are a few principles that underlie the design of both Hack and HHVM, which can help you understand how things came to be the way they are.

Program Types

There is a single observation about programs that informs both HHVM's approach to optimizing and executing code, and Hack's approach to verifying it. That is: behind most programs in dynamically typed languages, a statically typed program is hiding.

Consider this code, which works as both PHP and Hack:

```
for ($i = 0; $i < 10; $i++) {
  echo $i + 100;
}
```

Although it's not explicitly stated anywhere, it's obvious to any human reader that $i is always an integer. The computer science term for this is that $i is *monomorphic*: it only ever has one type. A typechecker could make use of this property to verify that the expression $i + 100 makes sense. An execution engine could make use of this property to compile $i + 100 into efficient machine code to do the addition.

A loop variable may seem like a trivial example, but it turns out that in real-world PHP codebases, most values are monomorphic. This makes intuitive sense, because you can't do much with a value—do arithmetic on it, index into it, call methods on it, etc.—without knowing what its type is. Most code, even in dynamically typed languages, does not check the type of each value before doing anything with it, which means that there must be hidden assumptions about the types of values. If the code mostly runs without runtime type errors, then those hidden assumptions must be true most of the time.

HHVM's approach is to assume that this observation usually holds, and to compile PHP and Hack to machine code accordingly. Because it compiles programs while they are running, it knows the types flowing through each piece of code it's about to compile. It outputs machine code that assumes those types: in the previous code example when compiling the expression $i + 100, HHVM would see that $i is an integer and use a single hardware addition instruction to do the addition.

The purpose of Hack, meanwhile, is to bring the hidden statically typed program into the light. It makes some types explicit with annotations, and verifies the rest with type inference. The idea is that Hack doesn't significantly constrain existing PHP programs; rather, it makes the behavior that the programs already had explicit, and exposes it to robust static analysis.

This point is worth repeating: Hack's static typing is *not* supposed to require a different style of programming. The language is designed to give you a better way to express the programs you were already writing.

Gradual Migration

Hack originated in the shadow of a multimillion-line PHP codebase. There's no way to convert a codebase of that size from one language to another in one fell swoop, no matter how similar the languages are, so Hack has evolved with very gradual migration paths from PHP. Hack code can use functions and classes written in PHP, and vice versa. For every feature of Hack, there is a seamless way for code that uses it to interact with code that doesn't use it.

In addition, the standard Hack/HHVM distribution comes with tools to do automated migration of PHP to Hack. It also includes a tool that transpiles Hack into PHP, for use by library authors who want to migrate to Hack while preserving a way for non-HHVM users to use their code. These tools are described in detail in Chapter 10.

HHVM, for its part, is intended to run PHP code identically to the standard PHP interpreter. The first step in migrating a PHP codebase to Hack is to switch to running that PHP code on HHVM. The only significant code changes that should be required in this step are around extensions: not all PHP and Zend extensions are compatible with HHVM. There should be no changes required because of differing behavior in the core language.

Make no mistake, though: despite its origins, Hack is an excellent choice if you're starting a new project from scratch. In fact, you'll get the most benefit out of Hack that way: the language is at its best when a codebase is 100% Hack.

How the Book Is Organized

The central feature of Hack is static typechecking. It cuts broadly across all of Hack's other features, and is the most significant difference between Hack and PHP. The book starts by exploring that topic in detail in Chapter 1. Almost everything else in the book depends on an understanding of the content in that chapter, so if you haven't seen Hack before, I very strongly recommend reading it thoroughly. That content is supplemented by Chapter 2, which discusses a particularly interesting part of Hack's type system.

The rest of Hack's features are mostly orthogonal to each other. Chapter 3 explains several of Hack's smaller features. Chapter 4 shows the few PHP features that are gone from Hack, and explains why. Chapter 5 explains how and why to use Hack's collection classes. Chapter 6 explains Hack's support for multitasking, and Chapter 7 explains Hack's syntax and library for generating HTML sanely and securely.

Chapter 8 covers the process of setting up, configuring, deploying, and monitoring HHVM. Chapter 9 covers the HHVM interactive debugger, hphpd. And finally, Chapter 10 explores some of the tools for working with Hack code, including a PHP-to-Hack migration tool and an interactive debugger.

Versions

This book is about Hack and HHVM version 3.9, which was released on August 18, 2015. (HHVM and the Hack typechecker live in the same codebase, and are released as a single package.) By the time you read this, there will already be newer versions available. However, 3.9 is a long-term support release; it will be updated with security and bug fixes for 48 weeks after its release.

HHVM 3.9 implements PHP 5.6 semantics. It supports all of the features new in PHP 5.6—constant scalar expressions, variadic functions, the exponentiation operator, etc. These features are present in Hack 3.9 as well. In general, as new versions of PHP come out, HHVM adds support for the new features and semantics, for Hack code as well as PHP code.

Conventions Used in This Book

The following typographical conventions are used in this book:

Italic
> Indicates new terms, URLs, email addresses, filenames, and file extensions.

`Constant width`
> Used for program listings, as well as within paragraphs to refer to program elements such as variable or function names, databases, data types, environment variables, statements, and keywords.

`Constant width bold`
> Shows commands or other text that should be typed literally by the user.

This element signifies a tip or suggestion.

This element signifies a general note.

This element indicates a warning or caution.

Safari® Books Online

 *Safari Books Online* is an on-demand digital library that delivers expert content in both book and video form from the world's leading authors in technology and business.

Technology professionals, software developers, web designers, and business and creative professionals use Safari Books Online as their primary resource for research, problem solving, learning, and certification training.

Safari Books Online offers a range of plans and pricing for enterprise, government, education, and individuals.

Members have access to thousands of books, training videos, and prepublication manuscripts in one fully searchable database from publishers like O'Reilly Media, Prentice Hall Professional, Addison-Wesley Professional, Microsoft Press, Sams, Que, Peachpit Press, Focal Press, Cisco Press, John Wiley & Sons, Syngress, Morgan Kaufmann, IBM Redbooks, Packt, Adobe Press, FT Press, Apress, Manning, New Riders, McGraw-Hill, Jones & Bartlett, Course Technology, and hundreds more. For more information about Safari Books Online, please visit us online.

How to Contact Us

Please address comments and questions concerning this book to the publisher:

O'Reilly Media, Inc.
1005 Gravenstein Highway North
Sebastopol, CA 95472
800-998-9938 (in the United States or Canada)
707-829-0515 (international or local)
707-829-0104 (fax)

We have a web page for this book, where we list errata, examples, and any additional information. You can access this page at *http://bit.ly/hack-and-hhvm*.

To comment or ask technical questions about this book, send email to *bookquestions@oreilly.com*.

For more information about our books, courses, conferences, and news, see our website at *http://www.oreilly.com*.

Find us on Facebook: *http://facebook.com/oreilly*

Follow us on Twitter: *http://twitter.com/oreillymedia*

Watch us on YouTube: *http://www.youtube.com/oreillymedia*

Content Updates

January 15, 2016

- Updated the book's reference version of HHVM and Hack to 3.9, released on August 18, 2015.

- Throughout the book, fixed errors in invocations of `array_map()` in code examples (the argument order was wrong).

- In Chapter 1, added documentation of the `noreturn` return type and the `class name` type. Updated section on `meth_caller()` to reflect lifting of restrictions. Rewrote some parts of the section on enforcement of type annotations at runtime to clarify some parts and reflect language changes.

- In Chapter 3, added documentation of type constants. Updated section on array shapes to reflect language changes. Updated section on silencing typechecker errors to reflect the addition of the `HH_IGNORE_ERROR` comment.

- In Chapter 4, noted that Hack does not allow returning from a `finally` block (which was true before version 3.9), and that PHP 7 has deprecated old-style constructors.

- In Chapter 5, fixed some minor errors in the collections API reference.

- In Chapter 6, updated section on async MySQL API to reflect addition of `%L` placeholders.

Acknowledgments

First and foremost, this book obviously wouldn't exist without the efforts, spanning many years, of everyone who has worked on HipHop, HHVM, and Hack. This includes both current and former Facebook employees, as well as members of the open source community. There are far too many to name them all here, but all of their contributions helped make Hack and HHVM what they are today.

Not only do these projects represent the product of a huge amount of effort, but they are also the rewards for significant risks. None of these projects were "sure things" when they were started, and all of them have spent a fair bit of time fighting for their own continued existence. The story I know best, from experience, is HHVM's. For the better part of two years, the HHVM team strove to get HHVM's performance up to parity with HipHop, knowing that if they didn't succeed, they would forfeit all of that work. The engineers and managers who drove the projects forward, despite such risks, deserve special recognition; it's never easy to stake years of one's own and others' careers on speculative things like this. Particular thanks are due to the creators: Haiping Zhao, of HipHop; Keith Adams, Jason Evans, and Drew Paroski, of HHVM; and Julien Verlaguet, of Hack.

Now, about this book. I'm grateful to have gotten the chance to write it; I suspect that not a lot of software companies or teams would be thrilled at the idea of letting one of their engineers spend seven months writing prose instead of software. A few individuals deserve credit for helping get this thing off the ground and shepherding it along. In alphabetical order, they are: Alma Chao, Todd Gascon, Joel Marcey, James Pearce, Joel Pobar, and Paul Tarjan.

Big thanks are also due to the Hack and HHVM team members who reviewed this book's early drafts. In alphabetical order, they are: Fred Emmott, Bill Fumerola, Eugene Letuchy, Alex Malyshev, Joel Marcey, Jez Ng, Jan Oravec, Dwayne Reeves, Julien Verlaguet, and Josh Watzman. This book was immensely improved by their feedback. Any mistakes are mine, not theirs.

CHAPTER 1

Typechecking

The typechecker is the flagship feature of Hack. It analyzes Hack programs statically (i.e., without running them) and checks for many different kinds of errors, which prevents bugs at an early stage of development and makes code easier to read and understand. To enhance the typechecker's ability to do this, Hack allows programmers to explicitly annotate the types of some values in their programs: function parameters, function return types, and properties. The typechecker will infer the rest.

The choice between statically typed languages and dynamically typed languages is endlessly debated among programmers. It's often presented as a choice between the robustness of static typing and the flexibility of dynamic typing. The philosophy of Hack rejects this as a false dichotomy. Hack retains the flexible, rapid-development character of PHP, a dynamically typed language, while adding a layer of robust, sophisticated typechecking.

In this chapter, we'll see why you should use the typechecker, how to use it, and how to write type annotations for it.

Why Use the Typechecker?

The argument in favor of Hack typechecking sounds similar to the argument often used in favor of statically typed languages. The typechecker is able to look for mistakes without running the program, so it can catch problems even with codepaths that aren't run during testing. Because it doesn't need to run the program, it catches problems earlier in development, which saves development time. Static analysis capability makes refactoring easier, as it can ensure that there are no breakages at module boundaries.

In the classic debate, the disadvantage that supposedly accompanies these features is a drag on development speed. Before you can run your program, you have to wait for it to compile, and depending on the language and the size of the program, that can take a long time. You also have to write out types everywhere, making your code more verbose and harder to change.

These downsides aren't present in Hack, for two reasons. First, the typechecker is designed for instant feedback, even when working in very large codebases. It uses a client/server model: the typechecking server runs in the background and monitors the filesystem for changes. When you edit a file, the server updates its in-memory analysis of your codebase. By the time you're ready to run your code, the analysis is already done; the client simply queries the server and displays results almost instantaneously. It can easily be integrated into text editors and IDEs, giving you feedback in real time.

Second, Hack type annotations are designed to be gradual. You can use as many or as few as you want. Type-annotated code can interoperate seamlessly with non-annotated Hack code and with PHP code. In addition, you don't annotate local variables; the typechecker infers their types from their surroundings.

Setting Up the Typechecker

Before we look at the syntax and semantics of Hack type annotations, we'll get the typechecker set up.

The first thing you need is an *.hhconfig* file. As well as holding project-wide configuration settings, this file serves to mark the top-level directory of your codebase, so the typechecker knows which files to include in its analysis.

For now, we don't need any configuration; our *.hhconfig* file can just be empty. So, navigate to the top-level directory of your project, and do this:

```
$ touch .hhconfig
$ hh_client
```

Running hh_client first checks for a running hh_server process. If there isn't one, the client will start one, so you should never have to start one yourself. The server will find the *.hhconfig* file and analyze every Hack file it finds in the directory containing that file and all directories below it.

A Hack file is one whose contents start with <?hh.[1] This is an adaptation of PHP's "opening tag" syntax. After the <?hh at the beginning (possibly supplemented by a *mode*, as described in "Typechecker Modes" on page 16), the rest of the file is Hack

---

[1] A Hack file is also allowed to start with a shebang line like #!/usr/bin/hhvm, but the <?hh must be the next non-blank line.

code. Unlike in PHP, the closing tag ?> is not valid in Hack; you can't use Hack with PHP's templating-language syntax.

Filename extensions are irrelevant: it's fine to name Hack files with the extension *.php*, although *.hh* is also conventional.

Once the typechecking server is started, if you have no Hack files in your project (i.e., all of your code is inside <?php tags instead of <?hh), running hh_client should simply print No errors!. This is because the typechecker only looks at Hack files; it doesn't do anything with PHP files.

Autoload Everything

One key assumption that the typechecker makes is that your project is set up so that any class, function, or constant in your codebase can be used from anywhere else in the codebase. It makes no attempt to analyze include or require statements to make sure that the right files have been included or required by the time their contents are used. Instead, it assumes that you have autoloading set up.

This both sidesteps a difficult static analysis problem and reflects modern best practice. "Autoload everything" is the approach taken by Composer, a popular package manager for PHP and Hack. Note that autoloading isn't mandatory—you can write your code using require and include, and the typechecker won't complain—but it's strongly recommended, because the typechecker won't protect you from missing require or include statements.

PHP provides autoloading for classes, and HHVM supports this, through both __autoload() and spl_autoload_register(). HHVM provides an additional feature that allows autoloading for functions and constants in both PHP and Hack, plus autoloading for type aliases (see "Type Aliases" on page 62) in Hack only. See "Enhanced Autoloading" on page 82 for full details on the HHVM-specific API.

Reading Error Messages

The typechecker's error messages are designed to be both detailed and easy to understand. Here's some example code with an error:

```
<?hh
function main() {
  $a = 10;
  $a[] = 20;
}
```

We'll put this in a file called *test.hh* and run the typechecker:

```
$ hh_client
/home/oyamauchi/test.hh:4:3,6: an int does not allow array append (Typing[4006])
    /home/oyamauchi/test.hh:3:8,9: You might want to check this out
```

Each line shows the full path to the file with the error, followed by the line number and the column numbers where the erroneous code starts and ends. The first error message line explains what the actual problem is—"an int does not allow array append"—and gives a number that uniquely identifies this error message (see "Silencing Typechecker Errors" on page 88 to find out how this is used). The line and column numbers are pointing to the code $a[].

The next line of the error message is indented, to show that it's not a separate error but is elaborating on the previous line. It explains why the typechecker thinks $a is an int: it's pointing to the code 10, which gets assigned to $a.

Type Annotation Syntax

This section explains the syntax for the three places where you can put type annotations. We haven't seen the full range of type annotations that Hack supports yet—that will be covered in "Hack's Type System" on page 6—but for now, all you need to know is that int and string are valid type annotations.

The three places where you can put type annotations are on function return types, function parameters, and properties.

Function Return Types

The syntax for function return types is the simplest. After the closing parenthesis of a function's parameter list, add a colon and a type name. You can do this with functions and methods, as well as body-less method declarations in interfaces and abstract classes. For example:

```
function returns_an_int(): int {
  // ...
}
function returns_a_string(): string {
  // ...
}
```

Whitespace is allowed between the closing parenthesis and the colon. It's common to put a newline between them in function signatures that are too long to fit on one line.

Closures can also have their return types annotated:

```
$add_one = function ($x): int { return $x + 1; };
$add_n = function ($x): int use ($n) { return $x + $n; };
```

This syntax is compatible with the return typehint syntax that will be released in PHP 7, except for the case of closures with lists of captured variables. In PHP 7, the return typehint goes after the list of captures, but in Hack, it goes after the list of parameters.

Function Parameters

Annotating function parameters uses exactly the same syntax as PHP uses for parameter typehints—just put the type name before the parameter name:

```
function f(int $start, string $thing) {
  // ...
}
```

Default arguments are supported as usual, but of course the default value must satisfy the type annotation. In regular PHP, there is a special allowance for a default value of `null` for a typehinted parameter, so that this is valid:

```
function f(SomeClass $obj = null) {
  // ...
}
```

This is *not* valid in Hack—it conflates the concept of an optional argument with that of a required argument that allows a placeholder value. In Hack, you can express the latter by making the parameter type nullable (see "Hack's Type System" on page 6).

Parameters Versus Arguments

These terms are often used interchangeably in casual talk among programmers, but they aren't the same thing. The difference between them is the same as the difference between variables and values. Parameters are variables, and arguments are the values that get assigned to parameters when a function is called. Consider this code:

```
function add_one($x) {
  return $x + 1;
}

echo add_one(10);
```

`$x` is a parameter of the function `add_one()`. `10` is an argument that gets assigned to the parameter `$x`.

We say that a function *has* parameters, but it's also correct to say that it *takes* arguments, because you pass arguments to a function when you call it.

Variadic functions

A variadic function is one that can take a variable number of arguments. In PHP, all functions are implicitly variadic; passing a function more arguments than it has parameters doesn't result in an error, and any function can access all arguments that were passed to it using the built-in functions `func_get_args()`, `func_get_arg()`, and `func_num_args()`.

In Hack, by contrast, passing excess arguments to a function is an error, unless the function is explicitly declared as variadic. The Hack syntax for making a function variadic is to put ... as the last argument in the function signature. Within such a function, you can access the arguments with func_get_args(), func_get_arg(), and func_num_args(), the same way as in PHP:

```
function log_error(string $format, ...) {
  $varargs = func_get_args();
  // ...
}
```

The variadic arguments are allowed to be of any type. The first argument to log_error() must be a string, but the subsequent arguments can be of any type and the typechecker will accept it.

Properties

In the declaration of a property (either static or non-static), the type annotation goes immediately before the property name:

```
class C {
  public static int $logging_level = 2;
  private string $name;
}
```

Initial values are supported (like 2 for $logging_level in the example), and the initial value must satisfy the type annotation.

 Initialization of properties with type annotations actually has several more rules, to avoid situations where code can access a property that hasn't been initialized. See "Property Initialization" on page 23 for details.

Hack's Type System

Hack provides a multitude of powerful ways to describe types. It builds on PHP's basic type system of booleans, integers, strings, arrays, etc., and adds many new ways to combine them or make them more expressive:

Primitive types
These are the same as PHP's primitive types: bool, int, float, string, array, and resource. All these are valid Hack type annotations.

In PHP, there are additional names for these types: boolean, integer, real, and double. These are *not* valid in Hack. The six mentioned above are the only acceptable primitive types in Hack.

There are two other types that express a simple combination of primitive types: num, which is either an integer or a float; and arraykey, which is either an integer or a string.

Object types

The name of any class or interface—built-in or non-built-in—can be used in a type annotation.

Enums

Enums are described more fully in Chapter 3. For our purposes here, it's enough to know that an enum gives a name to a set of constants. The name of an enum can be used as a type annotation; the only values that satisfy that annotation are the constants that are members of the enum.

Tuples

Tuples are a way to bundle together a fixed number of values of possibly different types. The most common use for tuples is to return multiple values from a function.

The syntax for tuple type annotations is simply a parenthesis-enclosed, comma-separated list of types (which may be any of the other types in this list, except void). The syntax for creating a tuple is identical to the array() syntax for creating arrays, except that the keyword array is replaced by tuple, and keys are not allowed.

For example, this function returns a tuple containing an integer and a float:

```
function find_max_and_index(array<float> $nums): (int, float) {
  $max = -INF;
  $max_index = -1;
  foreach ($nums as $index => $num) {
    if ($num > $max) {
      $max = $num;
      $max_index = $index;
    }
  }

  return tuple($max_index, $max);
}
```

Tuples behave like a restricted version of arrays. You can't change a tuple's set of keys: that is, you can't add or remove elements. You can change the values in a tuple, as long as you don't change their type. You can read from a tuple with array-indexing syntax, but it's more common to unpack them with list assignment instead of reading individual elements.

Under the hood, tuples really are arrays: if you pass a tuple to is_array(), it will return true.

mixed

> mixed means any value that can possibly exist in a Hack program, including null.

void

> void is only valid as a function return type, and it means that the function returns nothing. (In PHP, a function that "returns nothing" actually has a return value of null, but in Hack, it's an error to use the return value of a function returning void.)

> void is included within mixed. That is, it's legal for a function with return type mixed to return nothing.

noreturn

> noreturn is only valid as a return type, and it means that the function or method never returns normally: it always either throws an exception or terminates the program.

> The typechecker understands that code after a call to a noreturn function or static method (but not a non-static method[2]) can never be executed. This has consequences for the typechecker's type inference algorithm, which is control-flow-sensitive. For more details, see "Refining Types" on page 32.

this

> this is only valid as a method return type—it's not a valid return type for a bare function. It signifies that the method returns an object of the same class as the object that the method was called on.

> The purpose of this annotation is to allow chained method calls on classes that have subclasses. Chained method calls are a useful trick. They look like this:

> ```
> $random = $rng->setSeed(1234)->generate();
> ```

> To allow for this, the class in question has to return $this from methods that have no logical return value, like this:

> ```
> class RNG {
>   private int $seed = 0;
>
>   public function setSeed(int $seed): RNG {
>     $this->seed = $seed;
> ```

---

2 This is due to the order in which the typechecker's analysis phases happen. Before it can do type inference, it needs to analyze control flow, which includes accounting for noreturn calls. It can't determine the return type of a non-static method call during control flow analysis, because it needs to know the type on the left-hand side of the ->, and the results of type inference aren't available yet. This isn't an issue for calls to bare functions and static methods, since those can be resolved before types have been inferred.

```
    return $this;
  }

  // ...
}
```

In this example, if RNG has no subclasses, you can use RNG as the return type annotation of setSeed(), and there will be no problems. The trouble begins if RNG has subclasses.

The typechecker will report an error in the following example. Because the return type of setSeed() is RNG, it thinks that the call $rng->setSeed(1234) returns a RNG, and calling generateSpecial() on a RNG object is invalid; that method is only defined in the subclass. The more specific type of $rng (which the typechecker knows is a SpecialRNG) has been lost:

```
class SpecialRNG extends RNG {
  public function generateSpecial(): int {
    // ...
  }
}

function main(): void {
  $rng = new SpecialRNG();
  $special = $rng->setSeed(1234)->generateSpecial();
}
```

The this return type annotation solves this problem:

```
class RNG {
  private int $seed = 0;

  public function setSeed(int $seed): this {
    $this->seed = $seed;
    return $this;
  }

  // ...
}
```

Now, when the typechecker is calculating the type returned from the call $rng->setSeed(1234), the this annotation tells it to preserve the specific type of the expression to the left of the arrow. That way, the chained call to generateSpecial() is valid.

Static methods can also have the this return type, and in that case, it signifies that they return an object of the same class that the method was called on—that is, the class whose name is returned from get_called_class(). The way to satisfy this type annotation is to return new static():

```
class ParentClass {
  // This is needed to reassure the typechecker that 'new static()'
  // is valid
  final protected function __construct() {}

  public static function newInstance(): this {
    return new static();
  }
}

class ChildClass extends ParentClass {
}

function main(): void {
  ParentClass::newInstance();   // Returns a ParentClass instance
  ChildClass::newInstance();    // Returns a ChildClass instance
}
```

Type aliases
> Described fully in "Type Aliases" on page 62, type aliases are a way to give a new name to an existing type. You can use the new name as a type annotation.

Shapes
> Shapes, described in "Array Shapes" on page 71, are a way to tell the typechecker about the internal structure of arrays. A shape declaration can be used as a type annotation.

Type constants
> Described fully in "Type Constants" on page 66, type constants are analogous to class constants, but are types instead of values. Their names can be used as type annotations.

Nullable types
> All types except void, noreturn, and mixed can be made nullable by prefixing them with a question mark. A type annotation of ?int indicates a value that can be an integer or null. mixed can't be made nullable because it already includes null.

classname
> In PHP, but not in Hack, you can use a string containing the name of a class in any position where you can use a plain class name. The following code is valid PHP and invalid Hack:

```
class Thing {
}

function instantiate(string $clsname) {
  return new $clsname();   // OK in PHP; error in Hack
```

```
}

instantiate('Thing');
```

This is invalid in Hack because the typechecker won't always be able to determine the contents of $clsname, so it has no way to know what class is being instantiated, or even whether the named class exists.

However, there are often practical applications for code like this, so Hack offers the classname type. It allows you to pass around class names that aren't statically known, but in such a way that the typechecker has enough information to guarantee type safety.

The syntax for classname is simply the keyword classname followed by an angle-bracket-enclosed, unquoted class or interface name. A value of type classname<Thing> is a string containing the name of Thing *or* the name of any class or interface that inherits from Thing, through extends or implements relationships.

You can use such a value in any place where you could normally use the name of a class: in a new expression, on the righthand side of instanceof, on the lefthand side of :: in a static method call, etc.

```
function instantiate(classname<Thing> $clsname): Thing {
  return new $clsname();
}
```

The typechecker will use its knowledge of $clsname's contents to make sure the code is typesafe. For example, it will verify that Thing has a constructor that can be called with no arguments.

The only way to get a value of type classname is with the ::class construct:

```
class Thing {
  // ...
}

function takes_classname_thing(classname<Thing> $clsname): void {
  // ...
}

takes_classname_thing(Thing::class);    // OK
takes_classname_thing('Thing');         // Error
```

classname is aware of interface and inheritance relationships. For example:

```
class Thing {
  // ...
}
interface Iface {
```

```
  // ...
}
class SubThing extends Thing implements Iface {
  // ...
}

function takes_classname_thing(classname<Thing> $clsname): void {
  // ...
}
function takes_classname_iface(classname<Iface> $clsname): void {
  // ...
}

takes_classname_thing(SubThing::class);  // OK
takes_classname_iface(SubThing::class);  // OK

function returns_classname_iface(): classname<Iface> {
  return SubThing::class;  // OK
}
```

At runtime, a value of type `classname` is just a string. The typechecker recognizes this, and allows `classname` values to be implicitly converted to strings:

```
function takes_string(string $str): void {
  // ...
}

function takes_clsname(classname<Thing> $clsname): void {
  takes_string($clsname);  // OK
}
```

Callable types

Although PHP allows `callable` as a parameter typehint, Hack does not. Instead, Hack offers a much more powerful syntax that allows you to specify not only that a value is callable, but what types it takes as arguments and what type it returns.

The syntax is the keyword `function`, followed by a parenthesis-enclosed list of parameter types, followed by a colon and a return type, with all of that enclosed in parentheses. This mirrors the syntax of type annotations for functions; it is essentially a function signature without a name and without names for the parameters. In this example, `$callback` is a function taking an integer and a string, and returning a string:

```
function do_some_work(array $items,
                        (function(int, string): string) $callback): array {
  foreach ($items as $index => $value) {
    $string_result = $callback($index, $value);
    // ...
  }
}
```

There are four kinds of callable values that satisfy callable type annotations: closures, functions, instance methods, and static methods. Let's take a look at how to express them:

- Closures simply work as is:

```
function do_some_work((function(int): void) $callback): void {
  // ...
}

function main(): void {
  do_some_work(function (int $x): void { /* ... */ });
}
```

- To use a named function as a callable value, you have to pass the name through the special function fun():

```
function do_some_work((function(int): void) $callback): void {
  // ...
}

function f(int $x): void {
  // ...
}

function main(): void {
  do_some_work(fun('f'));
}
```

The argument to fun() must be a single-quoted string literal. The typechecker will look up that function to determine its parameter types and return type, and treat fun() as if it returns a callable value of the right type.

- To use an instance method as a callable value, you have to pass the object and the method name through the special function inst_meth(). This is similar to fun() in that the typechecker will look up the named method and treat inst_meth() as if it returns a callable value of the right type. Again, the method name must be a single-quoted string literal:

```
function do_some_work((function(int): void) $callback): void {
  // ...
}

class C {
  public function do_work(int $x): void {
    // ...
  }
}

function main(): void {}
  $c = new C();
```

```
    do_some_work(inst_meth($c, 'do_work'));
  }
```

- Using static methods is very similar: pass the class name and method name through the special function `class_meth()`. The method name must be a single-quoted string literal. The class name can be either a single-quoted string literal, or `::class` appended to an unquoted class name:

```
function do_some_work((function(int): void): $callback): void {
  // ...
}

class C {
  public static function prognosticate(int $x): void {
    // ...
  }
}

function main(): void {
  do_some_work(class_meth(C::class, 'prognosticate'));

  // Equivalent:
  do_some_work(class_meth('C', 'prognosticate'));
}
```

At runtime, `ClassName::class` simply evaluates to `'ClassName'`.

There's another way to create a callable value that calls instance methods, which is `meth_caller()`. It creates a callable value that calls a specific method on objects you pass to it.

Pass a class name and method name to `meth_caller()`. The returned value is callable; the first argument you pass to it is the object to call the method on, and the rest of the arguments are passed through to the underlying method.

```
class Greeter {
  function greet(string $name): void {
    echo 'Hi ' . $name';
  }
}

function main(): void {
  $caller = meth_caller(Greeter::class, 'greet');
  $obj = new C();
  $caller($obj, 'friend');  // Equivalent to calling
                            // $obj->greet('friend');
}
```

This is in contrast to `inst_meth()`, which bundles together a specific object and a method to call on it. `meth_caller()` is especially useful with utility functions like `array_map()` and `array_filter()`:

```
class User {
  public function getName(): string {
    // ...
  }
}

function all_names(array<User> $users): string {
  $names = array_map(meth_caller(User::class, 'getName'), $users);
  return implode(', ', $names);
}
```

There is one kind of value that is callable in PHP, but isn't recognized as such by the Hack typechecker: objects with an `__invoke()` method. This may change in the future.

Generics

Also known as *parameterized types*, generics allow a single piece of code to work with multiple different types in a way that is still verifiably typesafe. The simplest example is that instead of simply specifying that a value is an array, you can specify that it's an array of strings, or an array of objects of class `Person`, and so on.

Generics are an extremely powerful tool, and there's quite a bit to learn about them. They're fully described in Chapter 2.

For this chapter, though, it's enough to understand the syntax for generic arrays. It consists of the keyword `array` followed by either one or two types inside angle brackets. If there's just one type inside the angle brackets, that is the type of the *values* in the array, and the keys are assumed to be of type `int`. If there are two types, the first one is the type of the keys, and the second one is the type of the values. So, for example, `array<bool>` signifies an array with integer keys mapping to booleans, and `array<string, int>` signifies an array with string keys mapping to integers. The types inside the angle brackets are called *type parameters*.

One very important thing to note is that in Hack, you can't create any values that you can't create in PHP. The underlying bits are all the same between PHP and Hack; Hack's type system just gives you ways to express interesting unions and subsets of the possible values.

More concretely, consider this code:

```
function main(): void {
  f(10, 10);
}
```

```
function f(mixed $m, int $i): void {
  // ...
}
```

Within the body of f(), we say that $m is of type mixed and $i is of type int, even though they're storing exactly the same bits.

Or consider this:

```
function main(): void {
  $callable = function(string $s): ?int { /* ... */ };
}
```

Although we say that $callable is of type (function(string): ?int), under the hood, it's still just an object, like any other closure. It's not a magical "function pointer" value that is only possible in Hack, or anything like that.

In general, saying that some expression "is of type X" is a statement about what the *typechecker* knows, not about what the *runtime* knows.

Typechecker Modes

The Hack typechecker has three different modes: strict, partial, and decl. These modes are set on a file-by-file basis, and files in different modes can interoperate seamlessly. Each file declares, in a double-slash comment on its first line, which mode the typechecker should use on it. For example:

```
<?hh // strict
```

If there is no comment on the first line (i.e., the first line is just <?hh), then partial mode is used.

There are several differences between the modes, and we'll see many of them as we look at the typechecker's features. Here's the general idea of each mode:

Strict mode: `<?hh // strict`
> The most important feature of strict mode is that all named functions (and methods) must have their return types and all parameter types annotated, and all properties must have type annotations. In other words, anywhere there can be a type annotation, there must be one, with a few exceptions:
>
> - Closures don't need their parameter types or return types annotated.
> - Constructors and destructors don't need return type annotations—it doesn't make sense for them to return anything.
>
> There are three major restrictions in strict mode:

- Using any named entity[3] that isn't defined in a Hack file is an error. This means that strict-mode code can't call into PHP code. Note that strict-mode code *can* call into partial-mode or decl-mode Hack code.

- Most code at the top level of a file results in an error. The `require` family of statements[4] is allowed, as are statements that define named entities.[5]

- Using reference assignment (e.g., `$a = &$b`), or defining a function or method that returns by reference or takes arguments by reference, results in an error.

There are a few smaller differences, too; we'll cover those as we get to them.

To take full advantage of the typechecker, you should aim to have as much of your code in strict mode as possible. Strict-mode Hack is a sound type system. That means that if 100% of your code is in strict mode, it should be impossible to incur a type error at runtime. This is a very powerful guarantee, and the closer you can get to achieving it, the better.

Partial mode: `<?hh`
Partial mode relaxes the restrictions of strict mode. It does all the typechecking it can, but it doesn't require type annotations. In addition:

- If you use functions and classes that the typechecker doesn't see in a Hack file, there's no error. The typechecker leniently assumes that the missing entity is defined in a PHP file. See "Calling into PHP" on page 19 for details.

- Top-level code is allowed, but not typechecked. To minimize the amount of unchecked code you have, ideally you should wrap all your top-level code in a function and have your only top-level statement be a call to that function. That is, instead of this:

```
<?hh

set_up_autoloading();
do_logging();
$c = find_controller();
$c->go();
```

Do this:

```
<?hh

function main() {
  set_up_autoloading();
```

---

3 A named entity is a function, class, interface, constant, trait, enum, or type alias.
4 `require`, `include`, `require_once`, and `include_once`.
5 Defining constants with `const` syntax is allowed, but doing so with `define()` is not allowed.

```
    do_logging();
    $c = find_controller();
    $c->go();
}

main();
```

Even better, put the definition of `main()` in a strict-mode file.

- References are allowed, but the typechecker essentially pretends they don't exist and doesn't try to model their behavior. In this example, after the last line the typechecker still thinks `$a` is an integer, even though it is really a string:

```
$a = 10;
$b = &$a;
$b = 'not an int';
```

Put simply, you can use references in partial mode, but they break type safety, so it's best to avoid them.

Even in a project written in Hack from the ground up, there are uses for partial mode. In any script or web app, there has to be some amount of top-level code to serve as an entry point, so you'll always have at least one partial-mode file. You'll also need partial mode for access to superglobals like `$_GET`, `$_POST`, and `$argv`; we'll learn more about that in "Using Superglobals" on page 21.

Decl mode: `<?hh // decl`

In decl mode, code is not typechecked. All the typechecker does is read and index the signatures of functions and classes defined in the file. (There can still be errors in decl mode, for things like invalid type annotation syntax.)

The purpose of decl mode is to be a transition aid when migrating an existing PHP codebase to Hack: it provides a stepping stone between PHP and the other Hack modes. Changing a PHP file into decl-mode Hack is generally a very easy step, and has significant benefits over leaving the file as PHP. First, typechecking around calls to PHP code is very loose (see "Calling into PHP" on page 19), but calls to decl-mode Hack can be typechecked much more rigorously. Second, strict-mode Hack can't call into PHP at all, but it can call into decl-mode Hack.

If you're writing a new codebase that is 100% Hack from the beginning, you shouldn't use decl mode at all.

Code Without Annotations

There's one type that I didn't mention in the list earlier. It's the type signified by the absence of an annotation. For example, it's the type of `$x` inside this function:

```
function f($x) {
}
```

This type doesn't have a name that you can write in code. Among the Hack team, it's referred to as "any."

The typechecker treats this type specially. It can never be involved in a type error. Every value that can possibly exist in a Hack program satisfies this type "annotation," so you can pass anything at all to the function f() in this example without a type error. In the other direction, a value of this type satisfies every possible type annotation, so within f(), you can do anything at all with $x without a type error.

This may sound similar to mixed, but there is a very important difference. Every possible value satisfies mixed, but a value of type mixed does *not* satisfy every possible type annotation. If you want to pass a value of type mixed to a function that expects an int, for example, you must either make sure it's an integer (see "Refining Mixed Types to Primitives" on page 34) or cast it.

Values of the "any" type work the same way in all Hack modes. In strict mode, you can't *write* code without annotations, but you can *call into* code without annotations, defined in partial or decl mode. Another way to phrase the "everything that can be annotated must be annotated" restriction of strict mode is: code in strict mode may use values of this special type, but it's not allowed to produce them.

Calling into PHP

In partial and decl modes, if you use a named entity that the typechecker doesn't see defined in any Hack file, there will be no error. (In strict mode, there will be an "unbound name" error.) This may seem like a strangely loose behavior, but its purpose is rooted in Hack's easy migration path from PHP. This allows code in Hack files to use code in PHP files: to call functions, to use constants, and to instantiate and extend classes. You are on your own in cases like this—remember, the typechecker makes no attempt at all to analyze PHP files, not even to see what functions they define.

You can also make this an error in partial mode with a configuration option. The option is called assume_php (as in: "assume missing entities are defined in PHP"), and it's turned on by default. You can turn it off by adding this line to your *.hhconfig* file and restarting the typechecker server with the command hh_client restart:

```
assume_php = false
```

If you're just starting to migrate a large PHP codebase to Hack, it will be easier if you leave assume_php on. Later on, as more of the codebase becomes Hack, it's a good idea to turn it off, to get the benefit of stricter checking. If you're starting a new Hack codebase, you should turn it off (i.e., set `assume_php = false`) from the very beginning.

The use of unknown functions and classes hamstrings the typechecker somewhat, as it has to make generous assumptions around them:

- Calls to unknown functions are typechecked as if they could take any number of arguments of any type, and had no return type annotation.

- Unknown constants are assumed to be of the special "any" type—as if they were the result of calling a function with no return type annotation.

- Instantiating an unknown class results in a value that is known to be an object. Any method call on an object like this is valid, and is typechecked like a call to an unknown function. Any property access on an object like this is valid too, and returns a value of the special "any" type.

- A Hack class that has *any unknown ancestor,* or uses any unknown trait, or has any ancestor that uses an unknown trait, is very similar to an unknown class. A single unknown trait or class will cripple the typechecker in the entire hierarchy it's part of. Calling any unknown method on such a class is valid, and so is accessing any unknown property.

  However, if the typechecker can resolve a method call or property access to a method or property defined in Hack (even in decl mode), it will typecheck the call or access appropriately. For example:

```
class C extends SomeClassNotDefinedInHack {
  public int $known_property;

  public function known_method(string $s) {
    // ...
  }
}

function main(): void {
  $c = new C();
  $c->unknown_method();  // No error
  $c->known_method(12);  // Error: int not compatible with string

  $c->unknown_property->func();  // No error
  $c->known_property->func();    // Error: can't call method on an int
}
```

Rules

The rules enforced by the typechecker are largely quite straightforward, and its error messages are designed to explain problems clearly and suggest solutions. There are a few cases that are more subtle, though, and this section explains them.

Using Superglobals

Superglobals are global variables that are available in every scope, without the need for a `global` statement. There are nine of them, special-cased by the runtime:

- `$GLOBALS`
- `$_SERVER`
- `$_GET`
- `$_POST`
- `$_FILES`
- `$_COOKIE`
- `$_SESSION`
- `$_REQUEST`
- `$_ENV`

Hack's strict mode doesn't support superglobals; if you try to use one, the typechecker will say the variable is undefined. However, to write nontrivial web apps and scripts, you'll need to use them.

The simplest thing you can do is to write accessor functions in a partial-mode file, and call them from strict-mode files:

```
function get_params(): array {
  return $_GET;
}

function env_vars(): array {
  return $_ENV;
}

// ...
```

That approach doesn't contribute any type safety to your codebase, though, and it's easy to do better. With HTTP GET and POST parameters especially, you often know the type of the value you expect, and you can use this knowledge to get more strongly typed code:

```
function string_param(string $key): ?string {
  if (!array_key_exists($_GET, $key)) {
    return null;
  }
  $value = $_GET[$key];
  return is_string($value) ? $value : null;
}

// Alternative, stronger version: throw if wrong type
function string_param(string $key): ?string {
  if (!array_key_exists($_GET, $key)) {
    return null;
  }
  $value = $_GET[$key];
  invariant(is_string($value), 'GET param must be a string');
  return $value;
}
```

We'll see the `invariant()` function in more detail in "Refining Types" on page 32. For now, it's enough to know that it throws an exception if its first argument is `false`.

You can write similar accessors for other superglobals, and for other value types.

Types of Overriding Methods

Inheritance is one of the more complex interactions between pieces of code in Hack. The complexity arises from the action-at-a-distance phenomenon that inheritance creates. For example, if you have an object that has been type-annotated as `Some Class` and you call a method on it, you could enter a method in any class that descends from `SomeClass`. The call still has to be typesafe, though, which means there have to be rules around the types of methods that override other methods.

In an overriding method, parameter types must be exactly the same as in the overridden method. This is mainly due to a behavior inherited from PHP. In PHP, any method that is overriding an abstract method, or a method declared in an interface, must match the overridden method's parameter types exactly. This is likely to change in future versions of Hack, to instead allow overriding methods' parameter types to be more general.

Return types, on the other hand, do not have to be the same when overriding. An overriding method may have a *more specific* return type than the overridden method. For example:

```
class ParentClass {
  public function generate(): num {
    // ...
  }
}

class ChildClass extends ParentClass {
```

```
    public function generate(): int {  // OK
      // ...
    }
  }
```

Despite the changed return type, polymorphic callsites are still typesafe:

```
function f(ParentClass $obj) {
  $number = $obj->generate();
  // Even if $obj is a ChildClass instance, generate() still returns a num,
  // because ChildClass::generate() returns an int, and all ints are nums.
}
```

Overriding with a more general return type isn't valid—for example, if ChildClass's version of generate() were declared to return mixed, the typechecker would report an error.

Property Initialization

To maintain type safety, the typechecker enforces rules about how type-annotated properties are initialized, in both strict and partial modes. The overarching aim is to ensure that no property is ever read from before it is initialized to a value of the right type.

For static properties, the rule is simple: any non-nullable static property is required to have an initial value. Nullable properties without an explicit initial value are implicitly initialized to null.

Non-static properties have a more complex set of rules. The typechecker has to make sure that it's not possible to instantiate an object with an uninitialized non-nullable property. To that end, any non-nullable non-static property without an initial value must be initialized in the class's constructors:

```
class Person {
  private string $name;
  private ?string $address;

  public function __construct(string $name) {
    $this->name = $name;
  }
}
```

This code will pass the typechecker: the property $name is properly initialized, and $address is nullable so doesn't need to be initialized.

The typechecker will make sure that all possible codepaths through the constructor result in all properties being initialized. For this code:

```
class Person {
  private string $name;
```

```
    public function __construct(string $name, bool $skip_name) {
      if (!$skip_name) {
        $this->name = $name;
      }
    }
  }
```

the typechecker will report this error:

```
/home/oyamauchi/test.php:5:19,29: The class member name is not always properly
initialized
Make sure you systematically set $this->name when the method __construct is
called
Alternatively, you can define the type as optional (?...)
  (NastCheck[3015])
```

Another component of the typechecker's enforcement of this rule is that you aren't allowed to call public or protected methods from within the constructor until after all properties are initialized. For this code:

```
class C {
  private string $name;

  public function __construct(string $name) {
    $this->doSomething();
    $this->name = $name;
  }

  protected function doSomething(): void {
    // ...
  }
}
```

the typechecker will raise this error (you would, however, be allowed to call $this->doSomething() *after* the assignment to $this->name):

```
/home/oyamauchi/test.php:6:14,18: Until the initialization of $this is over,
you can only call private methods
The initialization is not over because $this->name can still potentially be
null (NastCheck[3004])
```

You *are* allowed to call private methods in that situation, but any private methods you call will be checked to make sure they don't access potentially uninitialized properties. Non-private methods can't be checked in this way, because they may be overridden in subclasses, so it's invalid to call them in this situation. For the following code:

```
class C {
  private string $name;

  public function __construct(string $name) {
    $this->dumpInfo();
    $this->name = $name;
```

```
  }

  private function dumpInfo(): void {
    var_dump($this->name);
  }
}
```

the typechecker will raise this error (again, however, you would be allowed to call $this->dumpInfo() after assigning to $this->name):

```
/home/oyamauchi/test.php:11:21,24: Read access to $this->name before
initialization (Typing[4083])
```

Properties declared in abstract classes are exempt from these rules. However, concrete child classes will be required to initialize their ancestors' uninitialized properties. For this code:

```
abstract class Abstr {
  protected string $name;
}
class C extends Abstr {
}
```

the typechecker reports this error:

```
/home/oyamauchi/test.php:5:7,7: The class member name is not always properly
initialized
Make sure you systematically set $this->name when the method __construct is
called
Alternatively, you can define the type as optional (?...)
  (NastCheck[3015])
```

Lastly, for simple cases like the examples in this section, where the property is simply initialized with a parameter of the constructor, you should use constructor parameter promotion (see "Constructor Parameter Promotion" on page 76). It cuts down on boilerplate code, and you don't have to think about property initialization issues:

```
class C {
  public function __construct(private string $name) { }
}
```

Typed Variadic Arguments

As we saw earlier, Hack has syntax to declare that a function is variadic:

```
function log_error(string $format, ...) {
  $args = func_get_args();
  // ...
}
```

PHP 5.6 introduced a different variadic function syntax, which has two features beyond Hack's—it packs variadic arguments into an array automatically, and it allows a typehint on the variadic parameter:

```
function sum(SomeClass ...$args) {
  // $args is an array of SomeClass objects
}
```

This syntax also exists in Hack. The typechecker supports the syntax, and typechecks calls to such functions correctly. HHVM supports the syntax too, but only *without* the type annotation. HHVM doesn't support checking the types of the variadic arguments, so it will raise a fatal error if it encounters a type annotation on a variadic parameter, to avoid giving the impression that the annotation is having an effect.

This creates a conflict. In strict mode, the Hack typechecker won't allow a parameter without a type annotation—even a variadic parameter—but HHVM won't run code that has an annotated variadic parameter.

There are two possible solutions to the conflict:

- Omit the annotation, and use partial mode.
- Omit the annotation, use strict mode, and add an HH_IGNORE_ERROR[4033] comment (see "Silencing Typechecker Errors" on page 88). This is the preferred solution, as strict mode should always be preferred over partial mode when possible.

Types for Generators

There are three interfaces you can use when adding return type annotations to generators: Iterator, KeyedIterator, and Generator. All three are generic. We won't cover generics in full until Chapter 2, but we'll see some basics here.

Use the first two when you don't expect to call send() on the generator. Use Iterator when you're only yielding a value, and KeyedIterator when you're yielding a key as well:

```
function yields_value_only(): Iterator<int> {
  yield 1;
  yield 2;
}

function yields_key_and_value(): KeyedIterator<int, string> {
  yield 1 => 'one';
  yield 2 => 'two';
}
```

The return type annotation Iterator<int> means that the generator is yielding values of type int, and no keys. The annotation KeyedIterator<int, string> means that the generator is yielding keys of type int and values of type string. This is similar to array types, which we've already seen; for example, array<int, string> means an array whose keys are integers and whose values are strings.

If you will be calling send() on the generator, use the annotation Generator:

```
function has_send_called(): Generator<int, string, User> {
  // Empty yield to get first User
  $user = yield 0 => '';
  // $user is of type ?User

  while ($user !== null) {
    $id = $user->getID();
    $name = $user->getName();
    $user = yield $id => $name;
  }
}

function main(array<User> $users): void {
  $generator = has_send_called();
  $generator->next();

  foreach ($users as $user) {
    $generator->send($user);
    var_dump($generator->key());
    var_dump($generator->current());
  }
}
```

The return type annotation Generator<int, string, User> means that the generator yields int keys and string values, and expects values of type User to be passed to its send() method.

Note that the value resulting from the yield is not of type User, but rather ?User. This is because it's always possible for the caller of the generator to call next() instead of send(), which makes the corresponding yield evaluate to null. You have to check that value against null before calling methods on it; see "Refining Nullable Types to Non-Nullable" on page 32 for details.

Fallthrough in switch Statements

There's a common mistake in switch statements of having one case that unintentionally falls through to the next. Hack adds a rule that catches this mistake—it's an error to have a case that falls through to the next case, unless the first one is empty:

```
switch ($day) {
  case 'sun':
    echo 'Sunday';  // Error
  case 'sat':
    echo 'Weekend';
    break;
  default:
    echo 'Weekday';
}
```

```
switch ($day) {
  case 'sun':  // OK: this case falls through, but is empty
  case 'sat':
    echo 'Weekend';
    break;
  default:
    echo 'Weekday';
}
```

If the fallthrough is intentional, put the comment // FALLTHROUGH as the last line of the falling-through case:

```
switch ($day) {
  case 'sun':
    echo 'Sunday';
    // FALLTHROUGH
  case 'sat':
    echo 'Weekend';
    break;
  default:
    echo 'Weekday';
}
```

This requires action on the part of the programmer, which greatly reduces the chances that the fallthrough is an oversight.

Type Inference

Type inference is central to Hack's approach to static typechecking. Like in PHP, local variables are not declared with types. However, being able to typecheck operations on locals is crucial to getting a useful amount of coverage.

Hack closes the gap with type inference. The typechecker starts with a small set of known types, from annotations and from literals, and then follows them through operators and function calls, deducing and checking types for everything downstream.

The way Hack's type inference works isn't always obvious at first glance. Let's take a look at the details.

Variables Don't Have Types

In most statically typed languages, a local variable is given a type when it comes into existence, and the variable can only hold values of that type for its entire lifetime. This example code could be C++ or Java, and in either case, there is a type error—because x was declared as an int, it can never hold values that aren't integers:

```
int x = 10;
x = "a string";  // Error
```

This is not the case in Hack. Like in PHP, local variables are not declared in Hack. You create a local variable simply by assigning a value to it. You can assign a new value to any local variable, regardless of what type of value the variable already holds:

```
$x = 10;
$x = "a string";   // OK
```

The key difference is that in Hack, local variables don't have types. Local variables hold values, which have types.

At each point in the program, the typechecker knows what type of value each variable holds *at that point*. If it sees a new value assigned to a variable, it will update its knowledge of what type of value that variable holds.

Unresolved Types

The fact that variables don't have types means that the typechecker needs a way to deal with code like the following:

```
if (some_condition()) {
  $x = 10;
} else {
  $x = 'ten';
}
```

This pattern is not uncommon in PHP code, and it's legal in Hack. The question, then, is: after the end of the conditional, what does the typechecker think the type of $x is?

The answer is that it uses an *unresolved type*. This is a construct that the typechecker uses to remember every type that $x *could* have. In this case, it remembers that $x could be an integer, or it could be a string.

After the conditional, you can do anything with $x that you could do with an integer *and* with a string, and you can't do anything that would be invalid for *either* an integer *or* a string. For example:

```
if (some_condition()) {
  $x = 10;
} else {
  $x = 'ten';
}

echo $x;            // OK: you can echo ints and strings
echo $x + 20;       // Error: can't use + on a string
echo $x->method();  // Error: can't call a method on an int or a string
```

Most importantly, $x will satisfy any type annotation that includes both integers and strings—like arraykey and mixed—and it won't satisfy anything else:

```
function takes_mixed(mixed $y): void {
}

function takes_int(int $y): void {
}

function main(): void {
  if (some_condition()) {
    $x = 10;
  } else {
    $x = 'ten';
  }

  takes_int($x);    // Error: $x may be a string
  takes_mixed($x);  // OK
}
```

This situation also commonly arises with class and interface hierarchies:

```
interface I {
}
class One implements I {
  public function method(): int {
    // ...
  }
}
class Two implements I {
  public function method(): string {
    // ...
  }
}

function main(): I {
  if (some_condition()) {
    $obj = new One();
  } else {
    $obj = new Two();
  }

  $int_or_string = $obj->method();  // OK

  return $obj;  // OK
}
```

Here, the call $obj->method() is valid, because both classes One and Two have a
method with the right name and the right number of parameters. The type returned
from the call is itself an unresolved type consisting of both possibilities: int or
string.

The return statement is also valid, because both possibilities for $obj satisfy the
return type annotation I.

We'll see unresolved types again when we discuss generics in "Unresolved Types, Revisited" on page 49.

Inference Is Function-Local

A fundamental restriction of Hack's type inference is that when analyzing one function, it will never look at the body of another function or method. For example, suppose the following code is your entire codebase:

```
function f($str) {
  return 'Here is a string: ' . $str;
}

function main() {
  echo f('boo!');
}

main();
```

Two facts are clear to a human reader: that `$str` is always a string, and that `f()` always returns a string. However, the Hack typechecker will not infer these facts. While inferring types within `f()`, it will not go looking for callers of `f()` to find out what types of arguments they're passing. While inferring types within `main()`, it will not go look at the body of `f()` to find out what type it returns. It will look at the signature of `f()` for a return type annotation, though, and find none, so it will treat `f()` as returning the special "any" type (see "Code Without Annotations" on page 18).

This restriction exists for performance reasons. Forcing inference in one function to stay within that function puts a strict upper bound on the amount of computation it takes to analyze one function, and by extension, an entire codebase. In computational-complexity terms, the type inference algorithm is superlinear in complexity, so it's important to give it many small inputs instead of one huge input, to keep the total running time manageable.

For large codebases—such as Facebook, the one Hack was originally designed for—this property is absolutely crucial. When the body of one function is changed (but not its signature), the typechecking server needs only to reanalyze that one function to bring its knowledge up to date, and it can do that almost instantaneously. When a function signature changes, the typechecking server reanalyzes that function and all of its callers, but not *their* callers, which puts a fairly low cap on the amount of work required.

There is one pseudoexception to this restriction: closures. Although a closure is technically a separate function from the one it's defined within, type inference on a function containing a closure is allowed to look inside the closure. Consider the following example:

```
$doubler = function ($x) { return $x + $x; };
var_dump($doubler(10));    // int(20)
var_dump($doubler(3.14));  // float(6.28)
```

Even though the closure has no annotations (which is valid even in strict mode), the typechecker can infer that the type of $doubler(10) is int—it analyzes the closure's body under the assumption that $x is an integer, and infers the return type because the addition operator applied to two integers results in an integer.[6] Similarly, it can infer that the type of $doubler(3.14) is float.

Incidentally, it's because type inference can look inside closures that strict mode allows closures to forgo type annotations.

Refining Types

Suppose you have a value of type ?string, and you want to pass it to a function that has a parameter of type string. How do you convert from one to the other? Or suppose you have an object that may or may not implement the interface Polarizable, and you want to call polarize() on it if it does. How can the typechecker know when the polarize() call is valid?

The task of establishing that a value of one type is also of another type is common in well-typed code. It may seem like a chore that you have to do to placate the type-checker, but this is really the key to how Hack catches mistakes early in development. This is how Hack prevents things like calling methods that don't exist, finding null in unexpected places, and other common annoyances of debugging a large PHP codebase.

You refine types using three constructs that the typechecker treats specially: null checks, type-querying built-in functions like is_integer(), and instanceof. When these constructs are used in control flow statements like loops and if statements, the type inference engine understands that this means types are different on different control flow paths.

Refining Nullable Types to Non-Nullable

Null checks are used to refine nullable types into non-nullable types. This example passes the typechecker:

```
function takes_string(string $str) {
  // ...
}
```

---

6 Except when it doesn't. See "Integer Arithmetic Overflow" on page 85.

```
function takes_nullable_string(?string $str) {
  if ($str !== null) {
    takes_string($str);
  }
  // ...
}
```

Inside the `if` block, the typechecker knows that `$str` is a non-nullable string, and thus that it can be passed to `takes_string()`. Note that null checks should use the identity comparison operators `===` and `!==` instead of equality comparison (`==` and `!=`) or conversion to a boolean; if you don't use identity comparison, the typechecker will issue an error.[7] The built-in function `is_null()` also works, as do ternary expressions:

```
function takes_nullable_string(?string $str) {
  takes_string($str === null ? "(null)" : $str);
  // ...
}
```

You can also use this style, where one branch of control flow is cut off:

```
function processInfo(?string $info) {
  if ($info === null) {
    return;
  }
  takes_string($info);
}
```

The typechecker understands that the call to `takes_string()` will only be executed if `$info` is not `null`, because if it is `null`, the `if` block will be entered and the function will return. (If the `return` statement were a `throw` instead, or a call to a `noreturn` function, the effect would be the same.)

Here's a slightly bigger example that demonstrates more complex control flow sensitivity:

```
function fetch_from_cache(): ?string {
  // ...
}

function do_expensive_computation(): string {
  // ...
}

function get_data(): string {
  $result = fetch_from_cache();
  if ($result === null) {
    $result = do_expensive_computation();
```

---

7 This is because, for example, `null == "0"` is true, which makes the null check at least slightly nonsensical.

```
    }
    return $result;
}
```

At the point of the `return` statement, the typechecker knows that `$result` is a non-null string, so the return type annotation is satisfied. If the `if` block was entered, then a non-null string was assigned to `$result`; if the `if` block wasn't entered, then `$result` must have already been a non-null string.

Finally, Hack includes a special built-in function called `invariant()`, which you can use essentially to state facts to the typechecker. It takes two arguments—a boolean expression, and a string describing what's being asserted (for human readers' benefit):

```
function processInfo(?string $info) {
    invariant($info !== null, "I know it's never null somehow");
    takes_string($info);
}
```

At runtime, if the first argument to `invariant()` turns out to be `false`, an `InvariantException` will be thrown. The typechecker knows this and infers that in the code after the `invariant()` call, `$info` cannot be `null`, because otherwise an exception would have been thrown and execution wouldn't have reached that code.

Refining Mixed Types to Primitives

For each primitive type, there is a built-in function to check whether a variable is of that type (e.g., `is_integer()`, `is_string()`, `is_array()`). The typechecker recognizes all of them specially, except for `is_object()`.[8] You'll often be using them on values of type `mixed`, or of a generic type.

The way you use these built-ins to give information to the typechecker is largely the same as the way you use null checks—the typechecker is control flow–sensitive, you can use `invariant()`, and so on. However, the type information these built-ins carry is more complex than just "null or not null," so there's a bit more detail in how inference works with them.

First, the typechecker doesn't remember negative information like "this value is *not* a string." For example:

```
function f(mixed $val) {
    if (!is_string($val)) {
        // $val is of type "mixed" here--we don't remember it's not a string
    } else {
```

---

8 This is because `is_object()` returns `true` for resources. The lack of support for `is_object()` isn't a problem in practice, because you can't really do anything useful with an object without knowing its class.

```
    // $val is of type "string" here
  }
}
```

In practice, this isn't much of a hindrance: there's little that could usefully be done with a value that we know is "anything but a string," other than refine its type further.

Second, the type-querying built-ins are the *only* way to refine types down to primitives. Even doing identity comparison against values of known type doesn't work:

```
function f(mixed $val) {
  if ($val === 'some string') {
    // $val is of type "mixed" here
    // Only is_string would tell the typechecker it's a string
  }
}
```

Refining Object Types

Finally, the typechecker understands using `instanceof` to check if an object is an instance of a given class or interface. Like null checks and type-querying built-ins, the typechecker understands `instanceof` in conditional statements and in `invariant()`:

```
class ParentClass {
}

class ChildClass extends ParentClass {
  public function doChildThings(): void {
    // ...
  }
}

function doThings(ParentClass $obj): void {
  if ($obj instanceof ChildClass) {
    $obj->doChildThings();  // OK
  }
}

function unconditionallyDoThings(ParentClass $obj): void {
  invariant($obj instanceof ChildClass, 'just trust me');
  $obj->doChildThings();  // OK
}
```

There are more details to cover here. Unlike null checks and the type-querying built-ins, `instanceof` deals with types that can overlap in complex ways, and the typechecker's ability to navigate them is slightly limited.

This example demonstrates the limitations—we have an abstract base class, with possibly many subclasses, some of which implement the built-in interface `Countable` and some of which don't:

```
abstract class BaseClass {
  abstract public function twist(): void;
}

class CountableSubclass extends BaseClass implements Countable {
  public function count(): int {
    // ...
  }
  public function twist(): void {
    // ...
  }
}

class NonCountableSubclass extends BaseClass {
  public function twist(): void {
    // ...
  }
}
```

Then we have a function that takes a `BaseClass`, calls `count()` on it if it's `Countable`, and then calls a method that `BaseClass` declares. This is a fairly common pattern in object-oriented codebases, albeit with interfaces other than `Countable`:

```
function twist_and_count(BaseClass $obj): void {
  if ($obj instanceof Countable) {
    echo 'Count: ' . $obj->count();
  }
  $obj->twist();
}
```

On the last line, there is a type error. This probably seems entirely unexpected, so let's go into detail about why.

The key to understanding the error is that when the typechecker sees an `instanceof` check, the information it derives from this is *exactly what the check says*, and it doesn't take inheritance hierarchies, interfaces, or anything else into account. It may even be the case that the condition is provably impossible to satisfy (e.g. if `Countable` were not implemented by `BaseClass` or any of its descendants), but the typechecker doesn't consider that.

At the beginning of the function, the typechecker thinks the type of `$obj` is `Base Class`, because of the annotation. But then, within the `if` block, the typechecker thinks that the type of `$obj` is `Countable`—not a `BaseClass` instance that implements `Countable`; just `Countable`. It has *forgotten* that `$obj` is also a `BaseClass`.

Then we come to the part after the `if` block. Here, the type of `$obj` is an unresolved type (see "Unresolved Types" on page 29) consisting of either `BaseClass` or `Countable`. So when it sees `$obj->twist()`, it reports an error, because it thinks there are possible values of `$obj` for which the call isn't valid—ones that are `Countable` but not `BaseClass`. You, the human reader, know that this isn't possible, but the type-checker doesn't.

The workaround for this is to use a separate local variable for the `instanceof` check. This prevents the typechecker from losing type information about `$obj`, which is the root cause of the problem:

```
function twist_and_count(BaseClass $obj) {
  $obj_countable = $obj;
  if ($obj_countable instanceof Countable) {
    echo 'Count: ' . $obj_countable->count();
  }
  $obj->twist();
}
```

In all of the situations just described, the condition in the `if` statement or `invariant()` call must be just a single type query. Combining multiple type queries with logical operators like `||` isn't supported by the typechecker. For example, this is a type error:

```
class Parent {
}
class One extends Parent {
  public function go(): void {}
}
class Two extends Parent {
  public function go(): void {}
}

function f(Parent $obj): void {
  if ($obj instanceof One || $obj instanceof Two) {
    $obj->go();  // Error
  }
}
```

A good way to work around this is with interfaces. Create an interface that declares the `go()` method, make `One` and `Two` implement it, and check for that interface in `f()`.

Inference on Properties

All our examples of inference so far have been on local variables. This is easy: the typechecker can be confident that it can see all reads and writes of local variables,[9] so it can make fairly strong guarantees when doing type inference on them.

---

9 As we've seen, the typechecker pretends that references don't exist; if you pass a local variable as a by-reference argument to a function, the typechecker assumes that it won't be changed.

Doing inference on properties is more difficult. The root of the problem is that, whereas local variables can't be modified from outside the function they're in, properties can. Consider this code, for example:

```
function increment_check_count(): void {
  // ...
}

function check_for_valid_characters(string $name): void {
  // ...
}

class C {
  private ?string $name;

  public function checkName(): void {
    if ($this->name !== null) {
      increment_check_count();
      check_for_valid_characters($this->name);
    }
  }
}
```

This code will *not* pass the typechecker. It will report an error:

```
/home/oyamauchi/test.php:16:34,44: Invalid argument (Typing[4110])
  /home/oyamauchi/test.php:6:37,42: This is a string
  /home/oyamauchi/test.php:11:11,17: It is incompatible with a nullable type
  /home/oyamauchi/test.php:15:7,29: All the local information about the member
  name has been invalidated during this call.
This is a limitation of the type-checker, use a local if that's the problem.
```

The error points to the call to check_for_valid_characters(). The error message gives a brief explanation of the problem. After the null check, the typechecker knows that $this->name is not null. However, the call to increment_check_count() forces the typechecker to *forget* that $this->name is not null, because that fact could be changed as a result of the call.

You, the programmer, might know that the value of $this->name won't change as a result of the call to increment_check_count(), but the typechecker can't find that out for itself—as we've seen, inference is function-local. The workaround for this is, as the error message says, to use a local variable. Copy the property into a local variable and use that instead:

```
public function checkName(): void {
  if ($this->name !== null) {
    $local_name = $this->name;
    Logger::log('checking name: ' . $local_name);
    check_for_valid_characters($local_name);
  }
}
```

You could also make the copy outside of the `if` block, and null-check the local instead. Either way, the typechecker can be sure that `$local_name` is not modified, and so it can remember its inferred non-nullable type.

Enforcement of Type Annotations at Runtime

HHVM and the typechecker report errors in different situations. It is possible for the typechecker to report errors in a program, but for that program to work exactly as intended at runtime. However, in the default configuration, this doesn't happen: HHVM is configured to invoke the typechecker at runtime, and refuse to run a file with typechecker errors in it. (See "Important Options" on page 198 for more on how to change this, through the option `hhvm.hack.lang.look_for_typechecker`.)

Conversely, it's possible for a program that passes the typechecker to result in errors at runtime, because of the typechecker's leniency with non-annotated code in partial and decl modes (see "Code Without Annotations" on page 18). This example—note that it's in partial mode—will pass the typechecker, but will result in a catchable fatal error at runtime:

```
<?hh

function supposed_to_return_a_string() {
  return 123;  // OK: no return type annotation, so no error
}

function takes_a_string(string $str): void {
  // ...
}

takes_a_string(supposed_to_return_a_string());
```

In future releases, HHVM's own enforcement of types at runtime will become much stricter, but for now it has only partial support for checking type annotations at runtime.

First of all, HHVM ignores property type annotations. You can assign anything you like to a type-annotated property, and HHVM won't complain.

Parameter type annotations behave just like PHP typehints: if they're violated, a catchable fatal error will be raised.[10] Return type annotations behave the same way.

You can make any parameter or return type annotation raise a warning instead of a catchable fatal error if violated, by putting an @ before it. This is called a *soft* annotation. Soft annotations are meant solely as a transitional mechanism while adding new

---

10 "Catchable fatal" may sound like an oxymoron. These errors do have odd behavior: the only way to "catch" them is with a user error handler, which you can set using the built-in function `set_error_handler()`.

annotations to existing code (see "Inferring and Adding Type Annotations" on page 242). They shouldn't be used in new code, and existing hard annotations should certainly never be made soft.

In both parameter type annotations and return type annotations, some of the details of Hack type annotations are not enforced:

- Any annotation of a primitive type, object type, `num`, or `arraykey` is enforced exactly as is.

- The return type `void` is not enforced. That is, a function with return type `void` can return an actual value, and no error will occur at runtime.

- The `this` return type is not enforced.

- The `noreturn` return type is enforced. That is, returning normally from a `noreturn` function will result in a catchable fatal. However, the catchable fatal means that the function appears, to the caller, to have not returned normally. So violating `noreturn` will actually end up making the `noreturn` correct!

- Nullable types are enforced, as long as the type being made nullable is enforced.

- Callable type annotations are not enforced.

- Annotations of tuples and shapes are enforced as if they said only `array`. The inner types aren't checked.

- Annotations of enums are enforced as if they were the underlying type of the enum. At runtime, values will not be checked to make sure they're valid values of the enum.

- Generic type annotations are enforced without their type parameters. That is, an annotation of `array<string, MyClass>` is enforced as if it just said `array`. The inner types aren't checked.

- Annotations of type constants are not enforced.

CHAPTER 2

Generics

Generics are a powerful feature of Hack's type system that allow you to write typesafe code without knowing what types will be flowing through it. A class or function can be generic, which means that it lets the caller specify what types flow through it.

The best examples of generic constructs are arrays and collection classes (see Chapter 5 for more information on collection classes). Without the ability to specify the type of an array's contents, it would be impossible to infer a type for any value that results from indexing into an array, and setting a value in an array couldn't be typechecked. These operations are pervasive in PHP and Hack code, and generics let the typechecker understand and verify them.

In this chapter, we'll look at all the features that generics offer, and how to use them.

Introductory Example

We'll start with a very simple example: a class that just wraps an arbitrary value. You would probably never write such a thing in practice,[1] but it's a good gentle introduction to generics. We'll use it as a running example throughout this chapter.

To make a class generic, put an angle bracket–enclosed, comma-separated list of *type parameters* immediately after the name of the class. A type parameter is simply an identifier whose name starts with an uppercase T.

---

1 It's not as useless as it may seem, though—this is a good way to have something resembling reference semantics for primitive types. This is more useful in Hack than in PHP, because PHP-style references aren't allowed in Hack.

Inside the definition of a generic class, you can use the type parameters in type annotations, in any of the three normal positions (properties, method parameters, and method return types), *except* in the type of a static property.

Here's our example generic class:

```
class Wrapper<Tval> {
  private Tval $value;

  public function __construct(Tval $value) {
    $this->value = $value;
  }

  public function setValue(Tval $value): void {
    $this->value = $value;
  }

  public function getValue(): Tval {
    return $this->value;
  }
}

// There can be multiple type parameters
class DualWrapper<Tone, Ttwo> {
  // ...
}
```

To use a generic class, you simply instantiate it as normal, and use the resulting object like any other:

```
$wrapper = new Wrapper(20);
$x = $wrapper->getValue();
```

In this example, thanks to Wrapper being generic, the typechecker knows that $x is an integer. It sees that you're passing an integer to the constructor of Wrapper, and infers that it should typecheck usages of that particular Wrapper instance as though the class definition said int instead of Tval everywhere.

The typechecking that you get in this situation is just as strong as it would be if you used this class instead of Wrapper:

```
class WrapperOfInt {
  private int $value;

  public function __construct(int $value) {
    $this->value = $value;
  }

  public function setValue(int $value): void {
    $this->value = $value;
  }
```

```
    public function getValue(): int {
      return $this->value;
    }
  }
```

The generic version, though, has the significant benefit that you can use it with any type. If you pass a string to the constructor of `Wrapper`, the return type of `getValue()` on that instance is `string`. If you pass a value of type `?float` to the constructor of `Wrapper`, the return type of `getValue()` on that instance is `?float`. And so on, with any other type you can think of.

This is the true power of generics: you can write a single implementation of `Wrapper` that wraps a value of any type, but that is still completely typesafe.

As the final piece of this introduction, here's how to write a type annotation for an instance of a generic class. The syntax is the name of the class, followed by an angle bracket–enclosed, comma-separated list of type annotations. Each annotation in the list is called a *type argument*:

```
function wrapped_input(): Wrapper<string> {
  $input = readline("Enter text: ");
  return new Wrapper($input);
}
```

The relationship between type parameters and type arguments is the same as the relationship between function parameters and function arguments: the type arguments are substituted for the uses of the type parameters in the generic class definition. In this case, the function is returning an instance of `Wrapper`, telling the typechecker that it should typecheck usages of this object as if the class definition said `string` instead of `Tval` everywhere.

Other Generic Entities

Classes aren't the only kind of entity that can be made generic.

Functions and Methods

A generic function has a list of type parameters between its name and the opening parenthesis of its parameter list. It can be called like any other:

```
function wrap<T>(T $value): Wrapper<T> {
  return new Wrapper($value);
}

function main(): void {
  $w = wrap(20);
}
```

As this example shows, a generic function's type parameters can be used in the function's parameter types and return type.

Methods may also be generic. If a method is in a generic class or trait, it can use its enclosing class's type parameters, as well as introducing its own:

```
class Logger {
  public function logWrapped<Tval>(Wrapper<Tval> $value): void {
    // ...
  }
}

class Processor<Tconfig> {
  public function checkValue<Tval>(Tconfig $config, Tval $value): bool {
    // ...
  }
}
```

Traits and Interfaces

Both traits and interfaces can be generic. The syntax is very similar to generic class syntax, with the type parameter list after the name:

```
trait DebugLogging<Tval> {
  public static function debugLog(Tval $value): void {
    // ...
  }
}

interface WorkItem<Tresult> {
  public function performWork(): Tresult;
}
```

Anything that uses a generic trait, or implements a generic interface, must specify type arguments:

```
class StringProducingWorkItem implements WorkItem<string> {
  use DebugLogging<string>;

  // ...
}
```

A generic class can pass along its type parameters to interfaces that it implements or traits that it uses:

```
class ConcreteWorkItem<Tresult> implements WorkItem<Tresult> {
  use DebugLogging<Tresult>;

  // ...
}
```

Type Aliases

See "Type Aliases" on page 62 for full details on type aliases. They can be made generic by adding a list of type parameters immediately after the alias name:

```
type matrix<T> = array<array<T>>;
```

There is an interesting application of generics to type aliases in which you don't use the type parameter on the right hand side. A good example is serialization:

```
newtype serialized<T> = string;

function typed_serialize<T>(T $value): serialized<T> {
  return serialize($value);
}

function typed_unserialize<T>(serialized<T> $value): T {
  return unserialize($value);
}
```

This alias lets the typechecker distinguish between the serialized versions of various types, whereas the normal untyped `serialize()` API loses information about the type of the serialized value. It works without typechecker errors because it's essentially unchecked: `unserialize()` has no return type annotation, so the typechecker simply trusts that whatever you do with its return value is correct (see "Code Without Annotations" on page 18).

Here, the typechecker knows that `$unserialized` is a string:

```
$serialized_str = typed_serialize("hi");
$unserialized = typed_unserialize($serialized_str);
```

You can also make guarantees about the type of a serialized value:

```
function process_names(serialized<array<string>> $arr): void {
  foreach (typed_unserialize($arr) as $name) {
    // $name is known to be a string here
    // ...
  }
}
```

Type Erasure

Generics are a purely typechecker-level construct—HHVM is almost completely unaware of their existence.[2] In effect, when HHVM runs generic code, it's as if all type parameters and type arguments were stripped. This behavior is known as *type erasure*.

---

2 The lone exception is in the return types of async functions. See Chapter 6.

This has important consequences for what you can and can't do with type parameters inside the definition of a generic entity. The only thing you can do with a type parameter is to use it in a type annotation. Here are things you can't do with a type parameter that you can do with some other types:

- Instantiate it, as in `new T()`.

- Use it as a scope, as in `T::someStaticMethod()` or `T::$someStaticProperty` or `T::SOME_CONSTANT`.

- Pass it type arguments, as in `function f<T>(T<mixed> $value)`.

- Put it on the right hand side of `instanceof`, as in `$value instanceof T`.

- Cast to it, as in `(T)$value`.

- Use it in place of a class name in a `catch` block, as in:

  ```
  function f<Texc>(): void {
    try {
      something_that_throws();
    } catch (Texc $exception) {  // Error
      // ...
    }
  }
  ```

When type parameters are used as type annotations, they are not enforced at runtime. In this example, we use decl mode so that the typechecker doesn't report errors on the method calls in `f()`:

```
<?hh // decl

class GenericClass<T> {
  public function takes_type_param(T $x): void {
  }

  public function takes_int(int $x): void {
  }
}

function f(GenericClass<int> $gc): void {
  // Both calls below would be typechecker errors,
  // but this file is in decl mode

  // No runtime error
  $gc->takes_type_param('a string');

  // Runtime error: catchable fatal
  $gc->takes_int('a string');
}
```

Constraints

Within the definition of a generic entity, the typechecker knows nothing about the type parameters—that's the whole point of generics. This means you can't do much with a value whose type is a type parameter, other than pass it around. You can't call it, call methods or access properties on it, index into it, do arithmetic operations on it, or anything like that—the one significant exception is that equality and identity comparisons (==, ===, !=, and !==) are allowed.

You can change that, though, by adding a *constraint* to the type parameter. A constraint restricts what the type parameter is allowed to be. The syntax is to add the keyword as and a type annotation after the identifier in the type parameter list. Let's return to the introductory example of the Wrapper class, and add a constraint to its type parameter:

```
class Wrapper<Tval as num> {
  private Tval $value;

  public function __construct(Tval $value) {
    $this->value = $value;
  }

  public function setValue(Tval $value): void {
    $this->value = $value;
  }

  public function getValue(): Tval {
    return $this->value;
  }
}
```

With that, any code that uses the class can only do so with a value whose type is compatible with num:

```
function f(int $int, float $float, num $num,
          ?int $nullint, string $string, mixed $mixed): void {
  $w = new Wrapper($int);     // OK
  $w = new Wrapper($float);   // OK
  $w = new Wrapper($num);     // OK
  $w = new Wrapper($nullint); // Error
  $w = new Wrapper($string);  // Error
  $w = new Wrapper($mixed);   // Error
}
```

This also means that within the definition of Wrapper, the allowable operations on values of type Tval are the same as the allowable operations on values of type num. So we can add a method like this:

```
class Wrapper<Tval as num> {
  private Tval $value;
```

```
public function add(Tval $addend): void {
  // $this->value is known to be a num, so we can use the += operator on it
  $this->value += $addend;
}

// ...
}
```

You can use any valid type annotation as the constraint. The most common case is to use the name of a class or interface, which lets you call methods declared by the class or interface:

```
interface HasID {
  public function getID(): int;
}

function write_to_database<Tval as HasID>(Tval $value): void {
  $id = $value->getID();
  // ...
}
```

Each type parameter can have at most one constraint. If you want to restrict a type parameter to only classes that implement multiple specific interfaces, you can create an interface that combines them by extending all of them, and use that as your constraint:

```
interface HasID {
  public function getID(): int;
}
interface HasHashCode {
  public function getHashCode(): string;
}

interface HasIDAndHashCode extends HasID, HasHashCode {
}

function write_to_cache<Tval as HasIDAndHashCode>(Tval $value): void {
  $id = $value->getID();
  $hash_code = $value->getHashCode();
  // ...
}
```

There's no way to express a constraint like Tval must implement this interface *or* that interface.

As we've seen, a constraint type can be any valid type annotation; this includes other type parameters, and even type parameters from earlier in the same parameter list. For example, these usages of constraints are valid:

```
class GenericClass<Tclass> {
  public function genericMethod<Tmethod as Tclass>(): Tmethod {
```

```
    // ...
  }
}

function lookup<Tvalue, Tdefault as Tvalue>(string $key,
                                ?Tdefault $default = null): Tvalue {
  // ...
}
```

Unresolved Types, Revisited

In the introductory example, we saw that the typechecker is able to infer type arguments for generic classes when you use them. Here, the typechecker knows that Wrapper is being instantiated with int substituted for the type parameter Tval:

```
$w = new Wrapper(20);
```

The exact details of the inference algorithm are beyond our scope here, but it has some consequences that you need to know about.

Should the typechecker accept this code?

```
function takes_wrapper_of_int(Wrapper<int> $w): void {
  // ...
}

function main(int $n): void {
  $wrapper = new Wrapper($n);
  takes_wrapper_of_int($wrapper);
}
```

Intuitively, it seems like it should be allowed, and in fact it is. The typechecker knows, on the last line of main(), that $wrapper is a wrapper of an integer, and allows the call.

What about this?

```
function main(string $str): void {
  $wrapper = new Wrapper($str);
  takes_wrapper_of_int($wrapper);
}
```

It seems as if this shouldn't be allowed, and indeed it isn't.

What if we try the following instead?

```
function main(int $n, string $str): void {
  $w = new Wrapper($n);
  $w->setValue($str);
}
```

As we saw in the first example, the typechecker seems to understand that $wrapper is a Wrapper<int> after the first line. So it seems like the typechecker should report an error: you shouldn't be able to pass a string as an argument to setValue() on a Wrapper<int>. But in fact, this code is legal.

This is another place where the typechecker uses *unresolved types*. We first saw them in "Unresolved Types" on page 29, where they were used as a way for the typechecker to track a variable that could have multiple different types at a single point in a program, depending on the path taken to get there. With generics, the typechecker uses unresolved types to remember types that haven't been explicitly specified, while retaining the freedom to adjust them as it sees more code.

After the first line, the typechecker is certain that $w is a Wrapper, but there has been no explicit indication of what its type argument is. It remembers that it has seen this object being used in a way that's consistent with it having the type Wrapper<int>, but that type argument of int is an unresolved type. Then, upon seeing the call $w->setValue('a string'), the typechecker looks at the type of $w to see if the call is legal. When it sees the unresolved type argument, instead of raising an error, it adds string to the unresolved type. So, as far as the typechecker is concerned, $w could be either a Wrapper<int> or a Wrapper<string>.

To the human reader, this is unintuitive: obviously there's a string inside $w. But the typechecker is unaware of the semantics of Wrapper: it doesn't understand that Wrapper only holds a single value. All the typechecker knows is that it has seen $w being used as if it were a Wrapper<int>, and also as if it were a Wrapper<string>.

An unresolved type argument becomes *resolved* when it is checked against a type annotation. This example brings everything together:

```
function takes_wrapper_of_int(Wrapper<int> $w): void {
  // ...
}

function main(): void {
  $w = new Wrapper(20);
  takes_wrapper_of_int($w);
  $w->setValue('a string');  // Error!
}
```

This time, the typechecker reports an error on the last line. When $w is passed to takes_wrapper_of_int(), it has to be checked against the function's parameter type annotation. At that point, the type of $w is resolved; the typechecker has seen concrete evidence that $w is supposed to be a Wrapper<int>. Now that the type is resolved, the typechecker will not be lenient in checking calls to setValue(). Calling setValue('a string') on a Wrapper instance with resolved type Wrapper<int> is invalid, so the typechecker reports an error.

Generics and Subtypes

Let's return to the introductory example of the `Wrapper` class. Should the typechecker accept this code?

```
function takes_wrapper_of_num(Wrapper<num> $w): void {
  // ...
}

function takes_wrapper_of_int(Wrapper<int> $w): void {
  takes_wrapper_of_num($w);
}
```

The question is whether it's valid to pass a wrapper of an integer to something that expects a wrapper of a num. It seems like it should be: `int` is a subtype of `num` (meaning any value that is an `int` is also a `num`), so it seems that `Wrapper<int>` should likewise be a subtype of `Wrapper<num>`.

In fact, the typechecker reports an error for this example. It would be incorrect for the typechecker to assume that the subtype relationship of `int` and `num` transfers over to the subtype relationship between `Wrapper<int>` and `Wrapper<num>`.

To illustrate why, consider that `takes_wrapper_of_num()` could do this:

```
function takes_wrapper_of_num(Wrapper<num> $w): void {
  $w->setValue(3.14159);
}
```

That, by itself, is valid: setting the value inside a `Wrapper<num>` to a value of type `float`. But if you pass a `Wrapper<int>` to this version of `takes_wrapper_of_num()`, it will end up not being a wrapper of an integer anymore. So the typechecker can't accept passing a `Wrapper<int>` to `takes_wrapper_of_num()`; it's not typesafe. Note that that's a hard rule—the typechecker doesn't consider what `takes_wrapper_of_num()` is actually doing. Even if `takes_wrapper_of_num()` were empty, the typechecker would still report an error.

Now for another example: should the typechecker accept this?

```
function returns_wrapper_of_int(): Wrapper<int> {
  // ...
}

function returns_wrapper_of_num(): Wrapper<num> {
  return returns_wrapper_of_int();
}
```

Again, although this intuitively seems fine, the typechecker reports an error. The reasoning is similar. Suppose we fill in the blanks like this:

```
function returns_wrapper_of_int(): Wrapper<int> {
  static $w = new Wrapper(20);
  return $w;
}

function returns_wrapper_of_num(): Wrapper<num> {
  return returns_wrapper_of_int();
}

function main(): void {
  $wrapper_of_num = returns_wrapper_of_num();
  $wrapper_of_num->setValue(2.71828);
}
```

This is clearly invalid—after `main()` executes, any call to `returns_wrapper_of_int()` will return a wrapper of something that's not an `int`. So, again, the typechecker has to report an error for the `return` statement in `returns_wrapper_of_num()`.

Arrays and Collections

Arrays and immutable Hack collection classes—`ImmVector`, `ImmMap`, `ImmSet`, and `Pair`—behave differently. They follow the intuitive notion that, for example, `array<int>` is a subtype of `array<num>`. This usage of arrays, for example, is valid:

```
function takes_array_of_num(array<num> $arr): void {
  // ...
}

function takes_array_of_int(array<int> $arr): void {
  takes_array_of_num($arr);  // OK
}
```

Similar behavior holds for the value types[3] of immutable collection classes, regardless of whether you annotate them with their own names or (as is recommended) with interface names like `ConstVector`:

```
function takes_constvector_of_num(ConstVector<num> $cv): void {
  // ...
}
function takes_constvector_of_int(ConstVector<int> $cv): void {
  takes_constvector_of_num($cv);  // OK
}


function takes_constmap_of_arraykey_mixed(ConstMap<string, mixed> $cm): void {
  // ...
```

---

3 It doesn't hold for key types because of variance rules (see "Advanced: Covariance and Contravariance" on page 53). The key type parameter appears in contravariant positions, like the parameter of `get()`, so it can't be covariant. This is likely to change in the future, as a special case.

```
  }
  function takes_constmap_of_string_int(ConstMap<string, int> $cm): void {
    takes_constmap_of_arraykey_mixed($cm);   // OK
  }
```

Why is this valid for arrays and immutable collections, but not for `Wrapper`?

In the case of immutable collections, the reason is simply that they're immutable. Even if you pass an `ImmVector<int>` to a function that takes an `ImmVector<num>`, that function has no way to get a non-integer value into the vector. There's nothing it can do to violate the contract that the vector must only contain integers.

In the case of arrays, the reason is similar. For this purpose, arrays behave very much like immutable collections because of their pass-by-value semantics. In the previous example, from the perspective of `takes_array_of_num()`, the array in the body of `takes_array_of_int()` actually is read-only. `takes_array_of_num()` can't cause that array to have non-integers in it, because it doesn't have access to the original array; it only has access to a copy.

Advanced: Covariance and Contravariance

Unless you're writing some very general, collection-like library, it's very unlikely that you need to read past here. For the vast majority of use cases, all you need is to know that the rules just discussed exist, and to understand why. This section is about how to modify those rules when you need to.

The concept of how the subtype relationships of generic types are affected by the subtype relationships of their type arguments is called *variance*. There are three kinds of variance. Suppose we have a generic class called `Thing`, with a type parameter T. Then (using `int` and `num` as example type arguments):

- If `Thing<int>` is a subtype of `Thing<num>`, we say that `Thing` is *covariant on* T. Arrays are covariant on both their type parameters, and immutable collection classes are covariant on their value type parameters.

- If `Thing<num>` is a subtype of `Thing<int>`, we say that `Thing` is *contravariant on* T. Counterintuitive though it may be, there are real applications for contravariance.

- If neither of the above is true, we say that `Thing` is *invariant on* T.

Syntax

The syntax to make a generic type covariant on a type parameter is to put a plus sign before the type parameter. You only do this in the parameter list; within the definition, just use the type parameter's name as before. Similarly, to make a generic type contravariant on a type parameter, put a minus sign before the type parameter. For example:

```
class CovariantOnT<+T> {
  private T $value;  // No + here
  // ...
}

class ContravariantOnT<-T> {
  private T $value;  // No - here
  // ...
}

class InvariantOnT<T> {
  private T $value;
  // ...
}
```

A class is allowed to have type parameters with different variances:

```
class DifferentVariances<Tinvariant, +Tcovariant, -Tcontravariant> {
  // ...
}
```

Here are some memory aids you can use to remember the terms and the syntax:

Covariance
> The prefix *co-* means "with," and the subtype relationship of a generic type goes *with*—"in the same direction as"—the subtype relationship of arguments to a covariant type parameter. Because they go together, the symbol is a plus sign.

Contravariance
> The prefix *contra-* means "against," and the subtype relationship of a generic type goes *against* the subtype relationship of arguments to a contravariant type parameter. Because they go in opposite directions, the symbol is a minus sign.

When to Use Them

Most classes you write won't use covariance or contravariance. These features are useful in a few specific situations:

- Covariance is for *read-only* types. For example, if we remove the setValue() method from Wrapper, then it's read-only with respect to its type parameter Tval —that is, it only outputs values of type Tval; it never takes them as input except in the constructor. So, Wrapper can be covariant on Tval.[4]

---

[4] Note that Wrapper could have read/write functionality that doesn't involve Tval, and Tval could still be covariant. The read-only nature of Tval is what counts, not the read-only nature of Wrapper.

- Contravariance is for *write-only* types. For example, a generic class that serializes values of type T to a logfile might be write-only with respect to values of type T—that is, it only takes values of type T as input; it never outputs them.

The typechecker enforces this by setting restrictions on how you can use covariant and contravariant type parameters. Specifically, each kind of type parameter is only allowed to appear in certain places in the code, called *covariant positions* and *contravariant positions*.

First, the simple part:

- Public and protected property types are restricted to invariant type parameters only.
- Return types are restricted to invariant or covariant type parameters. These are covariant positions.
- Function and method parameter types, except constructors, are restricted to invariant or contravariant type parameters. These are contravariant positions.
- Private property types and constructor parameter types have no type parameter restrictions.

Now, the slightly tricky part. It is possible to have a contravariant position *inside* another contravariant position, in which case the inner contravariant position is actually *covariant*. Here's an example:

```
class WriteOnly<-T> {
  private T $value;

  public function __construct(T $value) {
    $this->value = $value;
  }

  // Error!
  public function passToCallback((function(T): void) $callback): void {
    $callback($this->value);
  }
}
```

The contravariant type parameter T appears in a parameter type (the type of $call back) inside another parameter type (the type of passToCallback()). This is a contravariant position inside another contravariant position, so it's covariant, and thus invalid.

You can see why this is, intuitively: the way passToCallback() is written makes it possible for something outside of WriteOnly to get a value of type T out of a Write Only instance, which makes it not actually write-only.

A covariant position inside a covariant position is still covariant. Covariance and contravariance work somewhat like positive and negative numbers under multiplication: positive times positive is positive, but negative times negative is also positive.

Covariance

Let's remove `setValue()` from `Wrapper`, and make its type parameter covariant:

```
class Wrapper<+Tval> {
  private Tval $value;

  public function __construct(Tval $val) {
    $this->value = $val;
  }

  public function getValue(): Tval {
    return $this->value;
  }
}
```

The covariant type parameter `Tval` appears as the type of a private property, a parameter to the constructor, and a return type; all of these are positions where covariant type parameters are allowed. The typechecker will accept this code without error.

The next example is also accepted now. The restrictions placed on the covariant type parameter ensure that there's no way to break type safety while treating a `Wrapper<int>` as a `Wrapper<num>`:

```
function takes_wrapper_of_num(Wrapper<num> $w): void {
  // ...
}

function takes_wrapper_of_int(Wrapper<int> $w): void {
  takes_wrapper_of_num($w);   // OK
}
```

If you add a method to modify the value, the typechecker will report an error, saying that a covariant type parameter is appearing in a non-covariant position:

```
class Wrapper<+Tval> {
  public function setValue(Tval $value): void {   // Error
    $this->value = $value;
  }

  // ...
}
```

Similarly, if you change the `$value` property's access modifier to `public` or `protected`, the typechecker will report an error, saying that a non-private property is always an invariant position—i.e., you can't use covariant or contravariant type parameters there.

Contravariance

Contravariant types are less common, simply because write-only types are less common than read-only types. We'll look at contravariance through a class that builds up a buffer of values and then writes them as JSON to a stream:

```
class JSONLogger<-Tval> {
  private resource $stream;
  private array<Tval> $buffer = array();

  public function __construct(resource $stream) {
    $this->stream = $stream;
  }

  public function log(Tval $value): void {
    $buffer[] = $value;
  }

  public function flush(): void {
    fwrite($this->stream, json_encode($this->buffer));
    $this->buffer = array();
  }
}
```

Note that the contravariant type parameter Tval only appears in a method parameter and a private property, so the typechecker accepts this code. If you were to make $buffer public or protected, or add a method with Tval in the return type, the typechecker would report an error.

The contravariant type parameter means that JSONLogger<num> is a subtype of JSONLogger<int>, which may seem counterintuitive. This code demonstrates:

```
function wants_to_log_ints(JSONLogger<int> $logger): void {
  $logger->log(20);
}

function wants_to_log_nums(JSONLogger<num> $logger): void {
  wants_to_log_ints($logger);   // OK
  $logger->log(3.14);
}
```

The code here is passing a JSONLogger<num> to something that expects a JSONLogger<int>. This is fine, because a JSONLogger<num> can do anything that a JSONLogger<int> can (and more). Because there's no way to get a value of type Tval back *out* of a JSONLogger, no code outside the class can get a value from it of a type that it doesn't expect.

CHAPTER 3

Other Features of Hack

Hack has four major features that make the language different from PHP in fundamental ways: typechecking, collections, asynchronous (async) functions, and XHP. Beyond those, though, there's a wide range of smaller features that are designed to simplify certain common patterns or to address minor gaps.

Enums

An enum (short for *enumeration*) is a collection of related constants. Unlike simply creating global constants or class constants, creating an enum results in a new type: you can use the names of enums in type annotations. They also offer functionality like getting an array of all valid names or values, without resorting to heavyweight reflection APIs.

The syntax for an enum is the keyword `enum`, followed by a name for the enum, then a colon, then either `int` or `string` (which will be the enum's *underlying type*), then a brace-enclosed, semicolon-separated list of enum members. Each member is a name, followed by an equals sign and then a value (which must match the enum's underlying type):

```
enum CardSuit : int {
  SPADES = 0;
  HEARTS = 1;
  CLUBS = 2;
  DIAMONDS = 3;
}
```

Enum names have the same restrictions as class names (with regard to what characters they may contain, etc.), and it's an error to have a class and an enum with the same name.

The names of enum members have the same restrictions as class constant names. The names must be unique within the enum; if there are two members with the same name, the typechecker will report an error, and HHVM will raise a fatal error.

The values of enum members must be scalars; that is, it must be possible to evaluate them statically. This is the same restriction that applies to class constants. The values don't have to be unique within the enum. The only wrinkle if you have non-unique values is that calling `getNames()` on the enum (see "Enum Functions" on page 61) will throw an `InvariantException`.

You access the values with syntax similar to the syntax for class constants:

```
function suit_for_card_index(int $index): CardSuit {
  if ($index < 13) {
    return CardSuit::SPADES;
  } else if ($index < 26) {
    return CardSuit::HEARTS;
  } else if ($index < 39) {
    return CardSuit::CLUBS;
  } else {
    return CardSuit::DIAMONDS;
  }
}
```

Enums are distinct types. For example, even though the underlying type of `CardSuit` is `int`, you can't treat an `int` like a `CardSuit`, and vice versa:

```
function takes_int(int $x): void {
}

function takes_card_suit(CardSuit $suit): void {
}

function main() {
  takes_int(CardSuit::SPADES);  // Error
  takes_card_suit(1);           // Error
}
```

To convert a value of enum type to its underlying type, just use a regular PHP cast expression. To convert in the other direction, use the special enum functions `assert()` or `coerce()`, described in "Enum Functions" on page 61.

You can make it so that an enum type can be implicitly converted to its underlying type by adding the keyword `as` and repeating the underlying type just before the opening curly brace:

```
enum CardSuit : int as int {
  SPADES = 0;
  HEARTS = 1;
  CLUBS = 2;
  DIAMONDS = 3;
```

```
}

function takes_int(int $x): void {
}

function main(): void {
  takes_int(CardSuit::HEARTS);  // OK
}
```

One benefit of enums over class constants is that when a value of enum type is used as the controlling expression of a `switch` statement, the typechecker can ensure that all cases are handled. If some cases aren't handled, the typechecker will report an error, telling you which cases are missing:

```
<?hh // strict
enum CardSuit : int {
  SPADES = 0;
  HEARTS = 1;
  CLUBS = 2;
  DIAMONDS = 3;
}

function suit_symbol(CardSuit $suit): string {
  switch ($suit) {
    case CardSuit::SPADES:
      return "\xe2\x99\xa4";
    case CardSuit::CLUBS:
      return "\xe2\x99\xa7";
  }
}
```

The typechecker reports the following error:

```
/home/oyamauchi/test.php:10:13,17: Switch statement nonexhaustive; the
following cases are missing: HEARTS, DIAMONDS (Typing[4019])
  /home/oyamauchi/test.php:2:6,13: Enum declared here
```

Adding a `default` label will silence the error; you don't have to explicitly handle all the enum members. Note that if you explicitly handle all cases and also have a `default` label, the typechecker will warn you that the `default` is redundant.

Enum Functions

As we've seen so far, enums act like pseudoclasses. They share classes' namespace, and their members are accessed with the same syntax. There's one more similarity: every enum has six static methods that are used for getting information about the enum's members and converting arbitrary values to the enum type.

For example, if you're passed an `int` and you want to use it as a `CardSuit`, you can do this:

```
function takes_card_suit(CardSuit $suit) {
  // ...
}

function legacy_function(int $suit) {
  $enum_suit = CardSuit::coerce($suit);
  if ($enum_suit !== null) {
    takes_card_suit($enum_suit);
  }
}
```

These are all the methods. The return types assume that the enum is named
ExampleEnum:

- `assert(mixed $value): ExampleEnum` returns `$value` cast to the enum type if
  `$value` is of the enum's underlying type and is a member of the enum. If it's not,
  this throws an `UnexpectedValueException`.

- `assertAll(Traversable<mixed> $value): Container<ExampleEnum>` calls
  `assert()` with every value in the given `Traversable` (see "Core Interfaces" on
  page 110) and returns a `Container` of the resulting correctly typed values (or
  throws an `UnexpectedValueException` if any of the values aren't members of the
  enum).

- `coerce(mixed $value): ?ExampleEnum` is like `assert()`, but returns `null` if
  `$value` isn't a member of the enum instead of throwing an exception.

- `getNames(): array<ExampleEnum, string>` returns an array mapping from the
  enum members' values to their names. This will throw an `InvariantException` if
  the values are not unique within the enum.

- `getValues(): array<string, ExampleEnum>` returns an array mapping from
  the enum members' names to their values.

- `isValid(mixed $value): bool` returns whether `$value` is a member of the
  enum.

Type Aliases

Type aliases are a way to give a new name to an existing type. There are two kinds of
type alias—*transparent* and *opaque*—corresponding to two different reasons why you
might want to rename a type.

Transparent Type Aliases

If you're frequently using a complex type, you can give it a simple alias, both to
reduce visual complexity and character count and to make its true meaning clearer.

For example, if you use the type `Map<int, Vector<int>>`, it may be clearer to give it an alias like `UserIDToFriendIDsMap`. This is what transparent aliases are for.

The syntax is simple, consisting of the keyword `type`, followed by the new name for the type, an equals sign, and the type you're renaming (which is called the *underlying type*):

```
type UserIDToFriendIDsMap = Map<int, Vector<int>>;
```

This declaration must be at the top level of a file, not inside any other statements. The type on the right of the equals sign can be any valid type annotation. Once the type alias is defined, the new name can be used in type annotations. Type aliases share a namespace with classes: it's an error to have a type alias with the same name as a class.

The underlying type is not allowed to be `void`, `noreturn`, or `this`; those are all special types that only make sense in certain contexts.

Transparent type aliases can be implicitly converted to their underlying types, and vice versa:

```
type transparent = int;

function make_transparent(int $x): transparent {
  return $x;   // OK: implicit conversion of int to transparent
}

function takes_int(int $x): void {
}

function main(): void {
  $t = make_transparent(10);
  takes_int($t);   // OK: implicit conversion of transparent to int
}
```

Opaque Type Aliases

The other reason to create a type alias is if you're using a primitive type with a special meaning. A very common example of this is using integers as user IDs. You can make a type alias called `userid` to distinguish integers being used as user IDs from other integers, which can help prevent mistakes where an integer representing something else, like a count or a timestamp, is used as a user ID.

Another example of this is with string types. You could define a type alias of `string` called `sqlstring` and use it in the interface to your SQL database, to prevent accidentally using a query string that hasn't been properly escaped. (Another example of this kind of distinction is in "Secure by Default" on page 167.)

Opaque aliases are meant for this purpose. The difference between transparent and opaque aliases is that an opaque type alias *cannot* be converted to its underlying type (or vice versa), *except* in the file where the alias is defined.

The syntax for opaque aliases is the same as for transparent aliases, except that the keyword type is replaced by newtype:

```
newtype userid = int;
```

The same restrictions apply: the type alias can't have the same name as a class, and the declaration must be at the top level of a file.

To demonstrate how to use an opaque alias, suppose we have one file that defines the alias, plus a conversion function:

```
newtype opaque = int;

function make_opaque(int $x): opaque {
  return $x;
}
```

Note that the code in this file is allowed to implicitly convert the underlying type to the alias type—it returns a value of type int from a function whose return type is opaque, and the typechecker allows this.

In another file, we try to use it:

```
function takes_int(int $x): void {
}
function takes_opaque(opaque $x): void {
}

function main(): void {
  takes_int(make_opaque(10));     // Error
  takes_opaque(20);    // Error
}
```

As this example shows, if you want an opaque alias to be useful outside its file, you have to define some way to convert between the alias type and the underlying type, in the same file. Otherwise, there will be no way for code in other files to convert between them, or to create values of the alias type.

As opaque aliases are meant to be used for semantically significant aliases—like aliasing int as userid—forcing the use of an explicit conversion function is a feature, as it prevents accidental usage of a garden-variety integer as a user ID. The conversion function is also a good place to do verification: for example, you could check that the passed-in integer is a plausible user ID by making sure it's not negative.

If you're starting a new web app from scratch (i.e., with a blank database), here's a very simple thing you can do that will instantly eliminate a whole class of insidious bugs for the rest of the app's life. If you're allocating user IDs using an autoincrement column in a database table (which is a very typical, reasonable thing to do), set the autoincrement value to something astronomically high before adding any rows to it. By "astronomically high," I mean 2^{48} or something in that neighborhood. (You can express that in code as 1 << 48.)

This way, it's very unlikely that you'll have non–user ID integers that look like user IDs floating around your code. Array indices, array counts, and string lengths cannot be that high in PHP and Hack. Unix timestamps probably won't be that high either, unless you're dealing with dates 8.9 million years in the future. And there's no need to worry about wasting too much ID space—starting at 2^{48} still leaves you with 9 billion billion possible IDs.

Having done that, you can define an opaque type alias newtype userid = int, verify in the conversion function that the supposed user ID is greater than 2^{48}, and be almost certain that it's valid.

An opaque alias can have a *constraint type* added to it, which allows code outside the file where the alias is defined to implicitly convert the alias type to the constraint type, but *not* vice versa. Often, the constraint type is the same as the underlying type.

The syntax for this is to add, between the type alias name and the equals sign, the keyword as and a type annotation (the constraint type).

For example, in one file, we define aliases:

```
newtype totally_opaque = int;
newtype with_constraint as int = int;

function make_totally_opaque(int $x): totally_opaque {
  return $x;
}
function make_with_constraint(int $x): with_constraint {
  return $x;
}
```

In another file, we try to use them:

```
function takes_int(int $x): void {
}
function takes_totally_opaque(totally_opaque $x): void {
}
function takes_with_constraint(with_constraint $x): void {
}
```

```
function main(): void {
  takes_int(make_totally_opaque(20));   // Error
  takes_int(make_with_constraint(20));  // OK

  takes_totally_opaque(20);    // Error
  takes_with_constraint(20);   // Error
}
```

This feature is useful when bridging legacy code with new code that uses opaque aliases. You can make an opaque alias userid with underlying type int, but you may still have legacy code that passes around user IDs as integers. To make things easier, you can add a constraint to the type alias so you can seamlessly pass values of type userid to functions that expect int.

Restrictions

In general, you can only use type aliases in type annotations. You can't use them in other places, such as in new expressions:

```
class SomeClass {
}

type SomeAlias = SomeClass;

function f(): void {
  $obj = new SomeAlias();  // Error
}
```

The restrictions on type aliases are the same as the restrictions that generic type parameters have due to type erasure. The full list is in "Type Erasure" on page 45.

This is simply an artifact of the history of type aliases. Originally, they were a typechecker-only construct, erased at runtime, just like generic type parameters. This is no longer true; type alias support was added to HHVM to allow it to enforce type annotations that contained type aliases. That support hasn't yet been extended to other parts of the runtime that are aware of types.

Autoloading Type Aliases

Type aliases can be autoloaded by HHVM's enhanced autoloading system, which is described in "Enhanced Autoloading" on page 82.

Type Constants

There's a common situation in well-typed object-oriented code: an abstract super-class wants to define a well-typed interface, but needs to leave some of the types to be specified by subclasses. A common example is a base class representing a model object, with subclasses representing various kinds of model data. The subclasses deal with different types, but should all share a common interface.

It's possible to accomplish this with generics, but it results in awkward code. Type constants are a better solution. A base class can define an *abstract* type constant—essentially a name without a real type attached—and subclasses override it with *concrete* type constants, providing real types to go with the name.

Type constants are roughly analogous to abstract methods: base classes define method signatures without bodies, while subclasses provide bodies to go with them.

Defining Type Constants

Type constants may only be defined at the top level of the class. The syntax to define them is as follows:

- The syntax to define an *abstract* type constant consists of the three keywords `abstract const type`, followed by a name for the type constant. By convention, this name should start with an uppercase T, like type parameters do.

  ```
  abstract class C {
    abstract const type Tkey;
  }
  ```

  You can optionally add a *constraint* to an abstract type constant; we'll see how to do that, and what it means, in "Constraints" on page 68.

  Any abstract type constant can be overridden by a type constant of the same name in a descendant class.

- The syntax to define a *concrete* type constant consists of the two keywords `const type`, followed by the type constant name, an equals sign, and a type annotation.

  ```
  class DataObject {
    const type Tkey = int;
    const type Tvalue = ?string;
  }
  ```

  A concrete type constant may override a type constant of the same name, inherited from an ancestor class. They don't have to override, but they usually do; without overriding, type constants are essentially just type aliases.

  Concrete type constants may also have constraints, which we'll also cover in "Constraints" on page 68.

  A concrete type constant may *only* be overridden if it has a constraint.

Any class that defines an abstract type constant must be abstract itself, and any class that inherits an abstract type constant must either be abstract itself or override it with a concrete type constant. This is analogous to the rule for abstract method declarations.

There is one major restriction on what a type constant is allowed to be: it can't refer to a generic type parameter.[1] For example:

```
class GenericClass<Tparam> {
  const type Tconst = Tparam;  // Error!
}
```

Constraints

Constraints on type constants are similar to constraints on generic type parameters (see "Constraints" on page 47): they restrict what the type constant may be overridden by.

Constraints are added in the definition of a type constant. Add the keyword as and a type annotation—the *constraint type*—directly after the constant's name in the declaration (before the equals sign, in a concrete type constant):

```
abstract class One {
  abstract const type T as arraykey;
}

class Two {
  const type T as arraykey = int;
}
```

A constraint on an abstract type constant has a simple meaning: any type constant overriding it must be a subtype of the constraint type.

```
abstract class Base {
  abstract const type T as arraykey;
}

class One extends Base {
  const type T = string;  // OK: string is a subtype of arraykey
}

class Two extends Base {
  const type T = bool;  // Error: bool is not a subtype of arraykey
}
```

A constraint on a concrete type constant applies the same restriction, and is required in order for that constant to be overridden at all.

---

1 This is so that type constants can, in a future version, be known to the runtime, for runtime enforcement and reflection. (Currently, they are erased at runtime, like generic type parameters.)

```
class WrongBase {
  const type T = arraykey;
}

class Wrong extends WrongBase {
  const type T = int;  // Error: WrongBase::T has no constraint
}

class CorrectBase {
  const type T as arraykey = arraykey;
}

class Correct extends CorrectBase {
  const type T = int;  // OK
}
```

When overriding a concrete type constant, the overriding type must be a subtype of the overridden type.

Using Type Constants

Usually, you refer to a type constant from within the class hierarchy that defines it. In that context, you normally refer to a type constant (using it as a type annotation) by prefixing its name with `this::`. You can think of the prefix `this::` in the same way as the `this` return type (see "Hack's Type System" on page 6). In non-static methods and properties, it represents the class of the `$this` object; in static methods, it represents the called class. Here's an example:

```
abstract class Base {
  abstract const type T;
  protected this::T $value;
}

class StringSub extends Base {
  const type T = string;
  public function getString(): string {
    return $this->value;  // OK
  }
}

class IntSub extends Base {
  const type T = int;
  public function getInt(): int {
    return $this->value;  // OK
  }
}
```

In the class `StringSub`, accessing `$this->value` results in a value of type `string`. It inherits `Base`'s definition of the property, which is of type `this::T`. Since the property access is occurring in the context of StringSub, where T is defined to be string, the property is of type string.

Following the same line of reasoning, in the class IntSub, accessing $this->value results in a value of type int. This is the power of type constants: the property is defined in only one place, but can have different types depending on the context where it's being used.

You can also refer to class constants from within the hierarchy where they're defined by prefixing their names with self::. It differs from the this:: prefix in that it refers specifically to the version of the constant defined in the class where the reference appears, and ignores any overrides.

In a class that defines an abstract type constant, you should always refer to that type constant using the this prefix. It doesn't make sense not to: there's no purpose for having a value whose type is an abstract type constant. This is likely to be enforced by the typechecker in future.

Outside the class hierarchy[2] where a type constant is defined, you can refer to them by prefixing them with a class name and two colons. It's fairly uncommon to need to do this, and it's tricky to get it right when overriding is involved. One possible application is essentially to use type constants as scoped type aliases:

```
class Schema {
  const type Tname = string;
  const type Ttimestamp = int;
}

function validate_name(Schema::Tname $name): bool {
  // ...
}
```

There are some restrictions on where you can use type constants. You can use them in any type annotation, with one exception: you can't use a type constant prefixed by this:: in the type of a static property. (self:: is fine, as is this:: in the types of non-static properties.)

You can't use type constants anywhere else—for example, in new expressions, or on the righthand side of instanceof, among others. These restrictions are the same as the ones on type parameters in generic classes, which are fully documented in "Type Erasure" on page 45.

---

2 Like class constants, type constants behave as if they had public visibility. There's no way to change this.

Array Shapes

There's a very common pattern in PHP codebases of using arrays as pseudo-objects. For example, instead of defining a `User` class with properties for the user's ID and name, code will simply pass around arrays with keys `'id'` and `'name'` to represent users.

Array shapes are a way to tell the Hack typechecker about the structure of an array in cases like this. The typechecker can verify that the array has the right set of keys and that the keys map to values of the right types.

The syntax for a shape declaration is the keyword `shape`, followed by a parenthesis-enclosed, comma-separated list of key/value pairs. Each pair is a key—either a string literal or a class constant whose value is an integer or a string—followed by the token `=>`, followed by a type annotation.

```
type user = shape('id' => int, 'name' => string);

function returns_shape(): shape('id' => int, 'name' => string) {
  // ...
}

class C {
  private shape('id' => int, 'name' => string) $user;
}
```

Shape declarations can also be nested:

```
type recipient = shape(
  'name'    => int,
  'address' => shape(
    'street'   => string,
    'city'     => string,
    'postcode' => int
  )
);
```

A shape is really just an array with special tracking by the typechecker. To create a shape, use the same syntax as the `array()` syntax for creating arrays, but use the `shape` keyword instead:

```
type user = shape('id' => int, 'name' => string);

function make_user_shape(int $id, string $name): user {
  return shape('id' => $id, 'name' => $name);
}

// This works also
function make_user_shape(int $id, string $name): user {
  $user = shape();
  $user['id'] = $id;
```

```
    $user['name'] = $name;
    return $user;
}
```

The resulting value is an array whose keys and value types are tracked. If you pass a shape to is_array(), it will return true. If you use hh_client --type-at-pos on a shape, it will only say [shape].

Note that within the body of the second version of the function, the value $user doesn't conform to the user shape declaration until after the third line. This is not a problem; the typechecker only enforces conformance with the shape declaration when it's checked against a type annotation—in this case, at the point of the return statement.

All non-nullable fields are required; if such a field isn't set when the shape is checked, the typechecker will report an error, as in the following code:

```
function return_shape(): shape('id' => int, 'name' => string) {
    return shape('id' => 20);
}
```

The typechecker reports the following error:

```
test.php:4:10,14: Invalid return type (Typing[4057])
    test.php:4:10,14: The field 'name' is missing
    test.php:3:20,24: The field 'name' is defined
```

Nullable fields are optional, but there's a wrinkle in that. The typechecker won't report an error if a nullable field isn't set when the shape is checked, but reading directly from that field at runtime will result in an E_NOTICE-level error (undefined index). There are two ways to deal with this:

- Make sure, when creating a shape, to write null into optional fields that you don't have a real value for. This will avoid the runtime error, but it isn't recommended, since the typechecker won't help you ensure that you've always done it, and it somewhat defeats the purpose of optional fields.

- Use the Shapes library (see "The Shapes Library" on page 73) to check whether optional fields are set,[3] before reading from them. This is the recommended way.

---

3 The typechecker won't let you use isset() or array_key_exists() on shapes, which is why a separate interface is needed.

Structural Subtyping

The typechecker allows *structural subtyping* for shapes. This means that the type-checker can consider one shape to be a subtype of another, simply because its fields are a superset of the other shape's fields.

Consider this code:

```
type big_shape    = shape('a' => int, 'b' => string);
type little_shape = shape('a' => int);

function get_big_shape(): big_shape {
  // ...
}

function get_little_shape(): little_shape {
  return get_big_shape();  // OK
}
```

It's valid for `get_little_shape()` to pass a value of type `big_shape` to its `return` statement, because the fields of `big_shape` are a superset_of the fields of `lit tle_shape`. Note, though, that any code that calls `get_little_shape()` will only be able to access fields declared in `little_shape` in the returned value.

You don't have to explicitly tell the typechecker about this subtype relationship, as you do with classes and interfaces. The typechecker deduces the subtype relationship on its own—it recognizes that any value that conforms to `big_shape` must necessarily conform to `little_shape` too, and allows `big_shape` values to be passed where `lit tle_shape` values are expected. Apart from the way the typechecker deduces it, this is a subtype relationship like any other.

The Shapes Library

`Shapes` is an abstract final class that contains four static methods for dealing with shapes:

`Shapes::idx(shape() $shape, arraykey $key, $default = null)`
> Checks the whether $key is set in the given shape.[4] If so, it returns the associated value; if not, it returns $default.

`Shapes::keyExists(shape() $shape, arraykey $key): bool`
> Returns whether the key $key is set in the given shape.

---

4 Note the use of structural subtyping here. The parameter type shape() accepts any shape, because any shape's fields are a superset of shape()'s fields.

ables. The language runtime has to inspect the closure's body statically to determine which variables to capture, and in the presence of variable variables, it can't do so. Consider the following code:

```
$one = /* ... */
$other = /* ... */
$local_reader = function ($index) use ($one, $other) {
  $name = ($index === 0 ? 'one' : 'other');
  return $$name;
};
```

With a lambda expression, the language runtime would have no way of knowing it should capture $one and $other, and there would be no way to tell it. If you rewrote the closure in the example as a lambda expression, the variables $one and $other would be undefined in the lambda's body and reading from them would result in "undefined variable" warnings.

Constructor Parameter Promotion

Constructor parameter promotion is a simple feature designed to reduce boilerplate code in constructors. If your codebase uses classes heavily, you probably have a lot of code like this:

```
class Employee {
  private $id;
  private $name;
  private $department;

  public function __construct($id, $name, $department) {
    $this->id = $id;
    $this->name = $name;
    $this->department = $department;
  }
}
```

This is bad because everything the class needs to store is repeated in four places: once as a property, once as a parameter of the constructor, and twice in the assignment expression in the body of the constructor. Constructor parameter promotion reduces the four down to one. The preceding code can be rewritten like this:

```
class Employee {
  // Nothing needed here

  public function __construct(private $id, private $name, private $department) {
    // Nothing needed here
  }
}
```

The syntax is very simple: all you have to do is put one of the access modifier keywords `private`, `protected`, or `public` before a parameter of the constructor. Promoted parameters can coexist with regular parameters, and they can be interleaved.

In addition to declaring a parameter of the constructor, the syntax declares a property of the same name with the given access modifier, and assigns the argument to the property. You can still put code in the body of the constructor, and it will run after the assignments are done.

This is compatible with type annotations: just put the type annotation between the access modifier keyword and the name. The type annotation applies to both the property and the parameter. You can also add default values for promoted parameters:

```
class User {
  public function __construct(private int $id, private string $name = '') {
  }
}
```

Attributes

Attributes are a syntactic extension that let you add metadata to functions, methods, classes, interfaces, and traits. You can access this metadata through small additions to the normal PHP reflection APIs.

Attributes are a structured substitute for information that is often encoded in documentation comments. Instead of requiring a separate program to extract this information, it becomes available programmatically through reflection. Here is an example showing documentation comments versus attribute usage:

```
/**
 * MyFeatureTestCase
 *
 * @owner oyamauchi
 * @deprecated
 */
class MyFeatureTestCase extends TestCase {
  // ...
}

/**
 * MyFeatureTestCase with attributes
 */
<<Owner('oyamauchi'), Deprecated>>
class MyFeatureTestCaseWithAttributes extends TestCase {
  // ...
}
```

Attribute Syntax

Each attribute is a key mapping to an array of values. The keys are strings, and values are scalars (null, boolean literals, numeric literals, string literals, or arrays of those).

The syntax is very simple. Immediately before a function, method, class, interface, or trait, put attributes inside two pairs of angle brackets. Each attribute, at its simplest, is just a key (an unquoted string):

```
<<DarkMagic>>
function summon_demon() {
  // ...
}
```

 Attribute keys beginning with two underscores are reserved for special use by the runtime and typechecker. Three such attributes exist in Hack/HHVM 3.9 (described in the next section), and there may be more in the future.

To access this attribute, use the getAttributes() or getAttribute() method of ReflectionFunction (ReflectionClass and ReflectionMethod have the same methods):

```
$function = new ReflectionFunction('summon_demon');

echo "All attributes: \n";
var_dump($function->getAttributes());

echo "Just DarkMagic: \n";
var_dump($function->getAttribute('DarkMagic'));

All attributes:
array(1) {
  ["DarkMagic"]=>
  array(0) {
  }
}
Just DarkMagic:
array(0) {
}
```

If you call getAttribute() to read an attribute that isn't there, it will return null with no error. Aside from that, calling getAttribute($name) is otherwise equivalent to calling getAttributes() and indexing into the returned array with $name.

To add attribute values, include a parenthesis-enclosed, comma-separated list of scalars immediately after the attribute name:

```
<<Magic('dark')>>
function summon_demon() {
```

```
  // ...
}

<<Magic('curse', 'dark')>>
function banish_to_eternal_void() {
  // ...
}

$function = new ReflectionFunction('banish_to_eternal_void');

var_dump($function->getAttributes());

array(1) {
  ["Magic"]=>
  array(2) {
    [0]=>
    string(5) "curse"
    [1]=>
    string(4) "dark"
  }
}
```

You don't have to declare attribute names anywhere before using them. They're really little more than parseable comments.

Special Attributes

There are three attributes that are treated specially by the Hack typechecker and by HHVM. The two leading underscores in their names indicate that they're special (this convention is reserved for use by special built-in attributes):

__Override
> When this attribute is applied to a method, the Hack typechecker will check that the method is overriding a method from one of its ancestor classes. If it's not overriding, the typechecker will report an error. Note that the method being overridden must be in a Hack file; if the method being overridden is in a PHP file, the typechecker can't see it, and it will report an error.
>
> __Override can be applied to methods defined in traits. The restriction won't be enforced in the trait itself, but it will be enforced in any class that uses the trait—consistent with traits' copy-and-paste semantics.
>
> HHVM doesn't treat this attribute specially; it won't cause any runtime errors.

__ConsistentConstruct
> In Hack, a child class's __construct() method doesn't have to have a signature that matches its parent class's __construct() method. This is intentional; it's perfectly reasonable for a child class to have different needs for its constructor.

This can hide problems, though, in cases where constructors are being called polymorphically—as in new static().

A good example is in the factory pattern. The following example shows an abstract base class with several static factory methods, each of which calls new static(). Each child class is supposed to implement a constructor with the same signature:

```
<<__ConsistentConstruct>>
abstract class Reader {
  protected function __construct(resource $file) { }

  public static function fromFile(string $path): this {
    return new static(fopen($path, 'r'));
  }

  public static function fromString(string $str): this {
    $tmpfile = tmpfile();
    fwrite($tmpfile, $str);
    fseek($tmpfile, 0);
    return new static($tmpfile);
  }

  abstract public function readItem(): mixed;
}

class BufferedReader extends Reader {
  protected function __construct(resource $file) {
    // Fill buffer ...
  }

  public function readItem(): mixed {
    // ...
  }
}

class TokenReader extends Reader {
  // ...
}
```

Without __ConsistentConstruct, a child class could have the wrong constructor signature and the Hack typechecker wouldn't be able to report an error for it. Because the typechecker can't tell which constructor will be invoked by the new static() call, it can't fully typecheck the call. But with __ConsistentConstruct, the typechecker will report an error for constructors with non-matching signatures, so you know (indirectly) that the new static() call is typesafe.

This attribute is only significant to the typechecker; HHVM doesn't treat it specially.

__Memoize

Unlike the other two special attributes, this one is treated specially by HHVM but ignored by the Hack typechecker. It lets you use the common pattern of memoization, with assistance from the runtime that makes it more efficient than it can be with PHP or Hack code alone.

Memoization is a pattern of caching the result of a time-consuming computation. It's often implemented like this:

```
function factorize_impl($num) {
  // Some factorization algorithm
}

function factorize($num) {
  static $cache = array();
  if (!isset($cache[$num])) {
    $cache[$num] = factorize_impl($num);
  }
  return $cache[$num];
}
```

Most of the code shown in this example is boilerplate, and the __Memoize attribute lets you remove all of that. Here's the alternative, which lets the runtime manage the cache for you:

```
<<__Memoize>>
function factorize($num) {
  // Some factorization algorithm
}
```

You can memoize functions or methods, but there are a few restrictions:

- You can't memoize variadic functions (i.e., functions that take a variable number of arguments).

- You can't memoize functions that take any arguments by reference.

- All arguments to the memoized function must be one of these types: bool, int, float, string, the nullable version of any of the previous types, an object of a class that implements the special interface IMemoizeParam, or an array or collection of any of the previous types.

  IMemoizeParam declares a single non-static method: getInstanceKey(): string. The job of this method is to turn the object into a string that can be used as an array key in the memoization cache.

There are some things to watch out for when using __Memoize. First, be aware that it's a time/memory trade-off. It can make code faster by reducing the amount of computation it does, but it will also increase memory usage. This is not always desirable.

Second, HHVM makes no guarantees about when it will actually execute a memoized function, as opposed to simply returning a value from the cache. Don't assume that the body of the function will only execute once for a given argument. HHVM is allowed, for example, to delete entries from the cache to free up memory—in fact, this is an advantage of using __Memoize instead of implementing memoization yourself.

Finally, note that HHVM doesn't try to make sure that the function you're memoizing has no side effects, or that it returns the same result for the same arguments no matter how many times it's called. Both of these properties are important for a function being memoized; if they don't hold, memoization might visibly change the program's behavior.

Enhanced Autoloading

PHP provides autoloading for classes, and HHVM supports this, through both __autoload() and spl_autoload_register(). HHVM provides an additional feature that allows autoloading for functions and constants in both PHP and Hack, plus autoloading for type aliases (see "Type Aliases" on page 62) in Hack only.

This feature has another advantage over PHP's autoloading mechanisms: it can do its job without running any PHP code, so its performance is generally better. A successful autoload can be done entirely within the runtime, using just two hashtable lookups. For that reason, if you're using HHVM, using this feature instead of PHP autoloading is strongly recommended.

The interface to this enhanced autoloading is the function autoload_set_paths(), in the HH namespace. It takes two arguments: an autoload map (which is an array), and a root path (which is a string). When HHVM needs to autoload something, it will perform the lookups in the autoload map.

The autoload map is an array. There are five optional string keys that are significant:

- The keys 'class', 'function', 'constant', and 'type' each map to arrays. Those inner arrays—*submaps*—have keys that are names of entities (classes, functions, constants, and types, respectively), and values that are file paths where the corresponding entities can be found.
- The key 'failure' maps to a callable value—the *failure callback*—that will be called if lookup in the above keys fails.

Here's an example that sets up the autoload map and calls a function that isn't loaded:

```
function autoload_fail(string $kind, string $name): ?bool {
    // ...
```

```
}

function setup_autoloading(): void {
  $map = array(
    'function' => array('extricate' => 'lib/extricate.php')
  );

  HH\autoload_set_paths($map, __DIR__ . '/');
}

setup_autoloading();
extricate();
```

When the function `extricate()` is called, the runtime looks in the `'function'` sub-map of the autoload map for the `'extricate'` entry. When it finds the entry, it appends the file path to the root path, loads the file at that combined path, and continues execution.

If anything about that procedure fails—if the `'function'` submap isn't present, or the `'extricate'` entry isn't present, or the file doesn't exist, or the file doesn't actually contain a definition of `extricate()`—the failure callback is called. If it returns true, the runtime tries to call `extricate()` again, assuming the failure callback loaded it. If it didn't , or if the failure callback returns `false` or `null`, the runtime declares failure, and raises a fatal error for an undefined function.

The failure callback gets passed two arguments: first, a string identifying the kind of entity being autoloaded (`'class'`, `'function'`, `'constant'`, or `'type'`), and second, a string with the entity's name.

The most intuitive way to understand the whole algorithm is with a flowchart; see Figure 3-1.

There are two situations in which the algorithm is slightly different:

- If the entity being autoloaded is a class, returning `false` from the failure callback causes different behavior from returning `null`. If the callback returns `false`, the behavior is the same as in the function case: a fatal error is immediately raised. But if the callback returns `null`, HHVM falls back to the standard PHP autoload mechanisms: `__autoload()` and the SPL autoload queue.

- If the entity being autoloaded *might* be a type alias, HHVM will first try the `'class'` submap, then the `'type'` submap, then the failure callback with first argument `'class'`, then the failure callback with first argument `'type'`. This is because any entity that could be a type alias can also be a class.

  The only time an entity to autoload might be a type alias is during enforcement of a parameter type annotation or a return type annotation.

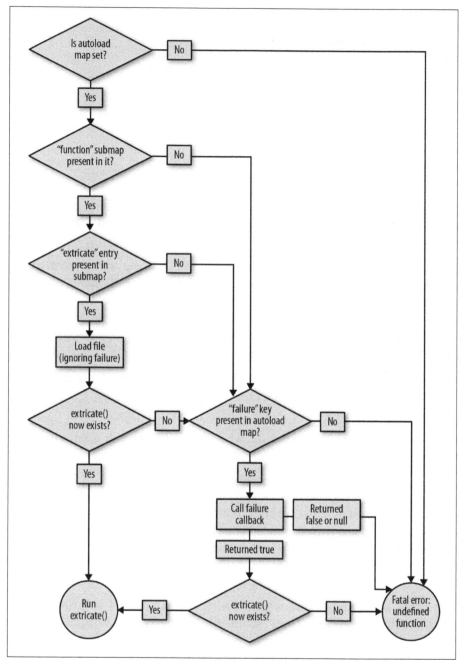

Figure 3-1. Autoloading a function

As a final note, the failure callback shouldn't be routinely used for actual loading; it should be used mostly for error logging. The whole autoloading process is slower if the runtime has to fall back to the failure callback.

Integer Arithmetic Overflow

In PHP, if integer arithmetic operations overflow, the result is a float:

```
var_dump(PHP_INT_MAX + 1);  // float (9.2233720368548E+18)
```

This is bad for performance: it means that almost every arithmetic operation in a program has to be checked for overflow, even though overflow is extremely unlikely in practice. It's also questionable from a program-logic standpoint: in the preceding example of PHP_INT_MAX + 1, the conversion to float causes an immediate loss of precision.

HHVM includes a mode to make integer arithmetic follow the rules of two's complement arithmetic at runtime. This means the result of adding, subtracting, or multiplying two integers is always an integer.[6] The configuration option to turn this mode on is hhvm.ints_overflow_to_ints.

The Hack typechecker, in fact, *always* treats integer arithmetic operations as if they followed the rules of two's complement arithmetic, and this is not configurable. The justification is that if the typechecker were to follow PHP's behavior, it would become very difficult to meaningfully typecheck anything involving the results of arithmetic operations. Besides that, the overflow-to-float behavior isn't used in any other mainstream programming language, and it often surprises newcomers to PHP.

Nullsafe Method Call and Property Access

Hack adds a new operator for calling methods and reading properties of an object that may be null. The operator is ?->, in contrast to the usual operator ->:

```
interface Reader {
  public function readAll(): string;
}

function read_everything(?Reader $reader): ?string {
  return $reader?->readAll();
}
```

If the value on the lefthand side of the operator is null, there is no warning or error, and the whole expression evaluates to null. Therefore, the type of this expression is the nullable version of the actual method's return type.

---

6 The mathematical phrase is "integers are closed under addition, subtraction, and multiplication."

The operator can't be used for writing to properties:

```
class Obj {
  public mixed $prop;
}

function write_prop(?Obj $obj): void {
  $obj?->prop = 123;  // Error
}
```

This operator is very well suited for chained method calls, because it allows any method in the chain to return `null` without requiring null checks everywhere, while still being safe from `BadMethodCallException`. For example:

```
$name = $comment?->getPost()?->getAuthor()?->getName();
```

Trait and Interface Requirements

Traits are one of the trickiest areas for the typechecker to navigate. A trait is essentially a bundle of code taken out of context. To be useful, traits must be able to refer to properties and methods that they don't define—the classes that use the traits will supply them.

To allow for stronger typechecking of traits, Hack provides a feature that allows you to restrict what classes may use a trait. Inside the definition of a trait, you can specify that any classes using it must extend a certain class, or implement a certain interface. This way, the typechecker can verify a property access or method call in a trait by checking it in the context of the classes and interfaces that are allowed to use the trait.

The syntax is `require extends ClassName` or `require implements InterfaceName`. These statements go at the top level of the trait definition:

```
class C {
  public function methodFromClass(): void { }
}

interface I {
  public function methodFromInterface(): void;
}

trait NoRequire {
  public function f(): void {
    $this->methodFromInterface();  // Error: could not find method
    $this->methodFromClass();      // Error: could not find method
  }
}

trait HasRequire {
  require extends C;
  require implements I;
```

```
  public function f(): void {
    $this->methodFromInterface();  // OK
    $this->methodFromClass();      // OK
  }
}
```

If a class uses a trait and doesn't fulfill the trait's requirements, the typechecker will report an error. Continuing from the previous example:

```
class Bad {
  use HasRequire;  // Error: failure to satisfy requirement
}
```

Note that `require extends` really does mean *extends*; that is, it's an error for the class named in a trait's `require` extends declaration to use that trait. Any class using the trait must be a descendant:

```
trait T {
  require extends C;
}

class C {
  use T;  // Error
}
```

In addition to these declarations, Hack also allows traits to implement interfaces. When a trait that implements an interface is used, it behaves as if the "implements" declaration were transferred onto the class using the trait, and all the attendant restrictions are enforced. This is very similar to using `require implements` in the trait:

```
interface I {
  public function methodFromInterface(): void;
}

trait T implements I {
  public function f(): void {
    $this->methodFromInterface();  // OK
  }
}

class C {
  use T;  // Error: must provide an implementation for methodFromInterface()
}
```

Finally, `require extends` works in interfaces as well. Only classes that descend from the named class are allowed to implement the interface (again, this excludes the named class itself):

```
interface I {
  require extends ParentClass;
```

```
}

class ParentClass {
  // It would be an error for this class to implement I
}

class ChildClass extends ParentClass implements I {  // OK
}

class OtherChild implements I {  // Error
}
```

Silencing Typechecker Errors

Suppose you have a core function, without type annotations, used all over the code-base, and you want to add annotations to it. This might cause type errors at a lot of the function's callsites. The typechecker gives you a way to add the annotations to the core function anyway, and silence the errors at each callsite that turns out to have an error. That way, you get the annotations in (so that new code using that function will be well-typed) but remain error-clean, while the places you need to fix are easily searchable. This is the purpose of the HH_FIXME and HH_IGNORE_ERROR comments.

Every error message reported by the typechecker has a numerical error code, shown at the end of the message. For example, consider this code:

```
<?hh // strict

function core_function(): int {
  return 123;
}

function some_other(): string {
  return core_function();
}
```

This generates the following error from the typechecker:

```
/home/oyamauchi/hack/test.php:8:10,24: Invalid return type (Typing[4110])
  /home/oyamauchi/hack/test.php:7:24,29: This is a string
  /home/oyamauchi/hack/test.php:3:27,29: It is incompatible with an int
```

The error code is 4110, the number shown in square brackets. (The word "Typing" just denotes the general category of the error, and isn't part of the error code—there's only one error 4110 across all categories.)

To silence this error, add the comment /* HH_FIXME[4110] */ either before the function signature or before the return statement. You should also add an explanation of why the error needs to be silenced within the comment, after the closing square bracket.

Instead of HH_FIXME, you can also use HH_IGNORE_ERROR. The effect is exactly the same, but having two possible syntaxes lets human readers distinguish between two different use cases: HH_FIXME for errors that are produced by mass refactorings and are intended to be fixed at some point, and HH_IGNORE_ERROR for errors that are permanent or not necessarily intended to be fixed.

Any of the following versions of some_other() will silence the error:

```
function some_other(): int {
  /* HH_FIXME[4110] from core_function return type */
  return core_function();
}

function some_other(): string {
  /* HH_FIXME[4110] from core_function return type */ return core_function();
}

/* HH_FIXME[4110] from core_function return type */
function some_other(): string {
  return core_function();
}

/* HH_FIXME[4110] core_function return type */ function some_other(): string {
  return core_function();
}
```

The syntax of the comment is precise. It *must* be a C-style /* */ comment; shell-style # comments and C++-style // comments won't work. It has to start with HH_FIXME or HH_IGNORE_ERROR, immediately followed by the error code in square brackets.

An HH_FIXME will silence the given error on the line containing the first non-whitespace, non-comment character after the end of the HH_FIXME comment. (In the preceding example, there are two pieces of code that work together to cause the error: the return statement and the return type annotation. Silencing either piece silences the whole error.)

You can apply multiple HH_FIXME comments to a single line by putting them consecutively before the line in question. For example, this code:

```
function f(?void $nonsense): int {
  return 'oops';
}
```

produces the following error output:

```
/home/oyamauchi/test.php:2:12,16: ?void is a nonsensical typehint (Typing[4066])
/home/oyamauchi/test.php:3:10,11: Invalid return type (Typing[4110])
  /home/oyamauchi/test.php:2:26,28: This is an int
  /home/oyamauchi/test.php:3:10,11: It is incompatible with a string
```

To silence both errors, do this:

ence is function-local, as described in "Inference Is Function-Local" on page 31). This makes it impossible to ensure type safety around references, and difficult to execute code around them efficiently.

Another example of "action at a distance" making type inference difficult is the problem of object properties. As we saw in "Inference on Properties" on page 37, the type-checker must be very conservative with its inference around object properties, because there are so many ways to act upon properties at a distance. This problem is even worse with references, which is why Hack simply ignores them.

There's a separate, small way in which references are bad for performance: accessing a variable that is a reference requires an additional pointer dereference, compared to accessing a regular variable. This means an additional memory access, which puts pressure on cache memories and incurs more roundtrips to main memory.

Garbage Collection

Another thing that makes references troublesome is that they allow PHP code to observe the runtime's copy-on-write optimization of array copying, by taking a reference to an element in an array. Apart from any philosophical arguments about why this is bad, there's a practical one too: the fact that copy-on-write is observable by PHP code makes it hard, if not impossible, to implement tracing garbage collection in a PHP engine.

As it is, if PHP engines don't use naïve reference counting, they'll cause observable behavior differences (also known as "bugs"). This means that there's very little freedom to experiment with other memory management algorithms, which closes off a source of possibly significant performance gains.

The global Statement

The global statement is forbidden in Hack, because it's implemented with references under the hood. The statement global $x is syntactic sugar for $x =& $GLOBALS['x'].

In partial mode, you can read from and write to the $GLOBALS array without references, so you can use that to work around the lack of a global statement. (In strict mode, Hack will report an error, saying $GLOBALS is an undefined variable.)

Top-Level Code

As a corollary to the ban on the global statement, most top-level code is forbidden in strict mode. (It is allowed, but not typechecked, in partial mode.) You're allowed to define named entities (functions, classes, etc.) and use the `require/include` family of statements at the top level in all modes.

This is simply because top-level code exists in global scope,[1] so any read or write of a local variable is actually a read or write of a global variable.

You can get rid of top-level code that doesn't rely on being in global scope simply by wrapping it in a function. If it does rely on being in global scope, it'll need a more substantial rewrite to become valid Hack.

Every program, whether a script or a web app, starts execution in top-level code, so every program will need at least one partial-mode file to serve as an entry point. Ideally, that one partial-mode file will only have one top-level statement other than `require` and definitions—a function call that is the gateway to the bulk of the program's logic:

```
<?hh

require_once 'lib/autoload.php';

function main() {
  setup_autoload();
  do_initialization();
  $controller = find_controller();
  $controller->execute();
}

main();
```

Old-Style Constructors

An old-style constructor is a method that has the same name as its enclosing class:

```
class Thing {
  public function Thing() {
    echo 'constructor!';
  }
}

$t = new Thing();  // prints 'constructor!'
```

This design was presumably inspired by C++ and Java, but was replaced in PHP 5 by the "unified" constructor `__construct`. Hack's ban on old-style constructors is to avoid a potentially confusing, and in this case redundant, feature. The interactions of

---

1 Or not, depending on where the file is included from—another reason it's hard to typecheck.

old-style and new-style constructors, especially in the presence of inheritance, are complex and inconsistent, and there's no reason to have both.

This isn't just a Hack change; old-style constructors were deprecated in PHP 7.

Case-Insensitive Name Lookup

In PHP, function and class names are looked up case-insensitively. That is, if you define a function named `compute`, you can call it by writing `CoMpUtE()`. If you try to do that in Hack, however, the typechecker will report an error, saying the function `CoMpUtE` is undefined.

Note, however, that although Hack is case-sensitive, it's not valid to define two functions (or two classes, etc.) that have names differing only in casing. That's because Hack has to be able to interoperate with PHP, in which name lookups are still case-insensitive.

This restriction actually has nothing to do with either type safety or performance. It would have been very simple to implement case-insensitive name lookup in the Hack typechecker, and it wouldn't affect the typechecker's ability to do type inference.

Rather, it's a philosophical decision. Most general-purpose programming languages are case-sensitive, including PHP's spiritual ancestors: Perl, C, and Java. It makes code marginally easier to read, and makes it no harder to write.

On the performance side, case-insensitive lookup is slightly less efficient than case-sensitive lookup, because the target string must undergo case normalization before being used as the key in a hashtable lookup. In HHVM, it also incurs a small memory penalty, because each function and class must store both the original name from source code (for use in error messages and reflection) and a case-normalized version of the name (for use in hashtable lookups).

Variable Variables

Variable variables look like this:

```
$name = 'x';
$x = 'well this is silly';
echo $$name;   // Prints 'well this is silly'
```

This isn't allowed in Hack because, in general, it's impossible to infer types around a construct like that. When the typechecker sees an expression like `$$name`, it has no idea what the type of that expression is, or even whether that's a valid variable access.

And that's just in the case of reading a variable variable. An expression like `$$name = 10` could, in general, change the type of any local variable in scope, and the typechecker has no hope of understanding the possible effects.

This reasoning echoes the reasons why references aren't allowed in Hack. Variable variables allow action at a distance. They allow code to read and write local variables through a layer of abstraction that is opaque to the typechecker.

There's also a performance concern. While converting PHP and Hack to bytecode, HHVM assigns each local variable a number, starting at 0 and increasing. At runtime, it stores all of a function's local variables consecutively in memory, in numerical order, and it can access each one with a single machine instruction. If variable variables aren't involved, at runtime HHVM doesn't need to remember local variable names; each usage of a local variable is replaced with its number, and that number is all that's needed to find the variable's contents in memory. But if variable variables are involved, HHVM has to set up and tear down a mapping of local variable names to memory locations when entering and exiting the function. This takes extra time and memory.

Dynamic Properties

In PHP, you can create an object property by assigning something to it, in much the same way you can create a local variable:

```php
<?php

class C {
}

function f(): void {
  $c = new C();
  $c->prop = 'hi';
  echo $c->prop;  // Prints 'hi'
}
```

In Hack, this isn't valid; you have to declare all properties. If you know all the properties an object will have in advance, declare them; if you don't, use a shape (see "Array Shapes" on page 71) or a Map (see Chapter 5) instead of an object.

This is for both type safety and performance. In general, it's impossible for the typechecker to infer the types of dynamic properties, or even whether a given dynamic property exists when it's read from.

The performance concern is that HHVM reserves slots within an object's memory for declared properties, allowing it to access a declared property by looking at a known, constant offset from the beginning of an object's memory. No hashtable lookups are involved. It can't do this with dynamic properties; it has to store those in a hashtable, incurring hashtable lookups every time a dynamic property is read or written. (This is very similar to the performance concern around variable variables.)

Mixing Method Call Syntax

In PHP, you can call static methods with non-static method call syntax, and you can call non-static methods with static method call syntax:

```
class C {
  public function nonstaticMethod() { }
  public static function staticMethod() { }
}

C::nonstaticMethod();   // Allowed in PHP

$c = new C();
$c->staticMethod();     // Allowed in PHP
```

Both of these are invalid in Hack. Static methods can only be called with :: syntax, and non-static methods can only be called with -> syntax.

The main reason why Hack forbids this behavior is that if a non-static method is called with :: syntax, then $this is null inside the method. That's problematic; it's not reasonable to expect a non-static method to tolerate $this being null. There will be an error as soon as it tries to call a method or access a property on $this. If the method doesn't use $this, then it probably shouldn't be a non-static method in the first place.

The distinction between static and non-static methods exists for a reason—does the method need an object context to work in, or not? Allowing this distinction to be erased at callsites makes the distinction useless, and gains us nothing.

isset, empty, and unset

The isset, empty, and unset expressions are allowed in partial mode, but not in strict mode.

All three of them are irregularities in PHP's syntax and semantics. They look like normal functions, but they're not. They're special-cased in PHP's grammar so that it's possible to pass undefined variables and index expressions (like $nonexistent['nonexistent']) without incurring warnings. They are also unusual in that the arguments you pass to isset and unset cannot be arbitrary expressions;[2] you can only pass expressions that would be valid lvalues (i.e., expressions that could appear on the lefthand side of an assignment expression). This "looks-like-a-function-but-isn't" phenomenon hurts language cleanliness, which is one argument against these features.

---

2 This restriction applied to empty as well, until PHP 5.5.

In Hack, there's no reason to use isset or empty to test whether a variable is defined: it should be knowable, statically, whether a variable is defined at a given position.

For testing the existence of array elements, use the built-in function array_key_exists() instead of isset or empty. Don't worry about performance: HHVM heavily optimizes calls to array_key_exists().

unset is a bit different. There's simply no reason to use it on a variable in Hack. If you want to get the same effect, just assign null to the variable. In PHP, there's one other reason to use unset on a variable—to break a reference relationship—but in Hack this isn't necessary because references aren't supported.

The one hole in functionality that this restriction creates is that you can't remove elements from an array in strict mode. The preferred alternative is to use a collection (see Chapter 5) instead of an array. If that's not feasible, you can work around this by defining, in a partial-mode file, a helper function that uses unset.

Others

Other PHP features not supported in Hack include:

eval() *and its close relative,* create_function()
> The effects of these functions are, of course, impossible to analyze statically. It's also generally bad programming practice to use functions like these. Usages of eval() generally fall into two categories: simple enough that eval() isn't necessary (in which case, the code can just be written normally instead); or complex enough that they pose a significant correctness or security risk.

The extract() *function*
> Using this function won't result in an error from the typechecker, in any mode. However, the typechecker makes no attempt to track its effects on the local variable environment; it will assume that all local variables have the same value after a call to extract() as they did before.

The goto *statement*
> This statement is the subject of a famous old debate among programmers, many of whom have strong opinions one way or the other. There's no point in rehashing the whole debate here; the important thing is that the Hack team comes down on the "no" side, so Hack doesn't allow goto.

Arguments to break *and* continue
> The break and continue statements are not allowed to take arguments in Hack. (In PHP, arguments are used to break or continue out of multiple nested loops— e.g., break(2).)

Returning from a `finally` *block*

`return` statements aren't allowed inside `finally` blocks in Hack. HHVM also doesn't support this when running PHP files, which is a known and deliberate incompatibility.

Incrementing and decrementing strings

In Hack, the operators (`++` and `--`) can't be applied to strings. In regular PHP, doing this has a variety of interesting behaviors: `++` applied to `"9"` yields `"10"`, applied to `"a"` it yields `"b"`, and applied to `"z"` it yields `"aa"`. There is little practical use for this sort of behavior, but if you need it, your only option is to code it manually.

The `and`, `or`, *and* `xor` *operators*

Instead of the first two, use `&&` and `||`, respectively. Beware, though, they fall in a different place in the order of operator precedence. Use parentheses to make sure your expression is parsed the way you expect. There's no exact alternative to the `xor` operator. The closest alternative is the `^` operator, which implements bitwise XOR as opposed to logical XOR; it also has different precedence.

CHAPTER 5

Collections

PHP has only one built-in collection type: `array`. It presents an interface that is a set of ordered key/value pairs. This interface allows it to serve the purpose of several different data structures that programs in most languages typically use: vectors, sets, and maps (also known as dictionaries).

Hack has several classes that provide specialized vector, set, and map functionality. They allow for better understanding by both the Hack typechecker and human readers of code.

There are seven collection classes in Hack:

`Vector`

A mutable, ordered sequence of values, indexed by integers. The indices are the integers between 0 and $n-1$, where n is the number of elements in the vector.

`Map`

A mutable, ordered set of unique keys, each of which maps to a value. The keys may be integers or strings, and the values can be of any type. Unlike the map types in many other programming languages, Hack `Map`s remember the order in which their values were inserted. Of all the collection classes, `Map` is the most similar to PHP arrays.

`Set`

A mutable, ordered set of unique values. The values may be integers or strings.

`Pair`

An immutable sequence of exactly two values, indexed by the integers 0 and 1. `Pair`s are a detail of the API to the other collection classes, and you generally shouldn't create them yourself; use tuples instead (see "Hack's Type System" on page 6).

`ImmVector`, `ImmMap`, *and* `ImmSet`
> Immutable versions of `Vector`, `Map`, and `Set`, respectively.

`Vector`, `Map`, `Set`, and `Pair` represent the overwhelming majority of use cases for PHP arrays.

In this chapter, we'll see why and how to use Hack collection classes.

 I'll be using lowercase-v "vector" and capital-V `Vector` distinctly in this chapter, and similarly for "map," "set," and "pair." I'll use "vector" to refer to the general concept of an ordered sequence of values, common to many programming languages. I'll use `Vector` to refer specifically to the class that Hack provides.

When I use the word "array" in this chapter, it specifically means the PHP/Hack data type, used with the `array` keyword.

Why Does Map Retain Insertion Order?

This decision was a difficult one, and the factors behind it are a great demonstration of how the pragmatic concerns of software engineering can override principles.

When Hack collections were first being developed, `Map` did *not* retain insertion order. If an engineer needed to keep an ordering over the keys in a `Map`, the solution was a `Map` plus a `Vector`, or something similar. From a language and library designer's perspective, this was ideal, affording maximum flexibility in `Map`'s implementation.

Then, two factors led to the creation of a new class, `StableMap`, which was a `Map` that retained insertion order. The first factor was the desire to programmatically convert array usage sites into collection usage sites. It's practically impossible for a program to tell whether a given array usage site depends on the array retaining insertion order, so any such conversion would have had to use `StableMap`.

The second factor was interoperability. As with other Hack features, a primary goal for the design of Hack collections was to make it easy to interoperate with existing code that used arrays. We expected there to be a lot of conversions between arrays and `Map`s, and if `Map` didn't retain insertion order, these conversions would be lossy.

The presence of both `StableMap` and `Map` created a cognitive burden for engineers. In PHP, nobody had ever had to think about whether to use an array with order retention or without, because there was no choice. With collections, this became a significant choice. There was also API friction: if one module uses `Map`s and another module uses `StableMap`s, how do they talk to each other? (There are interfaces like `ConstMap` and `MutableMap` that could be used to mitigate this API friction, but that would only have been more complexity for PHP and Hack engineers to deal with.)

In view of all this, we ultimately decided to make Map retain insertion order, and delete StableMap. The calculus would have been quite different if retaining insertion order everywhere had been bad for performance, but fortunately, it turned out not to be. In HHVM, we were able to apply implementation tricks from regular PHP arrays to erase the performance difference between StableMap and Map.

There's an interesting nuance to the performance consideration: in practice, had we decided to keep both Map and StableMap, we would have had to go out of our way to make Map *not appear to* retain insertion order, to avoid people depending on that behavior. That would have had a performance cost too.

Why Use Collections?

There is a single underlying reason to use collections instead of arrays: PHP arrays are extremely flexible, but in practice, applications use them in one of a small number of highly specific patterns: vectors, maps, and sets. Using the right type of collection instead makes life easier for both humans and computers.

For human readers of code, seeing the names of specific collection classes makes it clearer what their purpose is. This advantage becomes much more potent when combined with Hack's type annotations: the purpose of a collection is made clear at every abstraction boundary it passes through. This prevents mistakes and makes development faster and easier.

For computers, the smaller a collection's set of functionality is, the easier it is to understand the code around it. Arrays are particularly difficult for the Hack typechecker to understand, because they can be used in such a wide variety of ways. For example, if you're using an array as a vector and you pass it to a function that expects a map-like array, that should be a type error, but the typechecker can't tell when this happens: it's not possible, in general, to tell how an array is being used.

Hack is gradually adding solutions to this problem—shapes (see "Array Shapes" on page 71) are part of this effort—but collections provide immediate relief.

There can be performance benefits to using specific collection classes too. As an example, arrays generally allocate more memory than they use, so that they don't have to allocate more memory every time a value is added. However, some arrays are never modified, so this extra capacity is wasted; there's no way for a programmer to express that an array is immutable. Hack collection classes do have this feature.

The higher-level reason to use collections is simply that collections are more in keeping with Hack's general pro–static typing philosophical stance. The more you can express a program's behavior through static types, the better, for both humans and computers. Collections are a wide-ranging, high-leverage way to do so.

Collections Have Reference Semantics

If you're writing a project in Hack from the ground up, the Hack collection classes should be your first choice when you need collection functionality, for the reasons documented previously.

If you're working with a significant amount of preexisting PHP code, though, converting it to use collection classes instead of arrays can be quite challenging. The reason is one major semantic difference between arrays and collections: arrays have *value semantics*, whereas collections have *reference semantics*.

These two concepts are represented by the two possible answers to this question: in the following example, does the last statement print 'original' or 'new'?

```
$var_one = array('original');
$var_two = $var_one;
$var_two[0] = 'new';
echo $var_one[0];
```

The answer is 'original', which is consistent with value semantics. When you assign the array to $var_two, the array is copied,[1] so modifications to $var_two are not reflected in $var_one (and vice versa).

Collections are the opposite; they have reference semantics, like all objects do in Hack and PHP. If $var_one in our example were a Vector instead, the last statement would print 'new'. The assignment $var_two = $var_one doesn't copy the Vector, so the modification to $var_two is reflected in $var_one.

This may seem like a fairly minor difference at first, but it has far-reaching implications, and you need to be aware of it if you're converting code that uses arrays to use collections instead. In typical code, the pseudo-copying of arrays (as in the preceding example) is ubiquitous: it happens any time you pass an array to a function, or return an array from a function.

Here's an example of a situation in which you need to consider this difference:

```
function get_items(): array<string> {
  static $cache = null;
  if ($cache === null) {
    $cache = do_expensive_fetch();
  }
```

---

1 It is not actually copied in memory at that point, either in standard PHP or in HHVM; instead, it is only copied when it is modified. This is called *copy-on-write*. You may have heard statements like "PHP arrays are copy-on-write," which is true but describes implementation rather than semantics. Well, sort of. Copy-on-write should be an implementation detail—it behaves *as if* the array were copied at the time of the assignment —but it's not quite. There are some obscure corner cases where the copy-on-write is detectable, although those cases are arguably bugs in the language.

```
    return $cache;
  }

  function main(): void {
    $items = get_items();
    $items[] = some_special_item();

    foreach ($items as $item) {
      // ...
    }
  }
```

`main()` is modifying the value returned from `get_items()`, which caches the result of `do_expensive_fetch()` in a static local variable. Because `get_items()` returns an array, this code is correct: `main()` is working on a separate copy of the array from the one stored in the static variable in `get_items()`.

However, if this code is mechanically converted to use collections instead, so that `do_expensive_fetch()` and `get_items()` return `Vector<string>` instead, the code breaks. The `Vector` is never copied, so `main()`'s modification of the `Vector` will be visible to any other caller of `get_items()`.

Note that this is an example of memoization; you need to be aware of this issue when using the special attribute `__Memoize` as well (see "Special Attributes" on page 79).

The first line of defense against this problem is immutability. `get_items()` should be returning an immutable `Vector`, capturing the contract that callers should not be modifying it. If they need to modify it, they should make a copy and modify that instead (which is what is implicitly happening in the array-based code).

This is how `get_items()` should be implemented using collections (we'll see the meaning of the `ConstVector` type annotation in "Type Annotations for Collections" on page 110):

```
  function get_items(): ConstVector<string> {
    static $cache = null;
    if ($cache === null) {
      $cache = do_expensive_fetch();
    }
    return $cache->immutable();
  }
```

Every collection class has a method called `immutable()` that returns an immutable version of itself. This doesn't copy the collection's underlying storage in memory—in fact, it results in behavior very similar to PHP arrays' copy-on-write—so it's cheap. This way, if any caller of `get_items()` tries to modify the `Vector` it returns, an `InvalidOperationException` will be thrown, clearly showing you what needs to be changed.

Using Collections

With HHVM, the collection classes can be used even in regular PHP files (i.e., non-Hack files). You have to prefix their class names with the `HH` namespace (e.g., `HH\Vector`), whereas in Hack files the namespace isn't necessary.

Code that uses collections looks almost identical to code that uses arrays. Collections are built into the language and runtime, so they work seamlessly with many of the language constructs you already use with arrays—we'll look at those in this section. Each collection class also has a full-featured object-oriented interface, the most important parts of which we'll see here and in "Type Annotations for Collections" on page 110.

Literal Syntax

Hack adds special syntax for creating instances of collection classes, called *collection literal syntax*. It consists of the name of the class, followed by a brace-enclosed list of items. The items are separated by commas. In `Map` literals, each item is the key, followed by =>, followed by the value, just as in PHP array literal syntax:

```
$vector = Vector {'one', 'two', 'three'};
$map = Map {'one' => 1, 'two' => 2, 'three' => 3};
$set = Set {'one', 'two', 'three'};
$pair = Pair {'one', 'two'};
```

Collection literal syntax is allowed in any position where regular PHP `array()` syntax is allowed, including in the initializer expressions of object and class properties. This is the reason why it exists: even though collection literal syntax entails object creation (which usually isn't allowed in these positions), it is legal anywhere `array()` is legal. For example:

```
class Pluralizer {
  private static Map<string, string> $cache = Map {};
}
```

Collection literals in this position are not allowed to contain any expression that is itself not allowed in this position. `array()` syntax has the same restriction. For example, this is not valid syntax, because function calls are not valid class property initializers:

```
class Pluralizer {
  // Syntax error
  private static Map<string, string> $cache =
    Map {'child' => fetch_plural_from_db('child')};
}
```

Note that although the collection classes are generic, there are no type arguments in literal syntax:

```
$vec = Vector<int> {1, 2, 3};   // Syntax error
```

Instead, the typechecker will silently track the types of the collection's contents, and only check for errors when you pass the collection through a type annotation (e.g., by assigning it to a property with a type annotation). See "Unresolved Types, Revisited" on page 49 for full details.

Reading and Writing

The square-bracket syntax that you use with arrays is also what you use with Vector, Map, and Pair:

```
$vector = Vector {'zero', 'one', 'two'};
echo $vector[1];   // Prints 'one'

$map = Map {};
$map['zero'] = 0;

$pair = Pair {'first', 'second'};
echo $pair[0];   // Prints 'first'
```

If you try to read an element that doesn't exist, or to set an element in a Vector that is beyond the Vector's bounds, an OutOfBoundsException will be thrown. Accessing elements by reference (as in $ref = &$array[0] in regular PHP) is not allowed with collections; doing so results in a fatal error.

You can't use this syntax to modify Sets. You can use it to read from Sets, but you shouldn't. The most common operation on a Set is to test whether a value is in it, and the square-bracket syntax is unsuitable for that: if the value is not in the Set, it will throw an OutOfBoundsException. For membership testing, use the contains() method (see "Type Annotations for Collections" on page 110) instead:

```
if ($the_list->contains($user_id)) {
  echo "You're on the list";
}
```

Arrays have a quirky behavior wherein keys that are strings containing the representation of an integer[2] are treated as the integer instead. For example:

```
$array = array('3' => 'three');
echo $array[3];   // Prints 'three'
```

---

2 This is actually not the same logic as is used when converting strings to integers. The string must be the decimal representation of an integer between -2^{63} and $2^{63} - 1$ inclusive, with no leading or trailing whitespace or leading zeros. This "feature" is very bad for performance: on every array lookup, which is one of the most common operations in any PHP or Hack program, the key has to be checked for these conditions. There are some possible micro-optimizations, but it still incurs a noticeable performance cost.

```
$array = array(3 => 'three');
echo $array['3'];  // Prints 'three'
```

Hack collections do not do this. Map and Set treat the string "3" and the integer 3 as distinct keys, and if you use anything other than an integer to index into a Vector or Pair, an InvalidArgumentException will be thrown.

To test whether a key exists in a Map or an element exists in a Set, you can use the containsKey() and contains() methods, respectively:

```
$map = Map {'one' => 'un', 'two' => 'deux'};
if ($map->containsKey('two')) {
  echo "We know how to say 'two' in French!";
}

$set = Set {'one', 'two'};
if ($set->contains('one')) {
  echo "'one' is in the set";
}
```

You can also use isset and empty to test if a key or element exists, but you should always use containsKey() or contains() if possible. isset and empty aren't allowed in Hack strict mode—see "isset, empty, and unset" on page 96 for the reasons why. The only reason you may want to use them on collections is so that you can write code that accepts both arrays and collections seamlessly.

Like empty arrays, empty collections of any type evaluate to false when converted to bool. In particular, they're treated as false in conditional statements like if and while, and in ternary expressions:

```
$vector = Vector {};
if ($vector) {
  // Code in here will not be executed
}

$description = ($vector ? (string)$vector : '[none]');
```

Iterating

You can iterate over collections with foreach:

```
$vector = Vector {'zero', 'one'};
foreach ($vector as $value) {
  echo $value;
}

$map = Map {'one' => 'un', 'two' => 'deux'};
foreach ($map as $eng => $fr) {
  echo $eng . ' in French is ' . $fr;
}
```

Adding or removing an item in a collection while iterating over it with `foreach` is not allowed; doing that will result in an `InvalidOperationException` being thrown.

`foreach` by reference, as in `foreach ($vector as &$value)`, is also not allowed; doing that will result in a fatal error. You can approximate this behavior by adding the key or index as an iteration variable, as in `foreach ($vector as $index => $value)`, and modifying the value that way:

```
// Old code with array
$array = array(0, 1, 2);
foreach ($array as &$value) {
  $value *= 10;
}

// Equivalent code with Vector
$vector = Vector {0, 1, 2};
foreach ($vector as $index => $value) {
  $vector[$index] = $value * 10;
}
```

Adding values

You can append values to `Vector`s, and add them to `Set`s, with the normal empty-square-bracket syntax. In the case of `Set`s, if the value already exists in the `Set`, there's no effect:

```
$vector = Vector {'zero'};
$vector[] = 'one';
print_r($vector);  // Prints: "HH\Vector Object( [0] => zero, [1] => one )"

$set = Set {'eins'};
$set[] = 'eins';  // Value is already in $set; nothing happens
print_r($set);    // Prints: "HH\Set Object( eins )"
```

The same syntax works with `Map`s, but because you have to specify both a key and a value, the righthand side of the expression must be a `Pair` of key and value:

```
$map = Map {};
$map[] = Pair {'one', 'eins'};
print_r($map)  // Prints: "HH\Map Object( [one] => eins )"
```

You can also use the `add()` method on `Vector`s and `Set`s, passing the value to be added as the only argument. `Map` has the `add()` method, too; pass it a `Pair` of key and value.

Deleting values

To delete a value from a `Vector`, use the `removeKey()` method:

```
$vec = Vector {'first', 'second', 'third'};
$vec->removeKey(1);
print_r($vec);  // Prints: "HH\Vector Object( [0] => first, [1] => third )"
```

Note that the elements that are after the removed one are all shifted down by one index, so that the index 1 now holds the value 'third'. This is in line with vector semantics, which state that all indices between 0 and *n–1*, inclusive, are valid (where *n* is the number of elements in the vector).

The method to remove a key from a Map is also called removeKey(). To remove a value from a Set, use the method remove().

You can also delete items from Maps and Sets using the unset statement:

```
$map = Map {'one' => 'un', 'two' => 'deux'};
unset($map['one']);
print_r($map);  // Prints: "HH\Map Object( [two] => deux )"
```

However, again, you should generally use the methods instead, as unset isn't allowed —for good reason—in strict mode. You can use unset if you need to write code that accepts both arrays and collections seamlessly.

unset does *not* work with Vectors. This is because the semantics of removing elements from Vectors don't match the semantics of removing elements from arrays. Unsetting an element of an array (even one that's being used like a vector) leaves a "hole," where the array's valid indices are not contiguous, thus breaking vector semantics:

```
$arr = array('zero', 'one', 'two');
unset($arr[1]);
print_r($arr);  // Prints: "Array( [0] => zero, [2] => two )"
```

Operators

Collections can be compared for equality with the == operator. This is how it works:

1. If the two sides are not the same kind of collection (disregarding mutability), the result is false. For example, a Vector may compare equal to an ImmVector, but it will never compare equal to a Map.

2. If the two sides are Vectors or ImmVectors, the result is true if and only if both sides contain the same number of values, and the values at each index compare equal using ==. For example:

    ```
    $vector = Vector {1, 2};
    $immvector = ImmVector {1, 2};
    $strings = Vector {'1', '2'};
    $wrong_order = Vector {2, 1};

    var_dump($vector == $immvector);    // true
    ```

```
var_dump($vector == $strings);     // true, because 1 == '1', 2 == '2'
var_dump($vector == $wrong_order); // false
```

3. If the two sides are `Pairs`, the result is `true` if and only if the values at each index compare equal using ==.

4. If the two sides are `Sets` or `ImmSets`, the result is `true` if and only if both sides contain the same number of values, and every element in one side exists in the other side. Unlike with `Vectors`, these existence tests are done with === identity comparison. Order is irrelevant. For example:

```
$set = Set {1, 2};
$immset = ImmSet {1, 2};
$strings = Set {'1', '2'};
$wrong_order = Set {2, 1};

var_dump($set == $immset);      // true
var_dump($set == $strings);     // false
var_dump($set == $wrong_order); // true
```

5. If the two sides are `Maps` or `ImmMaps`, the result is `true` if and only if both sides contain the same number of keys, every key in one side exists in the other side (using *identity* comparison), and identical keys map to *equal* values (using == comparison). Order is irrelevant. For example:

```
$map = Map {10 => 20, 20 => 40};
$string_keys = Map {'10' => 20, '20' => 40};
$string_values = Map {10 => '20', 20 => '40'};

var_dump($map == $string_keys);   // false
var_dump($map == $string_values); // true
```

Collections can be compared for identity with the === operator. This only evaluates to `true` if both sides of the operator are the *same object*. If they are distinct objects, === comparison will evaluate to `false` even if the two objects have the same contents:

```
$vector = Vector {1, 2};
$another_variable = $vector;
var_dump($vector === $another_variable);  // true

$other = Vector {1, 2};
var_dump($vector === $other);  // false
```

List assignment with a collection on the righthand side works just as if the collection were an array. List assignment is shorthand for indexing into the array or collection on the righthand side with integer keys, so this is the behavior for `Maps` and `Sets` (the internal ordering of the `Map` or `Set` doesn't matter):

```
$vector = Vector {'one', 'two'};
list($one, $two) = $vector;
```

```
$map = Map {1 => 'one', 0 => 'zero'};
list($zero, $one) = $map;  // $zero is 'zero' and $one is 'one'
```

Immutable collections

Vector, Map, and Set have immutable equivalents: ImmVector, ImmMap, and ImmSet, respectively. (Pair is immutable and has no mutable equivalent.) They don't implement any methods that modify their contents, and they can't be modified through square-bracket syntax or unset; if you try to do so, an InvalidOperationException will be thrown. The contents of immutable collections are fixed when they're created. They can be created with literal syntax—just use ImmVector, ImmMap, or ImmSet as the class name—or through their constructors or conversion from another collection (see "Concrete Collection Classes" on page 118).

You should generally use immutable collections whenever possible. If some data isn't supposed to change, enforcing that contract closes off a possible source of bugs. It also encodes more information about the program's behavior in the type system, which is always a good thing.

Type Annotations for Collections

Most of the time, you shouldn't use the collection class names themselves in type annotations. Hack provides a large set of interfaces that describe elements of a collection's functionality, and you should generally use those in type annotations.

For example, if you're writing a function that takes a set of values as an argument and doesn't modify it, you should annotate the argument as ConstSet, an interface, rather than Set, the concrete class. This increases expressiveness, which helps the type-checker catch more mistakes: if you try to modify the set within the function, there will be a type error. It also makes the function's contract clear to callers: it wants a set, and it won't modify it.

In this section, we'll see the interfaces that you're most likely to use. This will double as a natural way to present the object-oriented interfaces to the collection classes. If you just want to see the collection class APIs all in one, skip to "Concrete Collection Classes" on page 118; that section doesn't have explanations for the methods, but many of them are self-explanatory, especially with type annotations.

Core Interfaces

The core collection interfaces are:

Traversable<T>

Anything that can be iterated over using foreach without a key is Traversable. Within such a foreach, the iteration variable will have type T. This is the only thing Traversable guarantees; it does not declare any methods.

The most important thing about Traversable is that regular PHP arrays are Traversable. This is unusual, because arrays are not objects and, in general, only objects can implement interfaces. Traversable is special-cased in the runtime to have this behavior.

In addition to arrays and collections, Traversable includes objects that implement Iterator.

Traversable can help bridge the gap between arrays and collections. If the only thing you do with a function argument is iterate over it using foreach without a key, irrespective of whether it's an array, a collection, or something else, you should annotate it as Traversable.

Note that if you're implementing your own class that you want to be usable with foreach, you should *not* make it implement Traversable. Use Iterable (described shortly) instead.

KeyedTraversable<Tk, Tv> extends Traversable<Tv>

KeyedTraversable is similar to Traversable, but additionally indicates that it's valid to include a key in the foreach statement. Regular PHP arrays are KeyedTraversable. The following example shows the difference between Traversable and KeyedTraversable:

```
function notKeyed(Traversable<T> $traversable): void {
  // Not valid
  foreach ($traversable as $key => $value) {
    // ...
  }
}

function keyed(KeyedTraversable<Tk, Tv> $traversable): void {
  // Valid
  foreach ($traversable as $key => $value) {
    // $key is of type Tk
    // $value is of type Tv
  }
}
```

Container<T> extends Traversable<T>

Container is exactly like Traversable, except that it does *not* include objects that implement Iterator. In other words, it includes only arrays and instances of col-

lection classes. The only thing you can do with a `Container` is to iterate over it
with `foreach`.

`KeyedContainer<Tk, Tv>` extends `KeyedTraversable<Tk, Tv>`
Similarly, `KeyedContainer` is like `KeyedTraversable`, except that it is restricted
to arrays and collection classes other than `Set` and `ImmSet`.

`Indexish<Tk, Tv>` extends `KeyedTraversable<Tk, Tv>`
`Indexish` signifies anything that can be indexed into using square-bracket syntax: `$indexish[$key]`. It declares no methods. Like `Traversable` and `KeyedTraversable`, it is a special interface that is "implemented" by arrays as well as collections and other objects that support this syntax.

`IteratorAggregate<T>` extends `Traversable<T>`
This interface is for objects that can produce an `Iterator` object to iterate over their contents. Unlike the previous three interfaces, it is *not* implemented by arrays. It's very unlikely that you'll ever use `IteratorAggregate` in type annotations—either `Iterable` or `Traversable` is probably more appropriate. The interface declares a single method:

- `getIterator(): Iterator<T>` returns an iterator over the object's contents.
  The `Iterator` interface is the one from standard PHP.

`Iterable<T>` extends `IteratorAggregate<T>`
This is where the real capabilities of collections begin to come in. The `Iterable`
interface declares several methods:

- `toArray(): array` converts the collection to an array. Note that the return
  value does not have a type argument: it's simply `array` instead of `array<T>`.

- `toValuesArray(): array` converts the collection to an array but discards
  the keys, replacing them with the integers *0* to *n*–1, in order.

- `toVector(): Vector<T>` converts the collection to a `Vector`. This is very
  similar to `toValuesArray()`; if the collection has keys (i.e., is a `Map`), the keys
  will be discarded.

- `toImmVector(): ImmVector<T>:` converts to an immutable `Vector`.

- `toSet(): Set<T>` converts the collection to a `Set`, discarding the keys, if any.

- `toImmSet(): ImmSet<T>` converts to an immutable `Set`.

- `values(): Iterable<T>` returns an `Iterable` object yielding the collection's
  values (discarding keys).

- `map<Tm>(function(T): Tm $callback): Iterable<Tm>` returns an
  `Iterable` object yielding the collection's values after they have been passed

through the given function. It is much like the standard PHP `array_map()` function. Here's an example that multiplies the elements of a `Vector` by 10:

```
$nums = Vector {1, 2, 3};
print_r($nums->map(function($x) { return $x * 10; }));

HH\Vector Object
(
    [0] => 10
    [1] => 20
    [2] => 30
)
```

- `filter(function(T): bool $callback): Iterable<T>` returns an `Iterable` object yielding the values from the collection that make the given function return `true`. Here's an example of picking out even numbers from a `Vector`:

```
$nums = Vector {1, 2, 3, 4};
print_r($nums->filter(function($x) { return $x % 2 === 0; }));

HH\Vector Object
(
    [0] => 2
    [1] => 4
)
```

- `zip<Tz>(Traversable<Tz> $traversable): Iterable<Pair<T, Tz>>` returns an `Iterable` object that pairs up the values from this collection and the values from the passed-in `Traversable`. An example is the best way to explain it:

```
$english = Vector {'one', 'two', 'three'};
$french = Vector {'un', 'deux', 'trois'};
print_r($english->zip($french));
```

This will output:

```
HH\Vector Object
(
    [0] => HH\Pair Object
        (
            [0] => one
            [1] => un
        )

    [1] => HH\Pair Object
        (
            [0] => two
            [1] => deux
        )
```

```
        [2] => HH\Pair Object
            (
                [0] => three
                [1] => trois
            )

    )
```

If the two collections have different counts, the resulting `Iterable` will have the smaller count.

`KeyedIterable<Tk, Tv> extends Iterable<Tv>`

This is analogous to `Iterable`, but with the key's type included. It adds some new methods and overrides some from `Iterable` with different return types. The new methods are listed first:

- `toKeysArray(): array` returns an array of the `Iterable`'s keys.

- `toMap(): Map<Tk, Tv>` returns the `Iterable` converted to a Map.

- `keys(): Iterable<Tk>*` returns an `Iterable` over this `Iterable`'s keys.

- `mapWithKey<Tm>(function(Tk, Tv): Tm $callback): KeyedItera ble<Tk, Tm>` is like `map()` but passes keys to the callback function as well as values.

- `filterWithKey(function(Tk, Tv): bool $callback): KeyedItera ble<Tk, Tv>` is like `filter()` but passes keys to the callback function as well as values.

- `getIterator(): KeyedIterator<Tk, Tv>` is an override with a more specific return type.

- `map<Tm>(function(T): Tm $callback): KeyedIterable<Tk, Tu>` is an override with a more specific return type.

- `filter(function(T): bool $callback): Iterable<T>` is an override with a more specific return type.

- `zip<Tz>(Traversable<Tz> $traversable): Iterable<Pair<T, Tz>>` is an override with a more specific return type.

General Collection Interfaces

There are three core interfaces that declare the most basic collection functionality. You'll essentially never use these in type annotations, as they're too nonspecific to be useful that way, but we'll look at them here to learn these core functions:

ConstCollection<T>

A read-only collection of values of type T. It says nothing about uniqueness of values, ordering, underlying implementation, or anything.

Every concrete collection class implements this interface (indirectly). It may seem unsuitable for Map, because it only has one type parameter and Map needs two (one for keys and one for values), but Maps do implement ConstCollection: a Map with key type Tk and value type Tv implements ConstCollection<Pair<Tk, Tv>>.

This interface declares three methods:

- count(): int returns the number of values in the collection.
- isEmpty(): bool returns whether the collection is empty.
- items(): Iterable<T> returns a value that can be iterated over using foreach, and will yield every value in the collection.

OutputCollection<T>

This interface declares two methods that allow adding values to the collection (every mutable collection class implements this):

- add(T $value): this adds the given value to the collection and returns the collection itself.
- addAll(?Traversable<T> $values): this iterates over the given Traversable and adds each resulting value to the collection. It returns the collection itself.

Collection<T> extends ConstCollection<T>, OutputCollection<T>

This interface declares no methods; it just serves to combine the read-only behavior of ConstCollection and the write-only behavior of OutputCollection.

Specific Collection Interfaces

Now, at last, we'll get into specific collection functionality. We'll look at six collection interfaces and the methods they declare.[3] They're meant to describe functionality independent of implementation. For now, there's only one concrete implementation of each, but there may be others in the future—for example, one can imagine a linked list–based class that implements MutableVector.

---

3 This section is not telling the whole story. There are actually six other interfaces in the picture, called SetAccess, ConstSetAccess, and similar. I'm not going into all the details of those because they're not used in type annotations and aren't essential to using collections.

All of these interfaces either directly or indirectly extend `KeyedIterable`, which declares several methods with `KeyedIterable` as their return type, such as `map()` and `filter()`. All of these interfaces override such methods with specific return types—for example, `ConstVector<T>` declares `filter(function(T): bool $callback): ConstVector<T>`. These overridden methods are omitted in the following list:

`ConstSet<T> extends ConstCollection<T>, KeyedIterable<mixed, T>`
This represents a read-only set of values of type T.[4] It declares only one method directly:

- `contains(T $value): bool` returns whether the given value is in the set. The semantics are the same as === comparison: the result is `true` if and only if there is a value `in the set that compares identical to `$value` using ===.

`MutableSet<T> extends ConstSet<T>, Collection<T>`
This represents a modifiable set of values of type T. It extends `ConstSet` and declares two methods directly:

- `clear(): this` removes all values from the set, and returns the set.
- `remove(T $value): this` removes the given value from the set (doing nothing if the value is not in the set), and returns the set. As with `contains()`, the semantics are the same as === comparison.

`ConstVector<T> extends ConstCollection<T>, KeyedIterable<int, T>`
This represents a read-only sequence of values of type T, indexed by integers. It declares three methods directly:

- `at(int $index): T` returns the value at the given index, or throws an exception if the index is out of bounds.
- `containsKey(int $index): bool` returns whether the given index is in bounds.
- `get(int $index): ?T` returns the value at the given index, or `null` if the index is out of bounds.

---

4 You may wonder why this interface extends `KeyedIterable<mixed, T>` instead of `KeyedIterable<T, T>`. The reason is a subtle problem with the type of `map()`. `KeyedIterable<T, T>` would declare a `map<Tm>()` function that returned `KeyedIterable<T, Tm>`. Then, `ConstSet<T>` would override it with a version that returned `ConstSet<Tm>`. The problem is that these are not compatible: in `KeyedIterable<T, Tm>`, the key and value types may be different, but in `ConstSet<Tm>`, they cannot be different. Making the key type `mixed` is slightly inelegant, and this may change in the future with additional typechecker functionality.

`MutableVector<T> extends ConstVector<T>, Collection<T>`

This represents a modifiable sequence of values of type T. It extends `ConstVector` and adds these methods:

- `clear():` this removes all values from the vector.

- `removeKey(int $index):` this removes the value at the given index. In line with vector semantics, the values at higher indices will all be shifted down by one, so that the indices remain contiguous.

- `set(int $index, T value):` this sets the given value at the given index, throwing an exception if the index is out of bounds. If you want to extend the vector, use `add()`.

- `setAll(KeyedTraversable<int, T> $kt):` this iterates over the given Key edTraversable and calls `set()` with each key/value pair in it.

`ConstMap<Tk, Tv> extends ConstCollection<Pair<Tk, Tv>>, KeyedItera ble<Tk, Tv>`

This represents a read-only mapping of keys of type Tk to values of type Tv. It declares methods that resemble those of `ConstSet` and `ConstVector`:

- `at(Tk $key):` Tv returns the value for the given key, or throws an exception if the key isn't in the map.

- `contains(Tk $key):` bool returns whether the given key exists in the map.

- `containsKey(Tk $key):` bool is the same as `contains()`. The duplication of methods is just a quirk of the inheritance hierarchy of these interfaces.

- `get(Tk $key):` ?Tv returns the value for the given key, or `null` if the key isn't in the map.

`MutableMap<Tk, Tv> extends ConstMap<Tk, Tv>`

This represents a modifiable mapping of keys to values. Again, the methods that it declares are a combination of the methods from `MutableVector` and `Mutable Set`:

- `clear():` this removes all keys and values from the map.

- `remove(Tk $key):` this removes the value at the given key.

- `removeKey(Tk $key):` this is exactly the same as `remove()`.

- `set(Tk $key, Tv $value):` this sets the given value at the given key.

- `setAll(KeyedTraversable<Tk, Tv> $kt):` this iterates over the given Key edTraversable and calls `set()` with each key/value pair in it.

Concrete Collection Classes

Finally, to bring all this together, we'll look at the full type-annotated APIs to all the collection classes. Each one implements one of the six interfaces from the previous section, and adds a few more useful methods.

Only methods defined by the classes themselves, and not declared by any of the interfaces we just saw, are listed here:

ImmVector<T> implements ConstVector<T>

- __construct(?Traversable<T> $values) creates a new ImmVector with the contents of the given Traversable.
- linearSearch(T $value): int performs a linear search for the given value within the ImmVector and returns the index at which the value was found, or -1 if it wasn't found.
- __toString(): string just returns "ImmVector".

Vector<T> implements MutableVector<T>

- __construct(?Traversable<T> $values) creates a new Vector with the contents of the given Traversable.
- linearSearch(T $value): int performs a linear search for the given value within the Vector and returns the index at which the value was found, or -1 if it wasn't found.
- pop(): T removes the last value from the Vector and returns it.
- reserve(int $size): void hints to the Vector that it should reallocate memory to hold the given number of values. The Vector may not do exactly that; this is just a hint.
- resize(int $size, T $value): void changes the size of the Vector to the passed size. If the new size is smaller than the current size, values at the end of the Vector are removed. If the new size is larger, the new values are set to $value.
- reverse(): void reverses the Vector in place.
- shuffle(): void randomly rearranges the values in the Vector.
- splice(int $offset, ?int $len = NULL): void removes $len values from the Vector, starting at $offset. If $len is not passed, it removes every value from $offset to the end of the Vector. This is similar to the built-in function array_splice().
- __toString(): string just returns "Vector".

`ImmSet<T> implements ConstSet<T>`

- `__construct(?Traversable<T> $values)` creates a new `ImmSet` with the contents of the given `Traversable`.

- `fromArrays(...): ImmSet<T>` is a `static` method that takes a variable number of arguments, which must all be arrays, and creates an `ImmSet` from all their contents.

- `fromItems(?Traversable<T> $items): ImmSet<T>` is a static method that creates an `ImmSet` from the given `Traversable`.

- `__toString(): string` just returns `"ImmSet"`.

`Set<T> implements MutableSet<T>`

- `__construct(?Traversable<T> $values)` creates a new `Set` with the contents of the given `Traversable`.

- `fromArrays(...): Set<T>` is a static method that takes a variable number of arguments, which must all be arrays, and creates an `Set` from all their contents.

- `fromItems(?Traversable<T> $items): Set<T>` is a static method that creates an `Set` from the given `Traversable`.

- `removeAll(?Traversable<T> $values): Set<T>` removes all the values in the given `Traversable` from the set, and returns the set itself.

- `__toString(): string` just returns `"Set"`.

`ImmMap<Tk, Tv> implements ConstMap<Tk, Tv>`

- `__construct(?KeyedTraversable<Tk, Tv> $values)` creates a new `ImmMap` with the contents of the given `Traversable`.

- `fromItems(?Traversable<Pair<Tk, Tv>> $items): ImmMap<T>` is a static method that creates an `ImmMap` from the given `Traversable`.

- `__toString(): string` just returns `"ImmMap"`.

`Map<Tk, Tv> implements MutableMap<Tk, Tv>`

- `__construct(?KeyedTraversable<Tk, Tv> $values)` creates a new `Map` with the contents of the given `Traversable`.

- `fromItems(?Traversable<Pair<Tk, Tv>> $items): Map<T>` is a static method that creates an `Map` from the given `Traversable`.

- `__toString(): string` just returns `"Map"`.

Interoperating with Arrays

Like other Hack features, collections were designed with interoperability in mind. A codebase can be gradually converted from using arrays to using collections.

Conversion to Arrays

All Hack collections can be converted to arrays with a cast expression, or with the `toArray()` method:

```
$vector = Vector {'first', 'second'};
print_r((array)$vector);        // Prints: Array( [0] => first, [1] => second )
print_r($vector->toArray());   // Same
```

The conversions are straightforward:

- Vectors and ImmVectors convert to arrays where the keys are the integer indices of the values, in the same order.

- Maps and ImmMaps convert to arrays with the same key/value pairs, in the same order.

- Sets and ImmSets convert to arrays with each key mapping to itself, in the same order.

- Pairs convert to arrays with the keys 0 and 1 (integers) in that order, mapping to the corresponding values.

There is a small wrinkle in the case of integer-like string keys (see "Reading and Writing" on page 105) in Maps and Sets. If the Map or Set contains keys that conflict with each other in this way, an E_WARNING-level error will be raised. The conflicting keys will reduce to one integer key in the resulting array, and it will map to the *last* value under the conflicting keys:

```
<?php
$map = Map {10 => 'int', '10' => 'string'};
$array = (array)$map;
// Warning: Map::toArray() for a map containing both int(10) and string('10')
var_dump($array);  // Prints: array(1) { [10]=> string(6) "string" }

$set = Set {10, "10"}
$array = (array)$set;
// Warning: Set::toArray() for a map containing both int(10) and string('10')
var_dump($array);  // Prints: array(1) { [10]=> string(2) "10" }
```

Use with Built-In and User Functions

Hack has a lot of built-in functions that can take arrays as arguments. There are several different ways in which these have been adapted to work with collections.

The sort built-ins

Hack has a wide variety of functions that are used to sort arrays. All of these have been adapted to work with collections as well, but each one only works with certain types of collections.

- Vectors only work with `sort()`, `rsort()`, and `usort()`. All the other sorting functions are concerned with keys, which doesn't make sense for a `Vector`.

- Maps and Sets only work with `asort()`, `arsort()`, `ksort()`, `krsort()`, `usort()`, `uasort()`, `uksort()`, `natsort()`, and `natcasesort()`. Note that for Sets, sorting by key is the same as sorting by value.

- Immutable collections and `Pairs` aren't supported because they're immutable, and these functions sort in place. Make a mutable copy of the collection and sort that instead.

Other built-ins

The remaining built-ins that deal with arrays take a variety of approaches. There are a few specific kinds to look at first:

- *Four built-ins that modify arrays* have been adapted to work with collections:
  - `array_pop()`
  - `array_push()`
  - `array_shift()`
  - `array_unshift()`

  The rest have not. Note that `array_push()` and `array_unshift()` support only Vector and Set.

- *Built-ins that read or modify arrays' internal pointers*, such as `current()` and `reset()`, don't work with collections at all, because collections don't have an equivalent of Hack arrays' internal pointers.

- *Debugging and introspection functions* produce output for collections similar to what they produce for arrays. For example, this:

  ```
  var_dump(array(10, 20));
  var_dump(Vector {10, 20});
  ```

  produces:

  ```
  array(2) {
    [0]=>
    int(10)
    [1]=>
    int(20)
  ```

```
  }
  object(HH\Vector)#1 (2) {
    [0]=>
    int(10)
    [1]=>
    int(20)
  }
```

The functions are:

— `debug_zval_dump()`

— `print_r()`

— `var_dump()`

— `var_export()`

- `serialize()` can serialize collections, but the resulting serialized string can only be unserialized by HHVM. (Collections aren't serialized the same way as other objects.)

The most common case among the remaining built-ins is that they have a parameter that *must* be an array and is *not* by-reference. Examples of this include `count()` and `array_diff()`. In cases like this, if you pass a collection as that parameter, it will be automatically converted to an array,[5] with no warning or error.

The last, and trickiest, category of built-ins consists of the ones that adapt their behavior based on the types of the arguments they're passed. `apc_store()` is an example: if the first argument is a string, a single value is stored in the Alternative PHP Cache (APC); but if it's an array, all the key/value mappings in the array are stored in APC. In general, built-ins like these do *not* support collections. The lone exception in HHVM 3.9 is `implode()`, which does support collections.

Non-built-in functions

Non-built-in functions with an `array` typehint will implicitly convert passed-in collections to arrays, but there will be an `E_NOTICE`-level error when doing so. The rationale for this behavior is that this code is likely under your control, so you can modify it to have a collection typehint, or `Indexish`, or `Traversable`, or whatever is appropriate. However, it may *not* be under your control (e.g., it could be in a third-party library), so making this a hard error like a fatal or an exception is too strict. For example, this code:

---

5 For efficiency, some of these built-ins have been adapted to use the collection directly, without converting it to an array, but the effect is exactly the same.

```
function examine(array $items) {
  if (is_array($items)) {
    echo "It's an array!";
  }
}

examine(Vector {1, 2, 3});
```

produces the following output:

```
Notice: Argument 1 to examine() must be of type array, HH\Vector given;
argument 1 was implicitly cast to array
It's an array!
```

By contrast, if you pass an array to a user function that expects a collection, no implicit conversion will happen, and the typehint will fail.

CHAPTER 6

Async

Typical web apps will need to start time-consuming external operations and wait for them to finish. They make queries to databases, which can involve waiting for a server across a network to read from a spinning disk. They might use external APIs, which can involve making HTTP or HTTPS requests across the Internet. These can take a lot of time, and if the app can't multitask, it will waste time waiting for those operations to finish, as it can't do anything useful in the meantime.

It gets worse: if a non-multitasking app has multiple time-consuming operations that could be done simultaneously (e.g., two independent database queries), it can't. It has to wait for one to finish, then start the next and wait for that to finish, and so on. This inefficiency adds up quickly and is tremendously wasteful; for high-traffic web apps, some form of multitasking that gets around these problems is a necessity. Some PHP extensions, like cURL and MySQLi, have support for executing multiple operations at a time, but they don't interoperate with each other.

In Figure 6-1, for example, the two queries could run in parallel, but with no way to multitask, they must run one at a time.

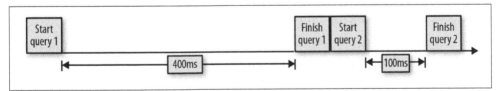

Figure 6-1. Two database queries, without async

Like PHP, Hack doesn't support multithreading, so web apps in Hack need some other form of multitasking.

That's the purpose of async. It offers a way to implement *cooperative multitasking*, in which tasks voluntarily and explicitly cede the CPU to one another. The opposite is *preemptive multitasking*, in which tasks are forcibly interrupted by the task manager.

Cooperative multitasking has several advantages over preemptive multitasking. Preemptive multitasking requires significant care to use safely. In the preemptive model, concurrency safety has to be pervasive; you have to protect critical sections and synchronize access to shared memory. In cooperative multitasking, none of that applies. Because each task gets to control when it yields to other tasks, it doesn't have to go out of its way to protect critical sections: all it has to do is avoid breaking them.

Async provides syntax for giving up the CPU to other async tasks, as well as infrastructure within HHVM (the *scheduler*) that manages the cooperative multitasking, deciding which async tasks to run and when. Figure 6-2 shows how cooperative multitasking can significantly reduce the end-to-end time of the two queries from Figure 6-1, by doing the second query while waiting for the first to complete.

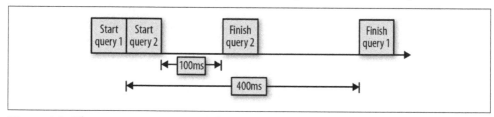

Figure 6-2. The same two queries, with async

In this chapter, we'll see what async functions look like, how to use them, how to structure your code around them, and how to use the async extensions that HHVM provides.

Introductory Examples

In this section, we'll look at a few small examples of async functions, just to give you an idea of what they look like and how async code is structured. We'll gloss over most of the details for now, and get into all the specifics in the rest of the chapter.

There are two syntactic differences between async functions and regular functions. Async functions have the `async` keyword immediately before the `function` keyword in their headers, and they can use the `await` keyword in their bodies. Here's the simplest possible example of an async function:

```
async function hello(): Awaitable<string> {
  return 'hello';
}
```

Methods, both static and non-static, can be async as well:

```
class C {
  public static async function hello(): Awaitable<string> {
    return 'hello';
  }
  public async function goodbye(): Awaitable<string> {
    return 'goodbye';
  }
}
```

Closures can also be async, whether they use PHP closure syntax or Hack lambda expression syntax (see "Lambda Expressions" on page 74):

```
$hello = async function(): Awaitable<string> { return 'hello'; };
$goodbye = async () ==> 'goodbye';
```

There are two important things to note about all these examples. First, async functions don't necessarily need to be inherently asynchronous at all; the examples are all returning a constant result. Second, async functions have a special return type. The bodies of these functions look as if they're returning strings, but at runtime, that's not what happens. A call to an async function returns an object that represents a result that may or may not be ready—an object that implements the interface Awaitable, as the return type annotations say. From that object, you can retrieve the value that the async function gives to its return statement.

 The return types of async functions are unique in that the type argument to Awaitable is not erased at runtime. The runtime checks values passed to return statements in async functions against that type argument, and raises catchable fatal errors if the checks fail, like it does with any other runtime type annotation failure:

```
<?hh // decl
// Decl mode to silence typechecker error

async function f(): Awaitable<string> {
  // Catchable fatal error at runtime
  return 100;
}
```

You get the value out of the Awaitable object by using the other part of the async function infrastructure: *awaiting*. An async function can use the keyword await to await the result of an asynchronous operation. The expression after the keyword must evaluate to an object that implements the interface Awaitable. An obvious example of such an object is the return value of another async function:

```
async function hello(): Awaitable<string> {
  return 'hello';
}
```

```
async function hello_world(): Awaitable<string> {
  $hello = await hello();
  return $hello . ' world';
}
```

In the function hello_world(), the first expression to be evaluated is the function call hello()—an ordinary function call. As you can see, this returns not the string 'hello', but an object that represents a result that may or may not be ready. Then the await keyword declares to the runtime, "Wait for that result to be ready, and then return it."

The runtime handles checking to see if the result is ready, and waiting if it isn't ready. If it's not ready, the runtime can *suspend* the execution of hello_world(): it stops executing the function, saves its execution state, and picks up execution somewhere else—in another async function that's waiting to run, if any.

Once the result is ready—that is, once the function hello() has executed a return statement—the scheduler can *resume* the execution of hello_world(). It restores the saved execution state of hello_world() and begins running the body of hello_world() at the point after the await expression. The await expression evaluates to whatever hello() passed to its return statement—that is, the string 'hello'. That value is assigned to the local variable $hello, and execution continues as normal from there.

This is a trivial example, though. Moving up from the syntax level, there are two things you have to do in order to reap benefits from async: use async extension functions, and await multiple asynchronous operations simultaneously.

HHVM provides async extension functions for four kinds of operations: queries to MySQL databases, queries to memcached, cURL requests, and reads and writes of stream resources. Here are examples of the async MySQL and cURL APIs:

```
async function fetch_from_web(): Awaitable<string> {
  return await HH\Asio\curl_exec('https://www.example.com/');
}

async function fetch_from_db(int $id): Awaitable<string> {
  $conn = await AsyncMysqlClient::connect(
    '127.0.0.1', 3306, 'example', 'admin', 'hunter2'
  );
  $result = await $conn->queryf('SELECT name FROM user WHERE id = %d', $id);
  return $result->mapRows()[0]['name'];
}
```

Note how similar this async code looks to equivalent non-async code—if you just removed the new keywords and changed the class and function names to use non-async extensions, it would *be* equivalent non-async code. There's no need to think about threading or synchronization. The async and await keywords are the only substantial differences: instead of simply calling a function that performs a long-running operation, you await it.

The other key to benefiting from async is to await multiple asynchronous operations at the same time. Running the two preceding async functions at the same time looks like this:

```
async function fetch_all(): Awaitable<string> {
  list($web, $db) =
  await HH\Asio\v(array(fetch_from_web(), fetch_from_db(1234)));
  return $web . $db;
}
```

We'll examine everything going on here in detail in the rest of this chapter, but now you have a high-level idea of how async code looks.

Async in Detail

Before getting started, if you're going to use async extensively, we highly recommend that you install `asio-utilities`, a library of async helper functions. We'll look at the contents of this library as we go. You can use async without it, but it makes code significantly more concise.

The recommended way to download and install the library is through Composer (*http://getcomposer.org*), a package manager for PHP and Hack. Add this to your *composer.json* file:

```
"require": {
  "hhvm/asio-utilities": "~1.0"
}
```

Wait Handles

The concept of a *wait handle* is central to the way async code works. A wait handle is an object that represents a *possibly asynchronous operation* that may or may not have completed. If it has completed, you can get a result from the wait handle. If not, you can await the wait handle.

Wait handles are represented by the generic interface `Awaitable`. There are several classes that implement this interface, but they're implementation details, and you shouldn't rely on their specifics.

The two most important kinds of wait handle are:

- Ones representing async functions. To get one of these, simply call an async function:

    ```
    async function f(): Awaitable<int> {
      // ...
    ```

```
  }
  async function main(): Awaitable<void> {
    $wait_handle = f();
    // $wait_handle is a wait handle; a value of type Awaitable<int>

    $result = await $wait_handle;
    // $result is an int; the await "unwraps" the Awaitable
  }
```

- Ones representing multiple other wait handles. To get one of these, use the async helper functions[1] HH\Asio\v() (when you have an indexed list of wait handles, like a Vector or an array with consecutive integer keys) or HH\Asio\m() (when you have an associative mapping of wait handles, like a Map or an array with string keys):

```
  async function triple(float $number): Awaitable<float> {
    return $number * 3.0;
  }

  async function triple_v(): Awaitable<void> {
    $handles = array(
      triple(3.0),
      triple(4.0),
    );
    $result = await HH\Asio\v($handles);

    var_dump($result[0]);  // Prints: float(9)
    var_dump($result[1]);  // Prints: float(12)
  }

  async function triple_m(): Awaitable<void> {
    $handles = array(
      'three' => triple(3.0),
      'four'  => triple(4.0),
    );
    $result = await HH\Asio\m($handles);

    var_dump($result['three']);  // Prints: float(9)
    var_dump($result['four']);   // Prints: float(12)
  }
```

HH\Asio\v() turns a Vector or array of awaitables into an awaitable Vector. Likewise, HH\Asio\m() turns a Map or array of awaitables into an awaitable Map.

---

1 These functions are built into HHVM; they're not part of asio-utilities. You can use them without installing the library.

For a non-async function to get a result out of a wait handle, there's a function in asio-utilities called HH\Asio\join().[2] It takes one argument, an Awaitable. The function waits for the awaitable to complete, then returns its result:

```
async function f(): Awaitable<mixed> {
  // ...
}

function main(): void {
  $result = HH\Asio\join(f());
}
```

You shouldn't call HH\Asio\join() inside an async function—if you do, that awaitable and its dependencies will run to completion synchronously, with none of your currently in-flight awaitables getting a chance to run. If you're in an async function, and you have a wait handle whose result you want, just await it.

Async and Callable Types

In "Hack's Type System" on page 6, we saw that Hack has syntax for annotating the types of callable values. In this example, you must pass f() a function that takes an integer and returns a string:

```
function f((function(int): string) $callback): void {
  // ...
}

function main(): void {
  $good = function (int $x): string { return (string)$x; };
  f($good);  // OK

  $bad = function (array $x): int { return count($x); };
  f($bad);  // Error
}
```

You might now ask: how do you do this for async functions? How would f(), in this example, specify that you must pass it an async function as a callback?

The answer is that you can't, for good reason. The async-ness of a function is an implementation detail of that function. Putting the async keyword on a function does two things:

- It allows the function to use the await keyword in its body—an implementation detail, and not something that should matter to any code outside the function.

---

2 HH\Asio\join() is part of asio-utilities, but in the future it will be built into HHVM. In general, asio-utilities is where the team tests new async APIs before building them into HHVM itself.

- It forces the function's return type to be `Awaitable`. The return type does matter to code outside the function, but what matters is *just* the return type, not the function's async-ness.

To return to the previous example, `f()` can specify that the callback must return an `Awaitable<string>`. This will *allow*, but not *require*, an async function to be passed as the callback:

```
function f((function(int): Awaitable<string>) $callback): void {
  // ...
}
```

To make the reason for this restriction clearer, consider another implementation detail of functions: whether they're closures or not. Allowing `f()` in our example to specify that you must pass it an async function would be just as silly as allowing it to specify that you must pass it a closure.

For the same reason, you can't declare abstract methods, or methods in interfaces, to be async. You can, of course, declare them as non-async, but with `Awaitable` as their return type:

```
interface I {
  public async function bad(): Awaitable<void>;   // Error
  public function good(): Awaitable<void>;         // OK
}

abstract class C {
  abstract public async function bad(): Awaitable<void>;   // Error
  abstract public function good(): Awaitable<void>;        // OK
}
```

await Is Not an Expression

Although `await` behaves like an expression in several ways, it's not a general expression. There are only three syntactic positions where it can appear:

- As an entire statement by itself:

```
async function f(): Awaitable<void> {
  await other_func();
}
```

- On the righthand side of a normal assignment or list assignment statement:

```
async function f(): Awaitable<void> {
  $result = await other_func();
  list($one, $two) = await yet_another_func();
}
```

- As the argument of a `return` statement:

```
async function f(): Awaitable<mixed> {
  return await other_func();
}
```

If you use `await` anywhere else, it's a syntax error. So, for example, you can't do this:

```
async function f(): Awaitable<void> {
  var_dump(await other_func());  // Syntax error
}
```

This restriction may be lifted in the future. It exists now because of implementation issues.[3]

Async Generators

Generators were introduced in PHP 5.5. On the surface, they look quite similar to async functions. Both features introduce a special kind of function that has the ability to stop executing partway through, in such a way that it can pick up where it left off later.

However, the two features are orthogonal: like any other functions, generators can be async. Here's an example that implements a countdown clock, yielding once per second (we'll see `HH\Asio\usleep()` in "Sleeping" on page 148):

```
async function countdown(int $start): AsyncIterator<int> {
  for ($i = $start; $i >= 0; --$i) {
    await HH\Asio\usleep(1000000);  // Sleep for 1 second
    yield $i;
  }
}
```

The most important thing to note here is the return type annotation: `AsyncIterator<int>`. This signifies that you can iterate over the value returned from `countdown()`, and the values you get out of the iteration are integers.

However, this is an async iterator, not a regular iterator. There's some new syntax to iterate over an async iterator—`await as`:

```
async function use_countdown(): Awaitable<void> {
  $async_gen = countdown();
  foreach ($async_gen await as $value) {
    // $value is of type int here
    var_dump($value);
```

---

3 As it is, with the restrictions on where `await` can appear, there's no way for an async function to get suspended in the middle of evaluating an expression. If `await` could appear anywhere, we would confront the issue of how to efficiently store the intermediate evaluation state of the expression, which isn't as straightforward as it may sound.

```
    }
  }
```

The `await as` syntax is shorthand for repeatedly doing `await $async_gen->next()`, just as the normal `foreach` syntax is shorthand for repeatedly calling `next()` on a normal iterator.

If you want to yield a key from an async generator as well, use the interface `AsyncKeyedIterator`. It has two type arguments: the key type and the value type. To iterate over one of these, you also use `await as`:

```
async function countdown(int $start): AsyncKeyedIterator<int, string> {
  for ($i = $start; $i >= 0; --$i) {
    await HH\Asio\usleep(1000000);
    yield $i => (string)$i;
  }
}

async function use_countdown(): Awaitable<void> {
  foreach (countdown(10) await as $num => $str) {
    // $num is of type int
    // $str is of type string
    var_dump($num, $str);
  }
}
```

Finally, if you want to call the `send()` or `raise()` methods on an async generator, you need to use the interface `AsyncGenerator` instead. It has three type arguments—the key type, the value type, and the type you want to pass to `send()`:

```
async function namifier(): AsyncGenerator<int, string, int> {
  // Get the first id
  $id = yield 0 => '';
  // $id is of type ?int

  while ($id !== null) {
    $name = await get_name($id);
    $id = yield $id => $name;
  }
}

async function use_namifier(array<int> $ids): Awaitable<void> {
  $namifier = namifier();
  await $namifier->next();

  // Note: this is poorly structured async code!
  // For demonstration only. Don't await in a loop.

  foreach ($ids as $id) {
    $result = await $namifier->send($id);
    // $result is of type ?(int, string)
```

```
    }
  }
```

There are some important things to point out here. First, even though the third type argument to AsyncGenerator is int, the result of a yield in the async generator is of type ?int. This is because it's always valid to pass null to send(). (Doing so is equivalent to calling next().)

Second, the result of await $namifier->send($id) is of type ?(int, string). The tuple contains the yielded key and value. The reason it's a nullable type is that the generator can always implicitly yield null, by means of yield break.

Third, remember that when calling next(), send(), and raise() on an async generator, you have to await them, not just call them.

Fourth, AsyncIterator and friends return actual values from their next() methods, rather than returning void (as the non-async Iterator and friends do). The same applies to the send() and raise() methods of AsyncGenerator.

Finally, this code is for demonstration purposes only. Don't write async code like this. In particular, don't await in a loop (see "Awaiting in a loop" on page 144 for details). Unfortunately, there are few compelling examples of async generator code now, because there aren't any extensions that use them. When there are, though, async generators will be an extremely powerful tool. For example, they could be used to implement streaming results from network services.

Exceptions in Async Functions

What we've seen so far is fairly straightforward: when you call an async function, it returns a wait handle. When you await a wait handle, you get its result: the value that the async function passed to its return statement. But what if the async function throws an exception?

The answer is that the same exception object will be rethrown when the wait handle is awaited:

```
async function thrower(): Awaitable<void> {
  throw new Exception();
}

async function main(): Awaitable<void> {
  // Does not throw
  $handle = thrower();

  // Throws an Exception, the same object thrower() threw
  await $handle;
}
```

If you're using HH\Asio\v() or HH\Asio\m() to await multiple wait handles simultaneously, and one of the component wait handles throws an exception, the combined wait handle will rethrow that exception. If multiple component wait handles throw exceptions, the combined wait handle will rethrow one of them. All of the component wait handles will complete, though (whether they finish normally or throw):

```
async function thrower(string $message): Awaitable<void> {
  throw new Exception($message);
}

async function main(): Awaitable<void> {
  // Does not throw
  $handles = [thrower('one'), thrower('two')];

  // Throws either of the two Exception objects
  $results = await HH\Asio\v($handles);
}
```

Often, this isn't what you want. In cases like this, you usually want to get the results of the wait handles that succeeded and just ignore the rest, or communicate failure in a different way.

asio-utilities provides an async function called HH\Asio\wrap(), which takes a wait handle as an argument. It will await the wait handle you pass in, catch any exception that it throws, and return an object containing either the result of the passed-in wait handle if no exception was thrown, or the exception object if one was thrown. It does this in the form of an HH\Asio\ResultOrExceptionWrapper.

HH\Asio\ResultOrExceptionWrapper is an interface in asio-utilities, defined like this:

```
namespace HH\Asio {
interface ResultOrExceptionWrapper<T> {
  public function isSucceeded(): bool;
  public function isFailed(): bool;
  public function getResult(): T;
  public function getException(): \Exception;
}
}
```

The four methods of ResultOrExceptionWrapper are:

- isSucceeded() indicates whether the inner wait handle exited normally (i.e., by means of return).

- isFailed() indicates whether the inner wait handle exited abnormally, by means of an exception.

- getResult() returns the inner wait handle's result if it exited normally, or rethrows the exception if not.

- `getException()` returns the exception that the inner wait handle threw, or throws an `InvariantException` if the inner wait handle didn't throw an exception.

Here's an example:

```
async function thrower(): Awaitable<void> {
  throw new Exception();
}

async function wrapped(): Awaitable<void> {
  // Does not throw
  $handle = HH\Asio\wrap(thrower());

  // Does not throw
  $wrapper = await $handle;

  if ($wrapper->isFailed()) {
    // Returns the same Exception object that thrower() threw
    $exc = $wrapper->getException();
  }
}
```

The examples in this section have had code like this:

```
$handle = thrower();
await $handle;
```

This is only to make it clear that calling the async function doesn't throw an exception, and awaiting the wait handle does. In general, you shouldn't separate the call from the `await` like this. "Dropping Wait Handles" on page 151 explains why in detail.

Mapping and Filtering Helpers

When creating multiple wait handles to await in parallel, you'll often have some collection of values that each need to be converted into wait handles, or you may need to filter some of them out. You can use the usual PHP and Hack built-in functions `array_map()` and `array_filter()` (or methods on Hack's collection classes) to do this, but this can make your code a bit verbose.

`asio-utilities` provides a whole slew of concisely named functions for processing arrays and collections with async mapping and filtering callbacks. They have names like `vm()`, `vfk()`, and `mmw()`. The names are terse, but these functions are so commonly used in async code that the conciseness is worth the loss of easy readability.

Here's how to decode the names:

- The first character is always v or m. This indicates what the function returns: a Vector or a Map.

- Next, you might see m, mk, f, or fk. These indicate whether the values in the collection will be passed through a mapping (m and mk) or filtering (f and fk) callback. If the k is present, this indicates that the key from the collection will be passed to the callback as well.

- Finally, there might be a w. If so, the values from the collection are passed through HH\Asio\wrap() after any mapping and filtering has been done.

The first argument is always the input array or collection. (The helpers actually accept Traversable or KeyedTraversable, as appropriate, so you can pass in iterators too.) If the function requires a callback for mapping or filtering, it is the second argument. (None of the functions require more than one callback.)

The mapping and filtering callbacks are *async* functions. Mapping callbacks must have either one parameter, of the collection's value type, or two parameters, of the collection's key and value types, respectively. They can return any type. Filtering callbacks have the same convention for parameters, and they must return booleans.

Mapping, especially, is very common: you'll have an async function that does an async operation on a single value, and you'll map that over an array or collection of values. For this, you would use vm(), vmk(), mm(), mmk(), or any of these with a w appended. The basic operation of each helper is: create a wait handle for each value by passing it to the async callback, then await all those wait handles in parallel, then put the results into a Vector. Here is an example showing what happens with both a Vector and a Map:

```
async function fourth_root(num $f): Awaitable<float> {
  if ($f < 0) {
    throw new Exception();
  }

  return sqrt(sqrt($f));
}

async function vector_with_mapping(): Awaitable<void> {
  $strs = Vector {16, 81};
  $roots = await HH\Asio\vm($strs, fun('fourth_root'));

  // $roots is Vector {2, 3}
}

async function map_with_mapping_wrapped(): Awaitable<void> {
  $nums = Map {
    'minus eighty-one' => -81,
    'sixteen' => 16,
```

```
    };
    $roots = await HH\Asio\mmw($nums, fun('fourth_root'));

    // $roots['minus eighty-one'] is a failed ResultOrExceptionWrapper
    // $roots['sixteen'] is a succeeded ResultOrExceptionWrapper with result 2
}
```

Filtering is less common. You'll have an async function that results in a boolean, and apply it to all elements of a collection in parallel. For this, you would use vf(), vfk(), mf(), mfk(), or any of these with a w appended. The basic operation of each helper is: create a wait handle for each value by passing it to the async callback, then filter the original array or collection with the resulting booleans. For example:

```
    async function is_user_admin(int $id): Awaitable<bool> {
      // ...
    }

    async function admins_from_list(Traversable<int> $ids): Awaitable<Vector<int>> {
      return HH\Asio\vf($ids, fun('is_user_admin'));
    }
```

Note that HH\Asio\v() and HH\Asio\m() are not part of asio-utilities—they are built into HHVM and always available for use in Hack code.

Table 6-1 shows the full range of helper functions and what they do.

Table 6-1. asio-utilities helper functions

Name	Returns a...	Callback	Passes key to callback?	Wraps exceptions?
v()	Vector	N/A		
vm()	Vector	Mapping	No	No
vmk()	Vector	Mapping	Yes	No
vf()	Vector	Filtering	No	No
vfk()	Vector	Filtering	Yes	No
vw()	Vector	N/A	N/A	Yes
vmw()	Vector	Mapping	No	Yes
vmkw()	Vector	Mapping	Yes	Yes
vfw()	Vector	Filtering	No	Yes
vfkw()	Vector	Filtering	Yes	Yes

Name	Returns a...	Callback	Passes key to callback?	Wraps exceptions?
m()	Map	N/A	N/A	No
mm()	Map	Mapping	No	No
mmk()	Map	Mapping	Yes	No
mf()	Map	Filtering	No	No
mfk()	Map	Filtering	Yes	No
mw()	Map	N/A	N/A	Yes
mmw()	Map	Mapping	No	Yes
mmkw()	Map	Mapping	Yes	Yes
mfw()	Map	Filtering	No	Yes
mfkw()	Map	Filtering	Yes	Yes

Lambda expression syntax (see "Lambda Expressions" on page 74) is very convenient in conjunction with these async helpers; lambdas cut down on the boilerplate required by closure syntax. To rewrite one of the previous examples:

```
async function fourth_root_strings(): Awaitable<void> {
  $strs = array('16', '81');
  $roots = await HH\Asio\vm($strs, async $str ==> fourth_root((float)$str));
  // $roots is Vector {2, 3}
}
```

Structuring Async Code

As we've seen, within a single function, async code looks very similar to naïve sequential code and is just as easy to reason about. On that level, you don't have to adapt to an unfamiliar new way of thinking.

To get the most benefit out of async, though, the higher-level organization of your code—what to put in which functions, and how to tie those functions together—requires some consideration with regard to *data dependencies*. This is the idea that in order to generate one piece of data, you need some other piece of data.

In this section, we'll look at how to break down a program's logic in terms of data dependencies, and how to translate typical data dependency shapes into async code. We'll also look at some common antipatterns, and why you should avoid them.

Data Dependencies

In a blogging application, generating a page of a single author's posts might require a series of queries like this:

1. Fetch the IDs of the author's posts—maybe all of them, maybe only the first 20 or so.

2. Fetch post data (title, excerpt, etc.) for each post ID.

3. Fetch the comment count for each post ID.

The most intuitive way to understand a set of data dependencies is with a graph. Figure 6-3 shows the dependency graph for this scenario. The arrows follow the direction of data flow; for example, each post ID flows into the fetching of post data, with the direction of the arrow.

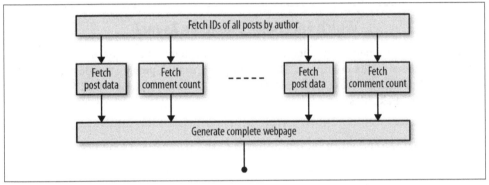

Figure 6-3. Dependency graph for "all posts by author" page

Learning how to structure async code well involves learning to recognize patterns in dependency graphs and translate them into async functions. This scenario has examples of some very common patterns:

1. Put each "chain"—a sequence of dependencies with no branching—into its own async function.

2. Put each bundle of parallel chains into its own async function.

3. Now that each bundle of parallel chains has been reduced to a single function, go back to the first step—there may be a new chain to reduce.

Note that "its own async function" doesn't have to mean a named function. It's often the best option, in terms of code cleanliness and readability, to use a closure (remember, closures can be async).

Your goal should be to fit *every* asynchronous operation that must happen in the course of a page request into this scheme. You should only have to call HH\Asio \join() once, at the very top level of your code, and its result should be all of the output for the page request.

For the "one author's posts" page, we'll use this scheme to break down the asynchronous operations into these async functions:

- One function for each underlying fetch operation: fetching all of the author's post IDs, fetching individual post data, and fetching comment counts.
- One function that bundles together a post-data-and-comment-count pair of chains. This will be a closure in the top-level function.
- One top-level function that coordinates all the data fetching.

Which Functions Should Be Async?

Don't be afraid to make a function async, even if it usually doesn't need to await anything (or never awaits anything). There's no performance penalty for doing so. If it helps the function fit better with your other code, or if it might ever need to be async in the future, make it async.

So, this is what the code for the "one author's posts" page might look like:

```
async function fetch_all_post_ids_for_author(int $author_id)
    : Awaitable<array<int>> {
  // Query database, etc.
  // ...
}

async function fetch_post_data(int $post_id): Awaitable<PostData> {
  // Query database, etc.
  // ...
}

async function fetch_comment_count(int $post_id): Awaitable<int> {
  // Query database, etc.
  // ...
}

async function fetch_page_data(int $author_id)
    : Awaitable<Vector<(PostData, int)>> {
  $all_post_ids = await fetch_all_post_ids_for_author($author_id);

  // An async closure that will turn a post ID into a tuple of
  // post data and comment count
  $post_fetcher = async function(int $post_id): Awaitable<(PostData, int)> {
```

```
    list($post_data, $comment_count) =
      await HH\Asio\v(array(
        fetch_post_data($post_id),
        fetch_comment_count($post_id),
      ));
    return tuple($post_data, $comment_count);
  };

  // Transform the array of post IDs into an array of results,
  // using the vm() function from asio-utilities
  return await HH\Asio\vm($all_post_ids, $post_fetcher);
}

async function generate_page(int $author_id): Awaitable<string> {
  $tuples = await fetch_page_data($author_id);

  foreach ($tuples as $tuple) {
    list($post_data, $comment_count) = $tuple;

    // Render the data into HTML
    // ...
  }

  // ...
}
```

Smart Data Fetching

It's important to note that this example is just meant to demonstrate how to structure async code, using an easy-to-grasp application. Depending on what your storage backends are and how you have them configured, it might be possible to do this in a single roundtrip to the database, using JOIN queries and such.

At the very least, this example should be establishing a database connection only once and passing the connection object around,[4] instead of having each fetching function, like fetch_post_data(), establish a connection itself.

It's quite possible to use async when communicating with your storage backends and still be very inefficient. Async doesn't give you license to stop thinking about things like caching intelligently, batching fetches, and constructing efficient SQL queries.

Antipatterns

There are a few ways to structure async code that may seem very tempting at first, but actually hamper the async code's ability to make efficient use of time.

---

4 See "MySQL" on page 155 for details on the async MySQL API.

These antipatterns are such because they create *false dependencies*; i.e., they cause one wait handle to wait for another (usually indirectly) even though it doesn't need to. Good async code faithfully translates the pure, ideal dependency graph into code.

Awaiting in a loop

Suppose you have an array of numerical user IDs, and an async function that loads data about a user (from a database, say) given a user ID. You want to turn the array of user IDs into an array of User objects. It's tempting to do something like this:

```
async function load_user(int $id): Awaitable<User> {
  // Call to memcache, database, ...
}

async function load_users(array<int> $ids): Awaitable<Vector<User>> {
  $result = Vector {};
  foreach ($ids as $id) {
    $result[] = await load_user($id);
  }
  return $result;
}
```

This is entirely defeating the purpose of async functions. All the users will be loaded in serial, one after the other, with no parallelism at all. This code is creating a dependency graph that is a single long chain:

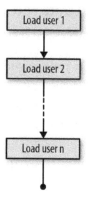

These are false dependencies, though: you don't need to finish loading the first user before you can start loading the second user. The real dependency graph, in which none of the individual user loads depends on any others, looks like this:

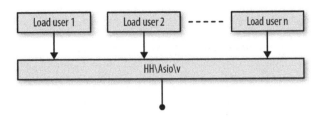

To express the real dependency graph in code, do this (the vm( ) function is explained in "Mapping and Filtering Helpers" on page 137):

```
async function load_users(array<int> $ids): Awaitable<Vector<User>> {
  return await HH\Asio\vm($ids, fun('load_user'));
}
```

In general, if you're tempted to await in a loop, that's probably because you have some collection of things to await. In that case, you should use one of the await-a-collection helpers (supplemented with `array_map()`, `array_filter()`, etc.) instead of iterating over the collection and awaiting in a loop.

This bears repeating: it's *never correct* to await in a loop. This is by far the easiest trap for async beginners to fall into, and it completely erases the benefits of async. Don't await in a loop.

The multi-ID pattern

Let's go back to the "all posts by one author" example. Suppose that instead of two parallel queries for each post, we need to do two *dependent* queries; that is, do one query, and use its result to construct another query.

Let's say, for example, that we want to display the text of the first comment on each post, instead of just the count. To start we need to fetch the ID of the first comment on each post, and then we need to fetch the content of those comments.[5]

It's tempting to implement that logic as follows:

```
async function fetch_first_comment_ids(array<int> $post_ids)
    : Awaitable<array<int>> {
  // Send a single database query with all post IDs
  // ...
}
```

---

5 This may seem odd, because a typical, normalized database schema wouldn't require the intermediate step of fetching comment IDs. However, in denormalized schemas—which have their merits, and are used in practice—this might not be possible.

```
async function fetch_comment_text(array<int> $comment_ids)
    : Awaitable<array<string>> {
  // Send a single database query with all comment IDs
  // ...
}

async function fetch_all_first_comments(int $author_id)
    : Awaitable<array<string>> {
  $all_post_ids = await fetch_all_post_ids_for_author($author_id);
  $all_comment_ids = await fetch_first_comment_ids($all_post_ids);
  return await fetch_comment_text($all_comment_ids);
}
```

This has the apparent advantage of guaranteeing only two trips to the database, regardless of how many posts you need to fetch data for. But this is poorly structured async code, again because it's creating false dependencies. Figure 6-4 shows the dependency graph created by this code. In particular, note that fetching the text for any comment indirectly depends on fetching *every* comment ID, which doesn't make sense.

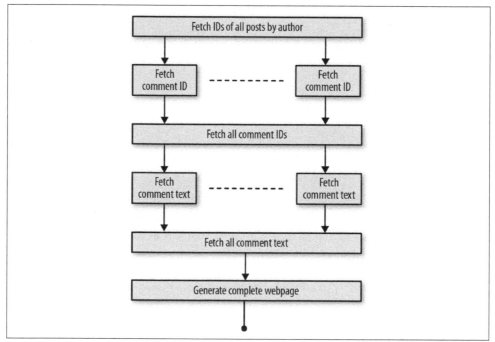

Figure 6-4. Dependency graph for bad first-comments code

The telltale sign of this antipattern is async functions that take multiple IDs, or lookup keys of any form, as arguments. They serve to create these horizontal false dependencies, which act as bottlenecks.

The real dependency graph that we should be creating doesn't have those horizontal dependencies: fetching each comment's text depends on fetching that comment's ID and nothing else. Figure 6-5 shows what the graph should look like.

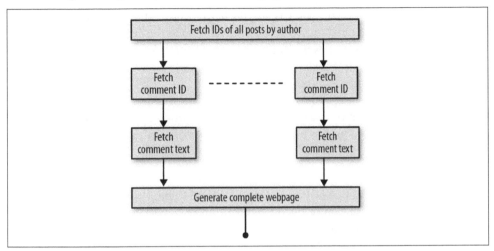

Figure 6-5. Correct dependency graph for first-comments page

We can translate this into code by following the guidelines given earlier and grouping chains of dependencies into their own functions. In this case, we group the chain for each post into a closure:

```
async function fetch_first_comment(int $comment_id): Awaitable<int> {
  // Send database query with a single post ID
  // ...
}

async function fetch_comment_text(int $comment_id): Awaitable<string> {
  // Send database query with a single comment ID
  // ...
}

async function fetch_all_first_comments(int $author_id)
    : Awaitable<Vector<string>> {
  $all_post_ids = await fetch_all_post_ids_for_author($author_id);

  $comment_fetcher = async function(int $post_id): Awaitable<string> {
    $first_comment_id = await fetch_first_comment($post_id);
    return await fetch_comment_text($first_comment_id);
  };

  return await HH\Asio\vm($all_post_ids, $comment_fetcher);
}
```

This code has the potential downside of incurring more roundtrips to the database, because it lacks the ability to send a query for more than one ID at a time. This problem can be solved fairly seamlessly with async; see "Batching" on page 149 for details.

The takeaway from these antipatterns should be to always think about the structure of the data first. Let the data inform how you structure the code; don't write code first and work out the dependencies it creates later.

Other Types of Waiting

Most of the wait handles you deal with will be representing async functions and multiple other wait handles, but there are two other kinds of waiting that can be useful.

Sleeping

You can use a wait handle to wait for a length of time to pass, while doing nothing on the CPU. This is akin to calling the usleep() built-in function, except that it allows other wait handles to run during the sleep period.

asio-utilities provides a function for sleeping: HH\Asio\usleep(). It takes one argument—the length of time to sleep for, in *microseconds*:[6]

```
async function sleepForFiveSeconds(): Awaitable<void> {
  echo "start\n";
  await HH\Asio\usleep(5000000);  // 5 million microseconds = 5 seconds
  echo "finish, at least five seconds later\n";
}
```

Note that the second echo happens *at least* five seconds later, not *exactly* five seconds later. When this wait handle sleeps, another one might run that uses the CPU for more than five seconds without awaiting, and the async scheduler can't interrupt it.

Rescheduling

To *reschedule* a wait handle means to send it to the back of the async scheduler's queue—to voluntarily wait until other pending wait handles have run. There are a couple of reasons you might want to do this: to interleave polling loops with other async operations, and to do batching.

---

[6] Measuring time on computers is always a tricky business. The timespan for which HH\Asio\usleep() actually sleeps may not be accurate to the microsecond, for various reasons, not least of which is the fact that the "clock" that underlies it varies according to what is available in the operating system and hardware where HHVM is running.

Polling

Ideally, your code would do all asynchronous work through async extensions. However, you may need to use some service that doesn't have a corresponding async extension. You may be able to use rescheduling to make such services work harmoniously with your async code.

The key is that you must be able to make nonblocking calls to the service. If you can, you can use rescheduling in your polling loop to allow other wait handles to run after unsuccessful polls.

`asio-utilities` provides a function for rescheduling: `HH\Asio\later()`. It takes no arguments. All you have to do is call and await it:

```
async function poll_for_result(PollingService $svc): Awaitable<mixed> {
  while (!$svc->isReady()) {
    await HH\Asio\later();
  }
  return $svc->getResult();
}
```

If there are no other wait handles running, this amounts to a busy loop of polling. Depending on how expensive it is to poll, and the expected latency of the service, you may want to sleep in this situation instead, using `HH\Asio\usleep()`.

Batching

If you're doing some high-latency operation that can benefit from batching—database queries are a good example—rescheduling can help you here too. The key is that you write an async function that does a batched operation after rescheduling, to give other wait handles a chance to add their items to the batch.

In this example, suppose that our underlying asynchronous operation is a key/value lookup that requires a roundtrip over a network to a storage server. Each roundtrip is high-latency, but you can send multiple keys in a single request without increasing the overall time taken. (`memcached` behaves somewhat like this, but we won't use its specific API.)

The code that uses this operation will look like this:

```
async function one(string $key): Awaitable<string> {
  $subkey = await Batcher::lookup($key);
  return await Batcher::lookup($subkey);
}

async function two(string $key): Awaitable<string> {
  return await Batcher::lookup($key);
}

async function main(): Awaitable<void> {
```

```
    $results = await HH\Asio\v(array(one('hello'), two('world')));
    echo $results[0];
    echo $results[1];
  }
```

If `Batcher::lookup()` simply did the lookup operation immediately, executing both `one()` and `two()` would result in a combined total of three roundtrips to the storage server. However, there's an optimization opportunity: if we could perform the first lookup in `one()` and the lookup in `two()` in a single roundtrip, we could complete everything with only two roundtrips, total.

Here's an implementation of the `Batcher` class that can do this:

```
class Batcher {
  private static array<string> $pendingKeys = array();
  private static ?Awaitable<array<string, string>> $waitHandle = null;

  public static async function lookup(string $key): Awaitable<string> {
    // Add this key to the pending batch
    self::$pendingKeys[] = $key;

    // If there's no wait handle about to start, create a new one
    if (self::$waitHandle === null) {
      self::$waitHandle = self::go();
    }

    // Wait for the batch to complete, and get our result from it
    $results = await self::$waitHandle;
    return $results[$key];
  }

  private static async function go(): Awaitable<array<string, string>> {
    // Let other wait handles get into this batch
    await HH\Asio\later();

    // Now this batch has started; clear the shared state
    $keys = self::$pendingKeys;
    self::$pendingKeys = array();
    self::$waitHandle = null;

    // Do the multi-key roundtrip
    return await multi_key_lookup($keys);
  }
}
```

The private static property `$waitHandle` represents a batched roundtrip that is about to start. The public method `lookup()` checks to see if a batched roundtrip is about to start; if not, it creates a new one by calling `go()`. It awaits the batched roundtrip, then retrieves the result it's interested in.

The await HH\Asio\later() in go() is the key to the batching. It functions as a "last call" for other wait handles that want to do lookups, causing go() to be deferred until other pending wait handles have run.

Consider the example of one() and two(). The proceedings start with this line:

```
$results = await HH\Asio\v(array(one('hello'), two('world')));
```

Both one() and two() are pending. Suppose one() gets to run first. It calls lookup(), which calls go(), which reschedules. The runtime looks for other wait handles it can run; two() is still pending, so that runs, calls lookup(), and gets suspended when it executes await self::$waitHandle (because that wait handle is already running).

After that, go() resumes, does its fetching, and returns its result. Both pending instances of lookup() receive their results, and pass them back to one() and two().

Common Mistakes

As we've seen, writing async code is broadly similar to writing normal sequential code. However, there are a few common traps you can fall into.

Dropping Wait Handles

When you call an async function, it returns a wait handle. When you await this wait handle, the async function's body will execute to completion. But what happens if you don't await the wait handle?

```
async function speak(): Awaitable<void> {
  echo "one";
  await HH\Asio\later();
  echo "two";
  echo "three";
}

async function f(): Awaitable<void> {
  $handle = speak();
  // Don't await or join it; just drop it
}

HH\Asio\join(f());
```

How much of speak() will execute? In other words, what will be echoed?

The possible answers are nothing, one, and onetwothree. In addition, the answer you get is not guaranteed to be consistent between runs. It can also change based on the version of HHVM you're running, the state of any other in-flight async functions, and the activities of butterflies flapping their wings on the other side of the world.

That is to say, the runtime has a lot of leeway to decide what to do. It is only allowed to suspend speak() when it encounters an await expression. Within that constraint, it may suspend and resume speak() as many times as it wants. This is to give the async scheduler the flexibility to arrange async execution as it sees fit, but it does mean that you have to be careful to await any wait handle that you create. Failing to await a wait handle will result in unpredictable behavior. Awaiting a wait handle guarantees that it will run to completion.

You may feel tempted to do something like this to implement detached tasks—that is, when you want to start a task and let it run, but you don't want to block anything else on waiting for it to finish. Nonessential logging in a web application is a common thing that tempts people to do this. Async doesn't provide a way to detach tasks. The only way to force a wait handle to run is to await it, and there's no way to await a wait handle without potentially blocking.

Even if you await all wait handles that you create, it's still possible to see their effects in different orders. In this example, any side effects (writing to the output buffer, network or disk I/O, etc.) of some_unrelated_stuff() may happen before or after any side effects of some_async_function():

```
async function f(): Awaitable<void> {
  $handle = some_async_function();
  some_unrelated_stuff();
  await $handle;
}
```

Generally, separating the creating of wait handles from awaiting them is discouraged; the creation and awaiting of a wait handle should happen as close together as possible. The preceding example would be better written as:

```
async function f(): Awaitable<void> {
  some_unrelated_stuff();
  await some_async_function();
}
```

Don't assume, because you observe the "correct" ordering of effects once, that they will always happen in that order. The ordering can change between two executions of the same code. To avoid having to be concerned about this, you should generally try not to write async functions that have side effects whose order is important. If you want to enforce that two things happen in a specific order, you must create a dependency between them using await.

Async Doesn't Create Threads

From the perspective of Hack code, the world is single-threaded, just like in PHP. An async function is not a thread; multiple async functions will not run in parallel. A single PHP/Hack environment's code will not run on multiple CPU cores. (HHVM does run multiple web requests in parallel using system-level threads, but the PHP/Hack environments in those threads can't substantively interact with each other.)

The async extensions may be using threads behind the scenes, but that's an implementation detail, not visible to Hack code.

Of course, there are times when you should use threads for parallelism—i.e., when you're doing CPU-intensive work that can be broken down into several tasks that need to synchronize with each other occasionally. In those cases, async will not help you, and in fact Hack is probably not the right language for the job.

Memoizing Async Functions

Because async functions are designed to be used with time-consuming operations, they are a natural fit with memoization. Memoization is a common programming pattern where the result of an expensive operation is cached, so that it can be returned cheaply the next time it's needed:

```
function time_consuming_op_impl(): string {
  // ...
}

function time_consuming_op(): string {
  static $result = null;
  if ($result === null) {
    $result = time_consuming_op_impl();
  }
  return $result;
}
```

The special attribute __Memoize (see "Special Attributes" on page 79) will behave correctly when applied to an async function. When you want memoization, you should generally use that attribute. If you have a good reason not to (needing fine control over the memoization cache, for example), read on.

When manually memoizing async functions, there is a serious potential mistake to be aware of, which can result in a race condition. The key thing to remember is: memoize the *wait handle*, not the *result*.

Memoizing the result is the most intuitively obvious thing to do, like this:

```
async function time_consuming_op_impl(): Awaitable<string> {
  // ...
}

async function time_consuming_op(): Awaitable<string> {
  static $result = null;
  if ($result === null) {
    $result = await time_consuming_op_impl();  // Wrong! Bad!
  }
  return $result;
}
```

There's a race condition here. Suppose there are two other async functions, one()
and two(), that are both in the async scheduler queue, and they are both going to
await time_consuming_op(). Then the following sequence of events can happen:

1. one() gets to run, and awaits time_consuming_op().

2. time_consuming_op() finds that the memoization cache is empty ($result is
   null), so it awaits time_consuming_op_impl(). It gets suspended.

3. two() gets to run, and awaits time_consuming_op(). Note that this is a new wait
   handle; it's not the same wait handle as in step 1.

4. time_consuming_op() again finds that the memoization cache is empty, so it
   awaits time_consuming_op_impl() again. Now the time-consuming operation
   will be done twice.

If time_consuming_op_impl() has side effects—maybe it's a database write—then
this could end up being a serious bug. Even if there are no side effects, it's still a bug;
the time-consuming operation is being done multiple times when it only needs to be
done once.

The root cause of the bug is that time_consuming_op() may get suspended between
checking the cache and *filling* the cache. By checking the cache and finding it empty, it
derives a fact about the state of the world: the operation has not yet completed. But
after awaiting, and thus possibly getting suspended, that fact may no longer be true:
the invariant that was supposed to hold inside the if block is violated.

As I said before, the correct solution is to memoize the wait handle, not the result:

```
async function time_consuming_op(): Awaitable<string> {
  static $handle = null;
  if ($handle === null) {
    $handle = time_consuming_op_impl();  // Don't await here!
  }
  return await $handle;  // Await here instead
}
```

This may seem unintuitive, because the function awaits every time it's executed, even on the cache-hit path. But that's fine: on every execution except the first, $handle is not null, so a new instance of time_consuming_op_impl() will not be started. The result of the one existing instance will be shared.

The race condition is gone. The sequence of events listed earlier is no longer possible: time_consuming_op() can't be suspended between finding the cache empty and filling the cache. one() and two() will end up awaiting the same wait handle: the one that's cached in time_consuming_op(). It's not an error for this to happen; they will both wait for it to finish, and will both receive the result once it's ready.

Async Extensions

In this section, we'll look at each of the four async extensions included with HHVM 3.9: MySQL, MCRouter, cURL, and streams.

The language-level components of async have been around for several versions prior to 3.9, but these extensions were new in 3.6.[7] Some of them aren't feature-complete yet, but they'll improve in future versions.

MySQL

The async MySQL extension is an object-oriented MySQL API, reminiscent of the mysqli extension that comes with PHP and HHVM. We won't cover it in full detail here; we'll just look at the most important parts—establishing connections, using connection pools, making queries, and reading results.

Connecting and querying

You start out with the class AsyncMysqlClient. It has a static async method connect() that creates a connection to a MySQL database. The signature looks like this:

```
class AsyncMysqlClient {
  public static async function connect(
    string $host,
    int $port,
    string $dbname,
    string $user,
    string $password,
    int $timeout_micros = -1
  ): Awaitable<?AsyncMysqlConnection>;
}
```

---

7 Async has been extensively used within Facebook for some time, but with internal-only async extensions.

The five required parameters are all the standard MySQL connection parameters: hostname, port, database name, username, and password. The last parameter is optional: the connection timeout in microseconds. A value of -1, the default, means to use the default timeout (which is 1 second in HHVM 3.9); a value of 0 means no timeout.

connect() results in an AsyncMysqlConnection (or null if there was an error establishing the connection). AsyncMysqlConnection has two async methods to query the database: query() and queryf(). query() just takes a string containing a query, and a timeout (following the same convention as connect()'s timeout, except that the default is 60 seconds).

queryf() is what you'll be using most of the time, because it takes a query string with placeholders and substitutes values for those placeholders after appropriate escaping. It's a variadic method—pass the query string as the first argument, and values for the placeholders as subsequent arguments:

```
async function fetch_user_names(Vector<int> $user_ids)
    : Awaitable<Vector<string>> {
  $conn = await AsyncMysqlClient::connect(
    '127.0.0.1',
    3306,
    'example',
    'admin',
    'hunter2',
  );
  if ($conn !== null) {
    $result = await $conn->queryf(
      'SELECT name FROM user WHERE id IN (%Ld)',
      $user_ids
    );
    // ...
  }
}
```

The full range of available placeholders is:

- %T: A table name.
- %C: A column name.
- %s: A string.
- %d: An integer.
- %f: A float.
- %LT, %LC, %Ls, %Ld, and %Lf: lists of the above five, respectively. Pass a Vector of values to have it expanded into a comma-separated list. Make sure to include parentheses around the placeholder in the query string, if necessary; they won't be added automatically.

- `%=s`: Nullable string comparison. If you pass a string, this will expand to = `'the string'`; if you pass `null`, it will expand to `IS NULL`.

- `%=d`: Nullable integer comparison.

- `%=f`: Nullable float comparison.

- `%Q`: Raw SQL; the string you pass will be substituted in unescaped. This can be very dangerous, as it opens the possibility of SQL injection, which can be a serious security vulnerability. Avoid using it if at all possible.

The Hack typechecker understands `queryf()` query strings, and typechecks calls to `queryf()` to ensure that you're passing the right number of arguments and that the arguments have the right types:

```
async function do_something(AsyncMysqlConnection $conn): Awaitable<void> {
  // Error: too few arguments
  $result = await $conn->queryf('SELECT * FROM user WHERE id = %d');
}
```

The typechecker intentionally doesn't recognize the placeholder `%Q`, to discourage its use. If you really need to use it, you can silence the error with an `HH_IGNORE_ERROR` comment (see "Silencing Typechecker Errors" on page 88).

`queryf()` will be getting support for more placeholder types in the future, such as the `%L` family (`%Ld` for a list of integers, `%Ls` for a list of strings, etc.).

Connection pools

An important restriction of `AsyncMysqlConnection` is that you can't make multiple queries over a single connection in parallel. That's something you'll often want to do when using async. The solution is to use `AsyncMysqlConnectionPool`. A connection pool is a collection of reusable connection objects; when a client requests a connection from the pool, it may get one that already exists, which avoids the overhead of establishing a new connection.

 In HHVM versions earlier than 3.6.3, connection pools have a significant bug that can cause spurious timeouts. If you use connection pools, make sure you're using HHVM 3.6.3 or later.

Create a connection pool like this:

```
$pool = new AsyncMysqlConnectionPool(array());
```

The constructor takes one argument, which is an array of configuration options. The possible options are:

per_key_connection_limit

> the maximum number of connections allowed in the pool for a single combination of hostname, port, database, and username. Default: 50.

pool_connection_limit

> the maximum number of connections allowed in the pool, total. Default: 5000.

idle_timeout_micros

> the maximum amount of time, in microseconds, that a connection will be allowed to sit idle in the pool before being destroyed. Default: 4 seconds.

age_timeout_micros

> the maximum age, in microseconds, that a connection in the pool will be allowed to reach before being destroyed. Default: 60 seconds.

expiration_policy

> a string, either 'IdleTime' or 'Age', that specifies whether connections in the pool will be destroyed based on their idle time or age. Default: 'Age'.

For example, to create a pool with at most 100 connections with expiration based on idle time:

```
$pool = new AsyncMysqlConnectionPool(
  array(
    'pool_connection_limit' => 100,
    'expiration_policy' => 'IdleTime',
  )
);
```

Once you have a pool created, you get connections from it by calling and awaiting its async method connect(), with the same set of arguments as you would pass to AsyncMysqlConnection::connect():

```
<<__Memoize>>
function get_pool(): AsyncMysqlConnectionPool {
  return new AsyncMysqlConnectionPool([]);
}

async function get_connection(): Awaitable<?AsyncMysqlConnection> {
  return await get_pool()->connect(
    '127.0.0.1',
    3306,
    'example',
    'admin',
    'hunter2',
  );
}
```

Query results

The results of query() and queryf() are instances of the class AsyncMysqlResult. This is an abstract class; its two most important concrete subclasses are AsyncMysql QueryResult and AsyncMysqlErrorResult.

AsyncMysqlQueryResult has four (non-async) methods for getting results: map Rows(), vectorRows(), mapRowsTyped(), and vectorRowsTyped(). All four methods return a Vector of rows. The "map" or "vector" part refers to how each row is represented. mapRows() and mapRowsTyped() return rows as Maps, mapping column names to values. vectorRows() and vectorRowsTyped() return rows as Vectors, containing values in the order they were specified in the query. For example:

```
async function fetch_user_name(AsyncMysqlConnection $conn,
                               int $user_id) : Awaitable<string> {
  $result = await $conn->queryf(
    'SELECT name FROM user WHERE id = %d',
    $user_id
  );
  invariant($result->numRows() === 1, 'exactly one row in result');

  $map = $result->mapRows();
  // The result you want is in $map['name']

  $vector = $result->vectorRows();
  return $vector[0];
}
```

The "typed" in the method names refers to how you want values from non-string columns represented. For example, if you have a column defined as type INTEGER in SQL, mapRowsTyped() and vectorRowsTyped() will return values from that column as integers in Hack, whereas mapRows() and vectorRows() will return values from that column as string representations of integers.

If the query resulted in an error, the result of query() or queryf() will be an Asyn cMysqlErrorResult object. This class has three important non-async methods for determining what happened:

failureType()
: Returns one of two strings, 'TimedOut' or 'Failed'. The latter signifies any failure other than a timeout.

mysql_errno()
: The numerical MySQL error code for the problem.

mysql_error()
: A human-readable string describing the problem.

Updated documentation for the async MySQL extension is available at the HHVM site (*http://docs.hhvm.com/manual/en/book.hack.async.mysql.php*).

MCRouter and memcached

MCRouter (*https://github.com/facebook/mcrouter*) is an open source project developed by Facebook. It is a memcached protocol routing library, providing a wide variety of features that aid in scaling a memcached deployment: connection pooling, prefix-based routing, online configuration changes, and many more. It speaks the memcached ASCII protocol and sits transparently between clients and memcached instances.

A full exploration of how to use MCRouter is beyond the scope of this book. Here, we'll simply be using the MCRouter library as a memcached client. The MCRouter extension mimics the Memcache and Memcached extensions that are part of PHP and Hack.[8] The MCRouter extension doesn't support all operations that memcached and MCRouter themselves support (cas, or compare-and-swap, being one of the major omissions), but this support will improve in future versions.

The extension is centered around the class MCRouter, which represents a memcached client. There are two ways to get an MCRouter object: through the constructor (more flexible), or through the static method createSimple() (more convenient). These are the signatures:

```
class MCRouter {
  public function __construct(array<string, mixed> $options, string $pid = '');
  public static function createSimple(ConstVector<string> $servers): MCRouter;
}
```

The constructor behaves differently depending on whether $pid (for *persistence ID*) is empty. If $pid is empty, the constructor starts a *transient* client and returns an object representing it. If $pid is not empty, the extension looks for a client that already exists with that persistence ID, and returns one if it finds it; if not, it starts a new client with that persistence ID. Generally, transient clients should only be used for debugging and testing, not production.

The $options parameter is used to configure any new clients that are started. It must have one of the keys 'config_str' (mapping to a JSON configuration string) or 'config_file' (mapping to a string containing the path to a JSON configuration file). More information on how to configure MCRouter is in the MCRouter source repository and on its GitHub page (*https://github.com/facebook/mcrouter*).

---

8 There are two extensions for talking to memcached. Memcached is newer and supports more memcached features, so it's generally recommended for use over Memcache.

`MCRouter::createSimple()` is a streamlined way to create a client; you can simply pass it a `Vector` (see Chapter 5) of strings with server addresses where memcached is running. The strings comprise a hostname, followed by a colon, followed by a port number, such as `'127.0.0.1:11211'`.

MCRouter, the class, has async methods with names that mirror commands in the memcached ASCII protocol. They throw exceptions on failure (which includes things like getting a key that doesn't exist), so the function `HH\Asio\wrap()` from asio-utilities comes in handy around this API. For example:

```
function fetch_user_name(MCRouter $mcr, int $user_id): Awaitable<string> {
  $key = 'name:' . $user_id;
  $cached_result = await HH\Asio\wrap($mcr->get($key));

  if ($cached_result->isSucceeded()) {
    return $cached_result->getResult();
  }

  // Fall back to querying database
  // ...
}
```

There are async methods for several core memcached protocol commands:

- `get()` to read the value for a given key
- `set()` to write a value, overwriting if a value already exists for the given key
- `add()` to write a value, but fail if a value already exists for the given key
- `replace()` to write a value, but fail if the value *doesn't* already exist for the given key
- `append()` and `prepend()` to append or prepend data to the value for a given key
- `incr()` to atomically increment a numeric value
- `del()` to delete a key
- `version()` to get the remote server's version

Updated documentation for the async MCRouter extension is available at the HHVM site (*http://docs.hhvm.com/manual/en/book.hack.mcrouter.php*).

cURL

cURL is a library for transferring data to and from resources identified by URLs. In practice, it's most often used to make HTTP and HTTPS requests.

The async cURL API in Hack consists of two functions:

```
async function curl_multi_await(resource $mh, float $timeout = 1.0)
  : Awaitable<int>;

namespace HH\Asio {
  async function curl_exec(mixed $urlOrHandle): Awaitable<string>;
}
```

HH\Asio\curl_exec() is a convenience wrapper around curl_multi_await(). You can pass it a cURL handle (i.e., something returned from curl_init()) or a string containing a URL (in which case, it will create the cURL handle for you), and it will execute the cURL handle asynchronously and return its result.

curl_multi_await() is the async equivalent of curl_multi_select(). It waits until there is activity on any of the cURL handles that are part of $mh, which must be a cURL multi handle (i.e., something returned from curl_multi_init()). When it completes, indicating that there was activity on at least one of the cURL handles, you process it with curl_multi_exec(), just as you do in non-async code.

Streams

This is the simplest of the async extensions. It consists of a single function, called stream_await(), whose job is to wait until a stream becomes readable or writable:

```
async function stream_await(resource $fp, int $events, float $timeout = 0.0)
  : Awaitable<int>;
```

stream_await() takes three parameters:

- $fp is the stream to watch for changes. It must be backed by a normal file, socket, tempfile, or pipe. Memory streams and user streams aren't supported.

- $events is one of the global constants STREAM_AWAIT_READ or STREAM_AWAIT_WRITE, or both of them bitwise-OR'ed together. It signifies what kind of change to watch for in the stream; that is, whether to watch for it to become readable (i.e., fread() on the stream will not block) or writable (i.e., fwrite() on the stream will not block). Note that a stream that is at end-of-file is considered readable, because fread() will not block.

- $timeout is the maximum length of time, in seconds, to wait. If this is zero, the async function completes immediately; it's really just a query for the status of the stream.

The result of the function is an integer indicating the current state of the stream, mapping to one of these four global constants:

- `STREAM_AWAIT_CLOSED`, indicating that the stream is now closed
- `STREAM_AWAIT_READY`, indicating that the stream is now readable or writable (depending on what was passed as `$events`)
- `STREAM_AWAIT_TIMEOUT`, indicating that the stream is in the same state as before, but the timeout triggered
- `STREAM_AWAIT_ERROR`, indicating that an error occurred

`stream_await()` is similar to `stream_select()` in functionality—waiting for a stream to enter an interesting state—but it doesn't have the multiplexing functionality of `stream_select()`. You can use `HH\Asio\v()` to await multiple stream wait handles simultaneously, but the resulting combined wait handle won't complete until *all* of its constituent stream wait handles have completed. You can work around this by wrapping the call to `stream_await()` inside another async function that uses the stream's result:

```
async function read_all(array<resource> $fps): Awaitable<void> {
  $read_single = async function(resource $fp) {
    $status = await stream_await($fp, STREAM_AWAIT_READ, 1.0);

    if ($status == STREAM_AWAIT_READY) {
      // Read from stream
      // ...
    }
  };

  await HH\Asio\v(array_map($read_single, $fps));
}
```

CHAPTER 7

XHP

XHP (named to resemble XHTML) is a feature of Hack that allows programmers to represent an HTML tree as PHP/Hack objects, by means of embedded XML-like syntax. This eliminates entire classes of bugs as well as a major source of security holes in web apps. It makes UI code cleaner, more maintainable, and more flexible.

Traditionally in PHP, you output web pages in one of two ways—either by using PHP templating within HTML:

```
<tt>Hello <strong><?= $user_name ?></strong>!</tt>
```

or by concatenating or interpolating strings:

```
echo "<tt>Hello <strong>$user_name</strong>!</tt>";
```

With XHP, the same example looks like this:

```
echo <tt>Hello <strong>{$user_name}</strong></tt>;
```

This is a normal echo statement, and there are no quotation marks. The HTML-like syntax is part of the grammar.

XHP is a great foundation for a modern, object-oriented web app UI library. In this chapter, we'll see why you should use it, how to use it, how to build on top of it, and how to convert a legacy codebase to use it.

Why Use XHP?

XHP can help improve the security and correctness of your UI code, with a variety of ways to prevent you from making common mistakes. It also helps organize your UI code more sanely, by providing an object-oriented interface to your HTML markup.

Runtime Validation

Can you spot the problem with this code?

```
echo '<div class="section-header">';
echo '<a href="#intro">Intro to <span class="metal">Death Metal</sapn></a>';
echo '</div>';
```

One of the closing tags is misspelled: `</sapn>`. In real code, you probably wouldn't detect a bug like this until you viewed the resulting webpage in a browser, and even then, depending on the bug, you might not notice it at all.

XHP eliminates this class of errors. The preceding example in XHP, including the typo, would look like this:

```
echo
  <div class="section-header">
    <a href="#intro">Intro to <span class="metal">Death Metal</sapn></a>
  </div>;
```

When you try to run, `include`, or `require` this file, you'll encounter a fatal error:

```
Fatal error: XHP: mismatched tag: 'sapn' not the same as 'span' in
/home/oyamauchi/test.php on line 4
```

XHP offers more sophisticated forms of validation as well. HTML has rules governing the allowed relationships between tags: which tags are allowed to have other tags inside them, which tags are allowed to have text inside them but no tags, and so on. XHP can check these constraints and raise errors if they're violated.

For example, the following is not valid HTML, because the `<select>` tag is not allowed to have tags inside it other than `<option>` and `<optgroup>`:

```
<select><strong>bold text!</strong></select>
```

If you try to do this in XHP, you'll encounter a fatal error, with details on what went wrong and where:

```
Fatal error: Element `select` was rendered with invalid children.

/home/oyamauchi/test.php:2

Verified 0 children before failing.

Children expected:
(:option|:optgroup)*

Children received:
:strong
```

XHP validates many of the rules imposed by the HTML5 draft specification, though not all. When you extend XHP with custom classes, you can add validation rules for them. We'll see how to do that in "children Declarations" on page 179.

Secure by Default

Here's some code that's meant to be used as the target of a web form submission. The user enters her name in a form field and this page displays a personalized welcome message. What is the problem with it?

```
$user_name = $_REQUEST['name'];

echo '<html>';
echo '<head><title>Welcome</title></head>';
echo '<body>Welcome, ' . $user_name . '</body>';
echo '</html>';
```

There is a security vulnerability. If the user submits a string containing HTML markup, that markup will end up being interpreted by the browser as part of the document object model (DOM). For example, if the user submits <blink>blinky text</blink> in the name query parameter, there will be blinking text on the resulting page, and that surely isn't what the site's author intended. This is known as a *cross-site scripting* (XSS) vulnerability.[1]

Without XHP, the XSS vulnerability is fixed by adding a call to htmlspecialchars(), like this:

```
$user_name = htmlspecialchars($_REQUEST['name']);
// ...
```

This is still troublesome: you have to remember to properly escape *every* string that could contain user input (including strings resulting from database queries and such). You also have to make sure they're escaped exactly once, or you'll see double-escaping bugs, which aren't security holes but are still undesirable.

This example is simple to fix, but it's also particularly egregious. XSS vulnerabilities in real code are likely to be quite a bit more subtle. Most codebases will have a large number of functions or methods that output pieces of a complete web page, and they are called in many different layers to assemble the final page; making sure that all the necessary escaping is done exactly once amid all the layers is a difficult and delicate task.

Here's the same code in XHP:

```
$user_name = $_REQUEST['name'];

echo
  <html>
  <head><title>Welcome</title></head>
  <body>Welcome, {$user_name}</body>
  </html>;
```

---

1 It's not CSS because that's Cascading Style Sheets.

There are no calls to `htmlspecialchars()` or any other escaping routines in this code, and yet there is no XSS vulnerability. XHP escapes reserved characters to HTML entities in the string before outputting it, replacing < with < and so on.

The root of the problem is that PHP and Hack make no distinction between *raw strings* and *HTML strings*. It's best to think of these as two completely different data types, with nontrivial algorithms to convert between them. A raw string is meant for display as is. An HTML string is a serialized DOM tree, meant to be used as input to an HTML rendering engine.

XSS vulnerabilities result from incorrectly treating raw strings as HTML strings. The string that the user types into the form field is a raw string, so it must be converted into an HTML string (i.e., reserved HTML characters must be escaped) before it gets used as input to an HTML rendering engine. To fail to do so is, in principle, a type error. XHP solves the problem by relieving you of the need to deal with HTML strings at all.

Thinking of HTML as a serialization format, rather than a markup language, makes this point clearer. Think of JSON, another commonly used serialization format. When you're writing code that has to output JSON, you don't do it by manually piecing together JSON characters; you build up a structure using PHP/Hack objects or arrays and then serialize it all to JSON by passing it to `json_encode()` as the last step. You, the application developer, are never dealing directly with strings containing JSON-encoded data.

Similarly, XHP gives you a way to build up a structure using PHP/Hack objects and then serialize it to HTML, without ever dealing with a serialized HTML string except to output it to a stream.

Why Is XSS Dangerous?

A full exploration of XSS vulnerabilities is beyond the scope of this book, but here's a quick overview. The most pressing danger posed by XSS is that it allows attackers to execute malicious JavaScript code in the context of a site that the user trusts.

JavaScript code running in a browser can generally access information in other windows and tabs of the same browser, but only if they are displaying the same site. This way, if you have your bank's website open in one tab and a malicious site open in another, the malicious site's JavaScript can't access your banking information. This restriction is called the *same-origin policy*.

However, if the bank's website has an XSS vulnerability, the attacker may be able to use it to execute JavaScript of his own devising, as if the bank's website had supplied it. The JavaScript will have access to the bank site's DOM, and may, for example,

---

make an HTTP request containing your bank account number to a site controlled by the attacker.

How to Use XHP

HHVM has support for XHP built in. You can turn it on and off with the configuration option `hhvm.enable_xhp`. You can enable XHP without enabling any other Hack features.

You'll also need the Hack library for XHP. This contains classes that form the infrastructure of XHP, as well as classes that mirror all the tags that HTML5 supports. The recommended way to integrate this with your project is to use Composer (*http:// getcomposer.org*). This will take care of fetching the source and setting up autoloading the necessary classes, so you can use XHP immediately.

A full guide to using Composer is outside the scope of this book, but here is what you'll need to add to your project's *composer.json* file:

```
"require": {
  "facebook/xhp-lib": "~2.2"
}
```

This specifies that we require version 2.2 or later.

Basic Tag Usage

We've already seen several examples of XHP usage, but we'll start from the very beginning here.

XHP is syntactic sugar for creating *XHP objects*. XHP objects are just like any other Hack objects: for example, you can call methods on them, and if you pass an XHP object to the built-in function `is_object()`, it will return `true`. The only difference is that instead of creating XHP objects with the keyword `new`, you create them with *XHP tags*, an HTML-like syntax extension.

XHP objects are instances of *XHP classes*, which again are like any other Hack classes except for two things: their names start with a colon (`:`), which is invalid in PHP and Hack; and they descend, possibly indirectly, from the core XHP library class `:xhp`.

XHP objects are meant to form a tree structure. Each object can have any number of *children*, each of which is either text or another XHP object. This mirrors the structure of HTML documents.

At its most basic, XHP tag syntax consists of an XHP class name *without* the leading colon, surrounded by angle brackets (`<` and `>`). This is an *opening tag*. Every opening tag must be balanced by a matching *closing tag*, which consists of the same class name, prefixed with a slash (/), all inside angle brackets. Between the opening and closing tags can be text, other tags, or embedded Hack code (see "Embedding Hack Code" on page 172).

This example creates a single XHP object, an instance of the class :strong, and passes it as an argument to the echo statement. It has a single child, which is the string bold text:

```
echo <strong>bold text</strong>;
```

Here is a more complex example that creates an XHP object of the class :div with two children. The first child is the string plain text. The second child is an XHP object of the class :strong with one child, the string bold text:

```
echo
  <div>
    plain text
    <strong>bold text</strong>
  </div>;
```

One important thing to learn from this example is that whitespace in XHP is mostly insignificant. In text within XHP, any sequence of whitespace characters (spaces, tabs, newlines, and carriage returns) will be collapsed into a single space. This is to allow for the linebreaking and indenting style used in this example, which we recommend for any XHP code that doesn't fit on a single line.

Remember that the syntax is meant to describe a tree structure. To make sure it does, opening and closing tags must be properly nested. That is, if you have a series of opening tags, their corresponding closing tags must appear in the opposite order. For example, this is invalid syntax:

```
echo <strong><em>bold italic text</strong></em>;
```

The opening tag <em> is inside the <strong> tag, but the closing tag </em> is outside it, which breaks the tree structure: one node in a tree cannot be partially a child of another one and partially not. In this example, the closing tag </em> must come before the closing tag </strong>. The HTML rendering engines in many web browsers are permissive about this kind of thing, but XHP is not.

Tags may also be self-closing; this is equivalent to an opening tag followed immediately by its closing tag, and is commonly used for XHP objects that don't have children. Just as in HTML, the syntax for a self-closing tag is a slash immediately before the closing angle bracket. The space before the slash isn't necessary; including it is a stylistic choice:

```
echo <hr />;
```

HTML character references

HTML character references are a way to encode characters in HTML, as an alternative to simply using the literal characters. This is useful when you need to encode a reserved HTML character like the ampersand (&), or when you need to use a character that is unsupported by the character set you're using.

You can use HTML character reference syntax in text within XHP, and it will be converted to the corresponding character during parsing. XHP supports every HTML entity from the HTML5 draft specification, as well as numeric character reference syntax.

This example will print a `<span>` tag containing three hearts. The first uses the entity, the second uses decimal notation, and the third uses hexadecimal notation. The resulting string is UTF-8-encoded:

```
echo <span>&hearts; &#9829; &#x2665;</span>;
```

Remember that XHP escapes all reserved HTML characters (there are five: & < > ' "), so if you use this syntax to generate one of those, it will be turned back into an entity when you convert the XHP object back to a string. This example will output ♥ &:

```
echo <span>&hearts; &amp;</span>;
```

There is no way to output a string like `&hearts;` directly from XHP.

Attributes

In addition to children, XHP objects can also have *attributes*. Attributes are key/value pairs that can hold data for an object. This is similar to HTML, where tags can have attributes that influence their behavior. Each XHP class defines the attributes that it can have; each attribute has a type and, optionally, a default value. Attributes may also be required; that is, it's an error to not set them.

XHP tag syntax supports attributes, and they look very similar to HTML attributes. After the tag name, there can be any number of attributes, separated by whitespace. Each attribute is a name, followed by an equals sign, followed by a value. There must be no whitespace around the equals sign. The value must be either a double-quoted string or a curly-brace-enclosed Hack expression (see "Embedding Hack Code" on page 172). For example:

```
echo <input type="button" name="submit" value="Click Here" />;
```

Note that although attribute values are double-quoted strings, they are *not* subject to variable interpolation as they are elsewhere. Dollar signs in attribute values have no special meaning. If you need variable interpolation, use embedded Hack code instead (see the next section).

Embedding Hack Code

You can embed Hack expressions within XHP syntax, to use the values of those expressions as attributes or children of XHP objects. The syntax is simple: enclose the Hack expression in curly braces. Here is an example with both ways you can use it, as an attribute value and as a child:

```
echo
  <a href={$user->getProfileURI()}>
    {$user->getName()}'s Profile
  </a>;
```

Apart from allowing you to insert dynamically generated data into XHP trees, this allows you to build up an XHP tree from individual pieces, instead of as a single mass:

```
$linked_profile_pic =
  <a href={$user->getProfileURI()}>
    <img src={$user->getProfilePicURI()} />
  </a>;

echo
  <div>
    <div class="profile-pic">{$linked_profile_pic}</div>
    {$user->getName()}
  </div>;
```

This is exactly equivalent to putting the code for the <a> tag directly inside the <div> tag.

Type Annotations for XHP

There are two interfaces that you'll use in type annotations when passing XHP objects around: XHPRoot and XHPChild.

XHPRoot is any object that is an instance of an XHP class. XHPChild is the set of things that are valid as the value of $xhpchild in this code:

```
echo <div>{$xhpchild}</div>;
```

That means XHP objects, as well as strings, integers, doubles, and arrays of any of these. It does *not* include non-XHP objects with __toString() methods. XHPChild is special in that it is "implemented" by primitive types, so, for example, 123 instan ceof XHPChild evaluates to true.

Here's an example of when you might use XHPChild—rendering a UI element that could be either a link or plain unlinked text:

```
function render_page_link(Page $page, bool $is_self): XHPChild {
  if ($is_self) {
    return $page->getTitle();
```

```
    } else {
      return <a href={$page->getURI()}>{$page->getTitle()}</a>;
    }
  }
```

If you have an XHPChild and you need to pass it to something that requires an XHPRoot, you can wrap it in the special XHP class x:frag. It's essentially a transparent wrapper for XHP content; adding an x:frag as a child to another XHP object is the same as adding each of the x:frag's children individually. This class is also what you'll use when you need to pass around a bundle of multiple XHP objects without anything to contain them:

```
function render_name_with_icon(User $user): XHPRoot {
  return
    <x:frag>
      <img src={$user->getIconURI()} />
       
      {$user->getName()}
    </x:frag>;
}
```

Object Interface

XHP objects have several public methods that can be used to inspect and modify their attributes and children. This gives you much more flexibility: when you create an XHP object, you don't need to have all of its children and attributes ready. You can create one and pass it around to other functions so that they can make modifications to it, or return one from a function so that the caller can customize it. The methods of an XHP object are:

appendChild(mixed $child): this
> Adds $child to the end of the object's array of children. $child can also be an array, in which case each of its contained objects will be passed to appendChild() recursively in turn.

prependChild(mixed $child): this
> Adds $child to the beginning of the object's array of children. $child can also be an array, in which case each of its contained objects will be passed to prepend Child() recursively in turn.

replaceChildren(...): this
> Takes a variable number of arguments, puts all its arguments in an array, and replaces the object's array of children with that array.

getChildren(?string $selector = null): Vector<XHPChild>
> If $selector is not passed, this simply returns all of the object's children. If $selector starts with %, this will return all children belonging to the category

named by $selector (see "Categories" on page 181). Otherwise, this will return all children that are instanceof the class named by $selector.

getFirstChild(?string $selector = null): ?XHPChild
If $selector is not passed, this returns the object's first child. Otherwise, it returns the first child that matches $selector (see getChildren() for details), or null if no such child exists.

getLastChild(?string $selector = null): ?XHPChild
If $selector is not passed, this returns the object's last child. Otherwise, it returns the last child that matches $selector (see getChildren() for details), or null if no such child exists.

getAttributes(): Map<string, mixed>
Returns the object's array of attributes. The returned Map is a copy of the object's internal attribute array; you can modify it without affecting the object.

getAttribute(string $name): mixed
Returns the value of the attribute named $name. If the attribute is not set, this returns null if the attribute is not required, or throws an XHPAttributeRequire dException if it is required. If $name is not the name of a declared attribute, this throws an XHPAttributeNotSupportedException.

You should only use this method if the name of the attribute you're reading isn't statically known. Otherwise, you should use the $this->:name syntax, because the typechecker understands it and can give the returned value the right type.

setAttribute(string $name, mixed $val): this
Sets the attribute named $name to $val. The value will be checked against the attribute's type, and if the type check fails, this throws an XHPInvalidAttribu teException. If $name doesn't contain the name of a declared attribute, this throws an XHPAttributeNotSupportedException.

Again, if you know the attribute name statically, you should use the $this->:name = $value syntax instead of this method.

setAttributes(KeyedTraversable<string, mixed> $attrs): this
Replaces the object's array of attributes with $attrs. The error conditions from setAttribute() apply to this method as well.

isAttributeSet(string $name): bool
Returns whether the attribute named $name is set.

categoryOf(string $cat): bool
Returns whether the object belongs to the category named $cat.

When using existing XHP classes, you'll mostly be using `appendChild()`, `prepend Child()`, and `setAttribute()`. When writing custom XHP classes (see "Creating Your Own XHP Classes" on page 176), you'll mostly be using `getChildren()` and `get Attribute()`.

Here's an example of using the object-oriented interface to build up an HTML list:

```
function build_list(array<string> $names): XHPRoot {
  $list = <ul />;

  foreach ($names as $name) {
    $list->appendChild(<li>{$name}</li>);
  }

  return $list;
}
```

Validation

XHP classes can declare the type and number of children they can have, as well as the types and names of the attributes they can have. These constraints are validated at various times:

- Children constraints are validated at render time; that is, when `toString()` is called. See "The Hack Library" on page 194 for more detail on this.
- Attribute names and types are validated when the attributes are set, either in an XHP tag or through `setAttribute()`.
- The presence of `@required` attributes is validated when the individual `@required` attributes are read.

Validation is on by default, and it can be turned off. We recommend that you keep it on during development and testing, to catch mistakes. If you want to save CPU cycles in production, though, turning XHP validation off is a quick and easy way to do it. All you have to do is make sure this line of code runs before you start using XHP:

```
:xhp::$ENABLE_VALIDATION = false;
```

Syntax highlighting

Generally, the PHP syntax highlighting modules that come with popular text editors will work fine on files that contain XHP. The main source of trouble is the use of apostrophes in text within XHP; syntax highlighters usually end up treating these as opening single quotes, resulting in text being incorrectly highlighted as a string literal. This won't cause a syntax error at runtime, but is confusing to read in a text editor.

The workaround is to put the apostrophe inside a double-quoted string inside an embedded code snippet. You can wrap just the apostrophe, or a larger part of the text, or anything in between:

```
echo <p>So text editors don{"'"}t get confused</p>;
echo <p>{"This'll work too"}</p>;
```

There's no technical advantage to either style, but the first style is more consistent with text that doesn't have apostrophes and thus doesn't need any kind of quoting.

Creating Your Own XHP Classes

The true power of XHP comes from its extensibility. It comes with classes for each standard HTML tag, but you can define your own classes to encapsulate your own rendering logic. For example, you can define an XHP class that represents an alert box on a web page, or a row in a list of users, or an entire navigation bar.

XHP class names always start with a colon (:) and may include colons in the middle, as long as there are never two adjacent colons. Colons aren't allowed in class names in PHP and Hack; this is one of the changes XHP introduces. XHP class names may also include hyphens (-), which is also invalid in PHP and Hack.

All you need to do to create a custom XHP class is to extend :x:element and implement the protected method render(), taking no arguments and returning an XHP object. Here's a minimal example:

```
class :hello-world extends :x:element {
  protected function render(): XHPRoot {
    return <em>Hello World</em>;
  }
}

echo <hello-world />;  // Prints <em>Hello World</em>
```

It's important to note that even when you're defining your own XHP classes, *you still never deal with HTML strings*. You implement everything in terms of other XHP classes, which can be your own classes or the built-in classes that mirror HTML tags.

The `render()` method's return type must be `XHPRoot`, so it must return an XHP object. If you want to return a plain string, wrap it in an `x:frag`:

```
class :hello-world extends :x:element {
  protected function render(): XHPRoot {
    return <x:frag>Hello world, plain as can be</x:frag>;
  }
}
```

Attributes

Your custom XHP classes can declare attributes that they can have. Inside the class definition, put the reserved XHP keyword `attribute`, followed by a type, followed by the attribute name, optionally followed by a default value. Attribute names are conventionally all lowercase, with no separators between words, mimicking the style used in HTML:

```
class :ui:profile-link extends :x:element {
  attribute int profileid;
  attribute bool showpicture = false;
}
```

XHP has special syntax for accessing the value of an attribute. It looks like regular property access syntax, with the attribute name as the property name, but the attribute name is prefixed with a colon:

```
class :hello extends :x:element {
  attribute string target;
  public function render(): XHPRoot {
    return <x:frag>Hello {$this->:target}!</x:frag>;
  }
}
```

If the attribute wasn't set, this returns `null`, or the default value if there is one.

You can make an attribute required by adding `@required` after the attribute name in the declaration. If you try to read a required attribute and that attribute hasn't been set, an `XHPAttributeRequiredException` will be thrown. Note that if the exception propagates out of the `render()` method, `:x:element` will catch it and turn it into a fatal error. If you want to catch the exception, you must do so inside `render()`, but this isn't recommended; instead, either make sure the attribute is set if it really is required, or don't make it required.

The syntax lets you combine `@required` and default values (put the `@required` after the default value), but that doesn't make sense semantically. If you don't pass the attribute, you'll still get an `XHPAttributeRequiredException` when you try to read it, so you'll never see the default value.

Attribute types

The types you can give to attributes are a subset of Hack type annotations. Every attribute *must* have a type, and attribute types are checked at runtime, even if the Hack typechecker is not being used.

Here is the set of acceptable attribute types and what they mean:

- `bool`, `int`, `float`, `string`, `array`, and `mixed` all mean the same as they do in Hack type annotations (see "Hack's Type System" on page 6). By default, there is no coercion; if you don't pass the exact type the attribute expects, an `XHPInvalidAttributeException` will be thrown.

- Hack enum names (see "Enums" on page 59) are allowed. They're checked at runtime with the `isValid()` enum function. If the check fails, an `XHPInvalidAttribute</span>Exception` will be thrown.

- There's another enum syntax that lets you list the acceptable values inline. It looks like this:

  ```
  attribute enum {'get', 'post'} formmethod;
  ```

  There's no limit to the number of possible values in the list. The values must be all be scalars (i.e., boolean, numeric, or string literals), and they will all be cast to strings. `enum` attributes are checked at runtime against the list of acceptable values with `===`. If the check fails, an `XHPInvalidAttributeException` will be thrown.

  These are entirely unrelated to Hack enums, and you should use Hack enums instead; they're more typesafe, and more consistent with non-XHP code.

- Class and interfaces names are allowed. They're checked at runtime with `instanceof`. If the check fails, an `XHPInvalidAttributeException` will be thrown.

  Of particular note is the special interface `Stringish`. It's special in the same way that `XHPChild` is: it's "implemented" by a primitive type, namely strings. It is also implicitly implemented by any class that has a `__toString()` method. This is in contrast to the attribute type `string`, which only accepts strings, and not objects.

Generic types (see Chapter 2), including `array`, can take type arguments when used as attribute types. Type erasure still applies, so although the Hack typechecker will make use of the type arguments, the runtime will not check them.

In attribute types, type aliases (see "Type Aliases" on page 62) are not resolved. Nullable types are not syntactically valid as attribute types, and neither are callable types.

Inheriting attributes

It's common to find that one class should support all the attributes that some other class does. The most common case is that you want your custom XHP class to support all of the attributes of a built-in parent class. For example, if you're designing an XHP class that renders a box with a drop shadow on a web page, you may want it to support all the attributes that the HTML <div> tag does.

The syntax for this is simple—you provide the `attribute` keyword followed by the name of another XHP class, including the leading colon:

```
class :ui:drop-shadow-box extends :x:element {
  attribute :div;
}
```

Be careful, though. This *only* declares attributes; it doesn't include any automatic transfer of :div attributes to <div> objects that :ui:drop-shadow-box returns from its render() method. To clarify, the implementation of :ui:drop-shadow-box might look something like this:

```
class :ui:drop-shadow-box extends :x:element {
  attribute :div;
  protected function render(): XHPRoot {
    return <div class="drop-shadow">{$this->getChildren()}</div>
  }
}
```

Code that uses :ui:drop-shadow-box may then do something like this:

```
echo <ui:drop-shadow-box id="mainBox">{$stuff}</ui:drop-shadow-box>;
```

In the resulting HTML output, the <div> will *not* have an id attribute set. The <ui:drop-shadow-box> has the id attribute set, but its render() method never reads that attribute, so it's simply lost. This is almost certainly not what you want.

To get automatic attribute transfer, you can use the XHPHelpers trait, which is fully described in "XHP Helpers" on page 184.

children Declarations

You can, and should, declare the types that your custom XHP class is allowed to have as children. The syntax for children declarations resembles regular expression syntax. To make these examples concrete, I'll show declarations from some real HTML tags.[2]

---

2 Note that you'll see classes extending :xhp:html-element instead of :x:element. See "The Hack Library" on page 194 for more details on that, but you should never need to do this with your own XHP classes.

If there is no `children` declaration, the class is allowed to have any number of children of any type. Having multiple `children` declarations in the same class is a syntax error.

The simplest `children` declaration is `empty`, meaning the element is not allowed to have children. For example, classes like `:br` and `:hr` would have declarations like this:

```
class :br extends :xhp:html-element {
  children empty;
  // ...
}
```

The next step is to name specific XHP classes (leading colon included) and put them in a sequence, separating them with commas:

```
class :html extends :xhp:html-element {
  children (:head, :body);
  // ...
}
```

This means that the `<html>` tag is required to have a `<head>` child and a `<body>` child, in that order, and no others.

There are two special pseudoclass names that you can use: `pcdata`, which stands for "parsed character data" and in practice means any Hack value that can be converted to a string; and `any`, which means anything is allowed, whether an XHP object or parsed character data. Note that these names do not have a leading colon:

```
class :option extends :xhp:html-element {
  children (pcdata)*;
}
```

The next step is to use the repetition operators * and +. Put these after another specifier to mean "zero or more of this" or "one or more of this," respectively:

```
class :ul extends :xhp:html-element {
  children (:li)*;
  // ...
}
class :dl extends :xhp:html-element {
  children (:dt+, :dd+)*;
  // ...
}
```

As you can see in the example of `:dl`, these constructs can be wrapped in parentheses and have other constructs applied to them. What `:dl`'s `children` declaration says is that a `<dl>`'s children must be zero or more groups of a nonempty run of `<dt>` followed by a nonempty run of `<dd>`. In plain English, this means that all of its children must be either `<dt>` or `<dd>`, the first one must not be `<dd>`, and the last one must not be `<dt>`.

There's one other postfix operator, which is ?, meaning "zero or one of this."

The next major concept is the alternation operator |, which means "this or that":

```
class :select extends :xhp:html-element {
  children (:option | :optgroup)*;
  // ...
}
```

This says a `<select>` can have any number of children, but they must all be either `<option>` or `<optgroup>`.

The last thing to discuss is the use of categories, which we'll look at in detail in the next section. In a `children` declaration, category names can be used anywhere an XHP class name can be used. They're prefixed with %:

```
class :strong extends :xhp:html-element {
  children (pcdata | %phrase)*;
  // ...
}
```

This means that `<strong>`'s children can be either text or instances of XHP classes with the category `%phrase`.

As a demonstration of how richly these constraints can be described, here's the `children` declaration of the `<table>` tag, which uses almost every possible construct and displays some deep nesting:

```
class :table extends :xhp:html-element {
  children (
    :caption?,
    :colgroup*,
    :thead?,
    (
      (:tfoot, (:tbody+ | :tr*)) |
      ((:tbody+ | :tr*), :tfoot?)
    )
  );
  // ...
}
```

Categories

Categories in XHP are similar to interfaces in regular object-oriented programming. An XHP class can be marked with any number of categories that can then be referred to from `children` declarations. They don't need to be declared anywhere before using them. The syntax is very simple—list the categories, each prefixed with % and separated by commas, after the `category` keyword:

```
class :strong extends :xhp:html-element {
  category %flow, %phrase;
```

```
    children (pcdata | %phrase)*;
    // ...
  }
```

The categories applied to the library-provided HTML tag implementations are taken directly from the HTML5 specification, and generally shouldn't be used for your custom classes. You may wonder, though, how you can get away with having your custom classes be children of built-in tags without adding these categories. For example, the following is valid:

```
class :hello-world extends :x:element {
  protected function render() {
    return <x:frag>Hello World</x:frag>;
  }
}

echo <strong><hello-world /></strong>;
```

It doesn't look like this will pass validation, though, because :strong requires its children to either be pcdata or have the category %phrase, and neither of those is true :hello-world does neither. The trick is that there are *two* separate children validation stages; this is discussed in much more detail in "The Hack Library" on page 194.

Context

You'll sometimes find that some XHP object deep down inside a tree needs access to a piece of information that's only available at the highest level. For example, a button on a website may need a different appearance depending on whether it's being viewed by an administrator or a regular user. The only way we've seen so far for the low-level object to get such information (if there's no global way to get it) is to have it passed down as an attribute through every level above it. This is far from ideal: not only does it require a lot of tedious duplicated code to define the attributes and pass them on, but it breaks encapsulation by forcing higher-level objects to have attributes simply for the sake of their low-level children.

Contexts were introduced to XHP to solve this problem. You can set context information on any XHP object, and when that object is rendered, it will pass its context down to all of its child objects:

```
$post_list = <ui:post-list posts={$posts} />;
$post_list->setContext('user_is_admin', $user_is_admin);
```

On the other end, in the lower-level object, simply call getContext() with the appropriate name to read the value. This class, farther down the stack, renders a post with a delete button only if the context item user_is_admin is true:

```
class :ui:post extends :x:element {
  protected function render() {
    $delete_button = null;
```

```
      if ($this->getContext('user_is_admin')) {
        $delete_button = <ui:button style="delete">Delete Post</ui:button>;
      }
      // ...
    }
  }
```

Other things to note:

- Context is only passed down the tree at *render time*. If you call setCon
  text('key', 'value') on an object and then immediately call getCon
  text('key') on its children, it will return null. In general, you should only call
  getContext() within a render() method.

- As an object is transferring context to its children during rendering, it does not
  overwrite the children's context if they have context items under the same key.
  For example:

  ```
  $inner = <inner />;
  $inner->setContext('key', 'inner-value');
  $outer = <outer>{$inner}</outer>;
  $outer->setContext('key', 'outer-value');
  ```

  If the inner object calls getContext('key'), it will return inner-value.

Async XHP

XHP integrates with Hack's async feature (see Chapter 6). When defining an XHP
class, you can use async in its rendering function with two steps:

1. Use the trait XHPAsync inside the class.

2. Implement the function asyncRender() instead of render(). asyncRender()
   should have no parameters, and return an Awaitable<XHPRoot>. For example:

   ```
   class :ui:external-api-status extends :x:element {

     use XHPAsync;

     protected async function asyncRender(): Awaitable<XHPRoot> {
       $status = await HH\Asio\curl_exec("https://example.com/api-status");
       return <x:frag>Status: {$status}</x:frag>;
     }
   }
   ```

The XHP infrastructure will detect that your element is async, and use asyncRen
der() instead of render().

XHP Helpers

XHP provides a trait called XHPHelpers that implements three very useful behaviors:

- Transferring attributes from one object to the object returned from its render() method
- Giving each object a unique id attribute
- Managing the class attribute

Transferring attributes

It's very common for an XHP class to inherit attributes from the XHP class that it will return from its render() method. For example, a class that implements a box with a drop shadow will probably inherit attributes from :div, because it will render the box as a <div>:

```
class :ui:drop-shadow-box extends :x:element {
  attribute :div;
  protected function render(): XHPRoot {
    return <div class="drop-shadow">{$this->getChildren()}</div>
  }
}
```

The problem with this code is that any attribute that you set on a ui:drop-shadow-box instance will simply be lost—the <div> returned from its render() method will not get those attributes automatically:

```
$box = <ui:drop-shadow-box title="the best box" />;

// Prints <div class="drop-shadow"></div>
echo $box->toString();
```

To get attributes transferred automatically, all you have to do is to use the trait XHPHelpers inside a class that you want this behavior for:

```
class :ui:drop-shadow-box extends :x:element {
  attribute :div;
  use XHPHelpers;

  protected function render(): XHPRoot {
    return <div class="drop-shadow">{$this->getChildren()}</div>;
  }
}
```

Now, after the ui:drop-shadow-box is rendered, XHPHelpers will iterate over all the attributes set on the ui:drop-shadow-box. For each attribute, if the object returned from render() declares that attribute, XHPHelpers will transfer it over:

```
$box = <ui:drop-shadow-box title="the best box" somename="somevalue" />;

// Prints <div class="drop-shadow" title="the best box"></div>
echo $box->toString();
```

Note that the attribute `somename="somevalue"` was *not* transferred. This is because `:ui:drop-shadow-box` box doesn't declare it, directly or indirectly (through inheriting attributes from `:div`).

When transferred, attributes set on the `ui:drop-shadow-box` will *overwrite* attributes of the same name that are set on the resultant `<div>`. For example:

```
class :ui:drop-shadow-box extends :x:element {
  attribute :div;
  use XHPHelpers;

  protected function render(): XHPRoot {
    return
      <div class="drop-shadow" title="title on the div">
        {$this->getChildren()}
      </div>;
  }
}

$box = <ui:drop-shadow-box title="title on the box" />;

// Prints <div class="drop-shadow" title="title on the box"></div>
echo $box->toString();
```

There is one exception to that overwriting behavior: the `class` attribute. Instead of simply overwriting the `<div>`'s value of this attribute, `XHPHelpers` will append to it (making sure the classes are separated by spaces):

```
$box = <ui:drop-shadow-box class="class-on-box" />;

// Prints <div class="drop-shadow class-on-box"></div>
echo $box->toString();
```

Unique IDs

In web programming, it's useful to give DOM nodes `id` attributes, so that CSS selectors and JavaScript code can refer to them. However, this is significantly less useful if node IDs aren't unique.

`XHPHelpers` provides a method that gets a unique ID for any element. Under the hood, it is generating random IDs.[3] In your `render()` function, just call `getID()`:

---

3 Yes, this means the IDS are not *guaranteed* to be unique, but the chances of generating the same ID twice on the same page are vanishingly small.

```
class :hello-world extends :x:element {
  protected function render() {
    return <span id={$this->getID()}>Hello world</span>;
  }
}
```

Managing the class attribute

As we just saw, the attribute-transferring logic of XHPHelpers treats the class attribute specially. That's because the class attribute of DOM nodes is unlike others: semantically, its value is a set, not a single value. XHPHelpers provides two methods in line with those semantics: addClass() and conditionClass().

addClass() takes a string as an argument, and appends that string to the object's class attribute. (Of course, the object's class must declare the class attribute, directly or indirectly.) It makes sure the existing value of the attribute and the new value being appended are separated by whitespace:

```
class :ui:drop-shadow-box extends :x:element {
  attribute :div;
  protected function render(): XHPRoot {
    $div = <div />;
    $div->addClass('drop-shadow');
    $div->appendChild($this->getChildren());
    return $div;
  }
}
```

conditionClass() takes two arguments, a boolean and a string. If the boolean argument is true, it simply calls addClass() with the string argument.

XHP Best Practices

HHVM gives you the syntax, and the Hack library gives you the infrastructure and HTML tags, but building a good UI library on top of these foundations is left as an exercise for the reader. There are some open source XHP UI frameworks, and there will be more over time, but you may find yourself needing to build all or part of one yourself.

One source of inspiration for good XHP design is XHP-Bootstrap (*http://github.com/ hhvm/xhp-bootstrap*). This is an XHP interface to Bootstrap (*http://getbootstrap.com*), a popular library of common web UI components like buttons, drop-down menus, navigation bars, etc.

XHP is an unfamiliar paradigm for most PHP and Hack developers, and because it's relatively new, there's not much folk wisdom in the world about how to design good XHP libraries. This section presents a collection of best practices distilled from experience at Facebook, where XHP originated. Facebook's usage of XHP dates back to 2009, and in 2015, 100% of its web frontend code uses XHP to generate HTML.

No Additional Public API

XHP classes represent UI components. A user of an XHP class should be able to create it using tag syntax and render it to a string, without calling any methods on it. (Even methods like `appendChild()` are just alternatives to tag syntax.)

You shouldn't put any public methods in XHP classes—that breaks the convention that they simply represent UI components. The only public API you should add to XHP classes are attribute and `children` declarations.

Composition, Not Inheritance

One of the key tenets of XHP class design is to avoid sharing functionality using inheritance. Facebook's original non-XHP UI library used inheritance extensively, and the battle scars we gained from it were what drove us to avoid heavy use of inheritance as we migrated to XHP.

The problem with using inheritance pre-XHP was that it resulted in one of two things: unmaintainable code, or suboptimal output. The root cause is the need for parent classes to allow for subclasses to influence their behavior or output. There are two options for exercising this influence:

- Specify some methods as "can/should be overridden." This approach does a decent job of preventing tight coupling between the classes, but can lack flexibility because the only possible customizations are those the designers of the parent class thought of.

- Don't allow or encourage overriding of protected methods, and instead force subclasses to modify the HTML returned from parent methods. With this approach, either the child class has to know details about the parent's implementation, which results in excessively tight coupling and a parent class that is very difficult to modify, or the child class simply wraps the parent's output with a `<div>` or `<span>` or similar, which results in poor output.

XHP mitigates the latter problem somewhat by providing an object-oriented interface to the objects being passed around, but inheritance still isn't ideal. The main problem is that it obscures control flow: someone reading the code may have to trace up through several levels of inheritance to find inherited methods.

A UI library using XHP shouldn't need inheritance at all. XHP classes can inherit attributes (see "Inheriting attributes" on page 179), and because of the "no additional public API" rule, this is all you need to be able to use XHP classes polymorphically—polymorphism being one of the main benefits of traditional inheritance.

There is one application for inheritance in a good XHP UI library. A single abstract base class, which all other classes extend *directly*, is generally a good idea. XHP-Bootstrap does this, in the form of `:bootstrap:base`.

Don't Make Control Flow Tags

After being introduced to XHP, most developers will eventually feel a very strong urge to create control flow tags in XHP. If this happens to you, resist the temptation. XHP isn't designed to be used for control flow, and trying to do so will result in awkward, inefficient constructs.

Here's an example of the usage of a hypothetical `<x:if>` tag that renders its first child if its condition is `true`, and its second child otherwise:

```
echo
  <x:if cond={is_logged_in()}>
    <ui:logged-in-nav-bar />
    <ui:logged-out-nav-bar />
  </x:if>;
```

This looks clean and elegant, but there are a couple of things wrong with it. First of all, you are guaranteed to instantiate a useless object in all cases. Remember that XHP is syntactic sugar for creating objects; in this case, the code would instantiate both a `:ui:logged-in-nav-bar` and a `:ui:logged-out-nav-bar`, keep them allocated until render time, and then throw one of them away without rendering it. This is inefficient, and it breaks the correspondence between the XHP tree and the eventual HTML tree.

The other problem is that it doesn't scale. The preceding example is clear and readable, but once the two children of `<x:if>` start to get complex, readability quickly diminishes:

```
echo
  <x:if cond={is_logged_in()}>
    <x:if cond={user_is_admin()}>
      <div>
        <ui:admin-link />
        <ui:logged-in-nav-bar />
      </div>
      <ui:logged-in-nav-bar />
    </x:if>
    <ui:logged-out-nav-bar />
  </x:if>;
```

So conditional constructs are awkward, but what about loops? Here's a hypothetical `<x:foreach>` class that mimics a `foreach` loop in Hack:

```
echo
  <ul>
    <x:foreach seq={$items} func={function ($item) {
      return <li>{$item}</li>;
    }} />
  </ul>;
```

This appears to be much more sensible. There are no useless XHP objects being instantiated, and it will scale well: the closure passed to the <x:foreach> object can increase in complexity without hurting clarity.

But remember, again, that XHP is just syntactic sugar for object creation. If you look at what's going on under the hood, it becomes clear that this <x:foreach> class is a bad idea. Here's a "de-sugared" version of the previous code:

```
echo new xhp_ul(array(
  new xhp_x__foreach(array(
    'seq' => $items,
    'func' => function ($item) {
      return new xhp_li(array($item));
    }
  ))
));
```

This scheme is creating an object to represent a loop, which is silly: don't create an object to represent a loop, just write the loop! The object superficially resembles a regular Hack foreach loop when dressed up in XHP syntax, but the reality is quite different.

The recommended way to do what was just shown is to use appendChild() inside a regular Hack loop. The result is still quite easy to understand:

```
$ul = <ul />;
foreach ($items as $item) {
  $ul->appendChild(<li>{item}</li>);
}
echo $ul;
```

Distinguish Attributes from Children

When you're designing XHP classes, you'll often have to choose what should be an attribute and what should be a child. The guidance for this choice comes from XHP's philosophy of trying to represent the eventual DOM tree: if a value corresponds to a node in the DOM tree, it should be a child; otherwise, it should be an attribute.

Here are some examples, inspired by XHP-Bootstrap and Facebook's internal UI library:

- A class that represents a button might have attributes for visual style ("cancel," "default," etc.) and for disabled-ness, and take its caption as a child.

- A class that represents a dialog box might have an attribute for visual style ("note," "warning," etc.) and take a header, body, and footer as children.

The main corollary to this is that no attribute should ever have a type that is an XHP class.

Style Guide

XHP has its own set of style guidelines:

- Separate words in XHP class names with hyphens. Class names should be all lowercase.

- Use colons in XHP class names as a form of namespacing. For example, if you have desktop and mobile versions of your website in the same codebase, you might have a class for the navigation bar in each version, named something like :desktop:nav-bar and :mobile:nav-bar. This is just a convention, however; there are no real namespacing semantics. For example, from within :mobile:nav-bar, you still have to include the prefix when referring to other XHP classes prefixed with :mobile.

- Each class should only have the attribute keyword once, and all attribute declarations should follow it, separated by commas:

```
class :photo-frame extends :x:element {
  attribute
    :div,
    string caption,
    string imgsrc @required,
    enum {'compact', 'full'} style;
}
```

Migrating to XHP

In an ideal world, we would never have to deal with ugly legacy code. We would be free to build beautiful, clean abstractions on top of beautiful, clean abstractions, always choosing the best design for the problem at hand, our code in perfect harmony with the present task.

But we live in the real world, where millions of lines of legacy code are still serving traffic, and are unlikely to go away any time soon. New tools and abstractions need to be able to work with old ones. This is fairly easy with XHP, but there are a few things to watch out for.

Converting Bottom-Up

The smoothest way to turn legacy UI code into XHP-using code is to work bottom-up. That is, take the most basic, low-level components—the ones that don't depend on any others—and convert them to XHP. For example, consider this:

```
function render_profile_link($user) {
  $uri = htmlspecialchars($user->getProfileURI());
  $name = htmlspecialchars($user->getName());
  return "<a href=\"$uri\">$name's Profile</a>";
}
```

The least-disruptive way to convert this to XHP is to build the HTML structure and convert it to a string, all inside the function:

```
function render_profile_link($user) {
  $link =
    <a href={$user->getProfileURI()}>
      {$user->getName()}'s Profile
    </a>;
  return $link->toString();
}
```

This change is very easy because it's self-contained—it doesn't require you to modify the function's callers—but it makes very little meaningful progress toward a broader conversion. The problem is that it does nothing to change the fact that data is crossing abstraction boundaries in the form of HTML strings, instead of XHP objects. Callers still have to be concerned about escaping, and can't sanely modify the content returned from render_profile_link(). If you want to convert the next level up—the components that use render_profile_link()—to use XHP, it's still awkward because you will need to bridge the gap between HTML strings and raw strings.

The best alternative is to convert render_profile_link() into an XHP class:

```
class :ui:profile-link extends :x:element {
  attribute User user @required;
  protected function render(): XHPRoot {
    $user = $this->:user;
    return
      <a href={$user->getProfileURI()}>
        {$user->getName()}'s Profile
      </a>;
  }
}
```

For convenience, you can keep around a version of render_profile_link() that just delegates to this XHP class:

```
function render_profile_link($user): string {
  return (<ui:profile-link user={$user} />)->toString();
}
```

Be aware that this function is a crutch, though. The real goal is to convert every former caller of `render_profile_link()` to use `<ui:profile-link>` instead, and then delete `render_profile_link()`.

Getting Around XHP's Escaping

As we saw in "Secure by Default" on page 167, any string that you embed in an XHP structure will have its reserved HTML characters escaped as the XHP object gets turned into a string. This is a very good thing, as it makes XHP secure by default and eliminates XSS vulnerabilities.

Sometimes, though, this behavior isn't what you want. For example, you may be using a function from a library that returns an HTML string—a library for rendering markup formats like Markdown, say—that must be output as is, without escaping.

There is a deliberate backdoor in XHP's infrastructure that allows the creation of classes (regular classes, not XHP classes) that are exempt from escaping and validation. This takes the form of two interfaces:

`XHPUnsafeRenderable`

> This interface declares one method, `toHTMLString()`. It takes no arguments and returns a string. You can put objects implementing this interface into an XHP object tree, and the XHP rendering infrastructure will put the result of calling `toHTMLString()` directly into the returned HTML string, without escaping.

`XHPAlwaysValidChild`

> A class that implements this interface is a valid child of any XHP object, unless it has a declaration of `children empty` (see "children Declarations" on page 179). The interface itself declares no methods.

The XHP library doesn't come with any classes that implement these interfaces because, ideally, they shouldn't be needed, and using them has security implications. We wanted to create a barrier to doing these unsafe things, so that they're still possible, but you have to know the risks before you can do them.

With that stern warning, here's an example of a class that gets HTML from an external syntax highlighting library, and lets it be added to an XHP tree:

```
class SyntaxHighlight implements XHPUnsafeRenderable {
  private string $content;

  public function __construct(string $source) {
    $this->content = external_highlighting_function($source);
  }

  public function toHTMLString(): string {
    return $this->content;
```

```
    }
  }
```
And here's how to use it:

```
$code = <div>{new SyntaxHighlight($source)}</div>;
```

XHP Internals

This section is optional reading for people who want to understand what's going on under the hood. You shouldn't need to understand any of this to be able to use XHP effectively.

There are two components to XHP: the parser-level transformation that turns tag syntax into new expressions, and the Hack library that contains the core objects-to-strings infrastructure and implementations of HTML tags.

The Parser Transformation

As XHP syntax is being parsed, the parser transforms it into regular Hack syntax:

- XHP class names (those starting with colons) are transformed into legal Hack class names as follows:

  1. The leading colon is replaced with xhp_.
  2. Colons other than the leading one are replaced with __ (two underscores).
  3. Hyphens are replaced with _ (a single underscore).

  So, for example, the class name :ui:nav-bar will be transformed to xhp_ui__nav_bar internally. This transformation applies to XHP class definitions and where those class names are used.

  Error messages will use these transformed names, which is why I've described the transformation in detail.

- children, category, and attribute declarations are transformed into definitions of protected methods. Each method does nothing but return an array that contains an encoding of the declaration. The format of this array is an implementation detail and should never matter to users of XHP.

- XHP tag syntax is replaced with a new expression. Two arguments will be passed to the XHP class's constructor: an array of attributes (names mapping to values), and an array of children. Here is an example:

  ```
  echo
    <a href="/signup.php">
      Subscribe to <span class="brand">The Dispatch</span>
    </a>;
  ```

```
// Is transformed into:
echo new xhp_a(
  array('href' => '/signup.php'),
  array(
    'Subscribe to ',
    new xhp_span(
      array('class' => 'brand'),
      array('The Dispatch')
    )
  )
)
```

In fact, you can write code in the second style manually, and it will work.

The Hack Library

The Hack library defines several abstract classes that form the core objects-to-strings infrastructure of XHP. The class hierarchy is illustrated in Figure 7-1.

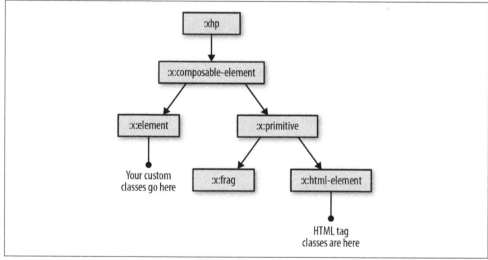

Figure 7-1. The hierarchy of XHP's core classes

Here are the details of the core classes shown in this hierarchy:

:xhp

> This defines the interface to XHP objects. It declares several abstract methods that define the interface to all XHP objects: getting and setting children and attributes. It has no properties and no non-static methods.

`:x:composable-element`

> This extends `:xhp` and is also abstract, but has a lot of concrete functionality: it provides implementations of child and attribute management methods, as well as validation of category, child, and attribute constraints. It has declared properties: arrays for children, attributes, and context.

`:x:primitive` *and* `:x:element`

> These both extend `:x:composable-element`, and are both abstract. The key distinction between them is that `:x:primitive` expects its subclasses to implement a method called `stringify()` that returns a *string*, whereas `:x:element` expects its subclasses to implement a method called `render()` or `asyncRender()` that returns an *XHP object*. This split is the key: it enables two separate validation stages, which allows built-in classes to seamlessly mix with custom ones while still performing meaningful validation.

The key operation is called *flushing*: converting an `:x:element` into an `:x:primitive` by repeatedly calling `render()` or `asyncRender()` on it, and recursively flushing its children, until it and all its children are `:x:primitive` objects. The rendering methods can return any XHP object, and your `:x:element`-extending custom classes may be built up in many layers, but at the bottom of the stack there must be the `:x:primitive`-extending classes from the XHP library, so this procedure is guaranteed to terminate eventually.

Flushing an `:x:element` tree creates an async dependency tree (see "Structuring Async Code" on page 140) by recursively calling and awaiting `asyncRender()` on each element. Multiple elements can be rendering in parallel this way, including ones from different levels of the tree.

You initiate the process of converting an XHP tree to a string by calling `toString()` (or calling and awaiting `asyncToString()`) on a single XHP object, which is the root of the tree:

- `:x:element`'s `toString()` validates the element's children (first stage of validation), flushes the element, and then calls `toString()` on the resulting `:x:primitive`.

- `:x:primitive`'s `toString()` flushes all of the element's children (awaiting them all simultaneously using `HH\Asio\m()`), validates the flushed children (second stage of validation), then calls `stringify()` on each child and concatenates the resulting strings together.

The last detail is the position of the library classes that represent HTML tags. These all extend `:xhp:html-element`, which extends `:x:primitive`. There are a few subclasses of `:xhp:html-element` that represent specific archetypes of HTML tags (e.g., `:xhp:html-singleton`, which is not allowed to have children), but these should be considered as internal to XHP, and not for use outside of the library.

Configuring and Deploying HHVM

At the language level, HHVM is meant to be a drop-in replacement for the standard PHP interpreter. When running scripts from the command line, this promise generally holds. However, the way you configure and deploy it to serve web apps is different, not least because of its just-in-time (JIT) compiler.

In this chapter, you'll learn the basics of setting up HHVM to serve web traffic. Of course, many details will depend on your specific application and infrastructure, so this chapter can't be a complete guide. The aim is to give you a good enough understanding of HHVM that you can figure out how to integrate it with your setup.

This chapter doesn't cover setting up the Hack typechecker, which is only used during development. For that, see Chapter 1.

Specifying Configuration Options

HHVM has a vast set of configuration options—far too many to cover them all in detail in this book. Many of them aren't meant for end users anyway; they're for people hacking on HHVM itself. In this section, we'll cover how to set configuration options, and what the most important ones are.

HHVM uses configuration files in INI format, which is the same format that the standard PHP interpreter uses. You can specify a configuration file with the -c flag:

```
$ hhvm -c config.ini file.php
```

INI format is very straightforward. Each option consists of a key/value pair. Each pair is on its own line in an INI file, with the key and value separated by an equals sign (whitespace is not significant):

```
hhvm.dump_bytecode = 1
hhvm.log.file = /tmp/hhvm.log
```

Some configuration options are associative arrays. hhvm.server_variables is an example; it sets the contents of the $_SERVER variable within PHP and Hack. You specify such options like this (in INI format):

```
hhvm.server_variables[ENVIRONMENT] = prod
hhvm.server_variables[A_NUMBER] = 314
```

Within a PHP or Hack program with this configuration, $_SERVER will have those values under those keys:

```
var_dump($_SERVER['ENVIRONMENT']);  // Prints: string(4) "prod"
var_dump($_SERVER['A_NUMBER']);     // Prints: int(314)
```

You can also specify options directly on the shell command line. Use the flag -d, followed by an INI-format key/value pair. Make sure that the pair either doesn't have whitespace in it or is quoted, or the shell will split it into multiple arguments and HHVM will misinterpret it:

```
$ hhvm -d hhvm.dump_bytecode=1 file.php
```

You can combine multiple config files and direct options in the same command:

```
$ hhvm -c config1.ini -d hhvm.dump_bytecode=1 -c config2.ini file.php
```

In this way, the same option can be specified multiple times. HHVM reads the command line left to right and config files top to bottom; the value of an option that it ends up with is the one that it reads last. For example, in the previous command line, the option -d hhvm.dump_bytecode=1 will override any setting of hhvm.dump_byte code in *config1.ini*. If the option is also specified in *config2.ini*, that setting will win.

Generally, for production use, it's best to specify all options in a single config file, simply to ensure consistency by avoiding this ordering dependence.

Important Options

The following are some of the most important HHVM configuration options:

hhvm.enable_obj_destruct_call *(boolean, default off)*
>   If this option is off, as it is by default, HHVM will not run __destruct() methods on objects that remain alive at the end of a request. (It will run __destruct() methods as normal at other times.) If your application can tolerate this, it can be a significant performance win: instead of having to traverse every array and object still alive at the end of a request, HHVM can simply deallocate all of the request's memory in one shot. If the option is on, HHVM will run all __destruct() methods as normal, at all times.

hhvm.hack.lang.look_for_typechecker *(boolean, default on)*
>   If this option is on, as it is by default, HHVM will refuse to run any Hack file unless it can find a Hack typechecker server process that is covering that file. In

production, you should turn this off, as you won't be running the Hack type-checker except in development environments. It will be automatically turned off if you are in repo-authoritative mode (see "Repo-Authoritative Mode" on page 202).

hhvm.jit_enable_rename_function *(boolean, default off)*
If this option is off, as it is by default, using the built-in rename_function() will raise a fatal error. Knowing that functions will not be renamed allows for some powerful optimizations, so if you don't rely on this functionality, you should keep this option off.

hhvm.server.thread_count *(integer, defaults to twice the number of CPU cores)*
This option specifies the number of worker threads that are used to serve web requests in server mode (see "Server Mode" on page 200). There's no one-size-fits-all formula for the ideal thread count. It depends, in complex ways, on the application's performance characteristics, and on the machine's CPU and memory specs.

Apps that don't use async (see Chapter 6) will likely benefit from thread counts much higher than the default, as threads will spend a good amount of wall time idle, waiting for I/O. A good starting point might be 15 times the core count.

Apps that use async heavily are likely to be OK with the default thread count, or slightly higher. Async can help HHVM use the CPU during time that would otherwise be spent idle.

The best way to tune this value is to experiment. Vary the thread count and observe the effects on CPU and memory utilization. As you raise the thread count, utilization of both resources should increase. Try doing this experiment at peak traffic times, since utilization at peak is the most important determiner of total capacity. Adjust the thread count to raise utilization up to some defined limit (70% CPU, say), and stop there.

HHVM uses OS-level threads, unlike PHP-FPM, which uses processes. The overhead of increasing HHVM's thread count is quite low, so don't worry about that when increasing it.

hhvm.source_root *(string, defaults to working directory of HHVM process)*
This option is only relevant in server mode, where it holds the path to the root directory of the code being served.

Server Mode

HHVM has two primary modes: command-line mode and server mode. Command-line mode is what's used when you run a command like `hhvm test.php`; it immediately executes the given script and exits when the script terminates.

Server mode is what you'll use to serve web requests. In this mode, the HHVM process starts up and doesn't execute anything immediately. It executes code in response to requests that come in via FastCGI, and stays running after requests finish. It can process multiple requests simultaneously. JIT-compiled code is kept in memory (in the *translation cache*) and shared across requests.

Start HHVM in server mode with the command-line flag `-m server`:

```
$ hhvm -m server -d hhvm.server.type=fastcgi -d hhvm.server.port=9000
```

This is a FastCGI server, so the port number 9000 is conventional.

The next step is to configure a web server to send requests to the HHVM FastCGI server. You can use any FastCGI-compatible web server software, such as Apache (*http://httpd.apache.org*) or nginx (*http://nginx.org*). We'll focus on nginx here, because it's simpler to configure, but won't cover configuring it from the ground up.

The bare minimum for sending FastCGI requests to HHVM is a `location` directive like this:

```
location ~ \.(hh|php)$ {
  include fastcgi_params;
  fastcgi_param SCRIPT_FILENAME $document_root$fastcgi_script_name;
  fastcgi_pass 127.0.0.1:9000;
}
```

`fastcgi_params` refers to a configuration file that comes with the standard nginx installation; it passes parameters of the request (HTTP method, content length, etc.) on to HHVM. The `fastcgi_param` directive tells HHVM which file to execute. The `fastcgi_pass` directive simply means that the request will be passed to the FastCGI server at the address `127.0.0.1` on port 9000. This configuration will be applied to any request for a path ending in *.hh* or *.php*.

The wrapper script

HHVM's command-line interface can be quite complex, so the package includes a script called `hhvm_wrapper` that puts a more convenient interface on some of the more common options.

Run `hhvm_wrapper --help` to see the options it provides. It can do things like run a script in repo-authoritative mode (see "Repo-Authoritative Mode" on page 202) with a single command:

```
$ hhvm_wrapper --compile test.php
```

To see what's going on behind the scenes, add the flag `--print-command` to any `hhvm_wrapper` command line. It will print out the underlying HHVM invocation, instead of running it.

Warming Up the JIT

The first few requests to an HHVM server will be slower than the rest, because it has to compile the PHP and Hack code into machine code before executing it. The effect is noticeable enough that you shouldn't immediately expose a newly started HHVM server to production traffic; you should warm it up first, by sending it a few synthetic requests.

In fact, the server starts out by not compiling code at all. The first few requests are run in HHVM's bytecode interpreter. The theory is that the first few requests to a web server are unusual—initialization is happening, caches are being filled, etc.—and that compiling those codepaths is bad for overall performance, as they won't be frequently taken once the server is warmed up. HHVM also uses these requests to collect some profiling data about the data types it sees the code using, so it can compile more effectively later. You can tune this threshold with the option `hhvm.jit_pro file_interp_requests`.

This characteristic sometimes confuses people trying to benchmark HHVM, as they see the first few requests being slower than they expect—in fact, often slower than running the same scripts from the command line. (HHVM always compiles code when running command-line scripts.)

To benchmark a JIT-based execution engine properly, you have to give it a warmup period. Because doing so is somewhat subtle, the HHVM team has released a tool that does a lot of it for you, enabling consistent benchmarking of server workloads. It's available on GitHub (*https://github.com/hhvm/oss-performance*).

Sending warmup requests can be as simple as using the command-line `curl` utility, from a shell script or similar. For best results:

- Use requests that are a representative mix of the most common requests you expect to see in production. For example, if you expect that about 40% of all requests in production will go to *index.php*, then about 40% of your warmup requests should be to *index.php*.

- Avoid sending multiple warmup requests in parallel. Nothing will break if you do send multiple parallel requests, but the JIT compiler tends to generate better code if it is not working on multiple requests at the same time.

Eventually you should have the warmup process scripted so that you can warm up a server with a single command, but initially, you'll need to have some manual involvement. There's some subtlety to working out a good number of requests to send—it varies depending on your application.

One way to work out a good number is to keep sending requests until you're seeing consistent response times for requests to the same endpoint. Sometime after the JIT compiler kicks in (after the last warmup request) you'll see another jump in performance, as it starts recompiling some code with the benefit of profile-guided optimization (PGO). There isn't a single request-count threshold for when PGO begins—it's based on how frequently individual pieces of code are run—so you should keep running warmup requests until response times level off.

You can also use the admin server (see "The Admin Server" on page 204) to monitor the sizes of the compiled-code caches. They will grow rapidly when the JIT compiler starts, but their growth will soon slow down significantly. When that happens, the server is sufficiently warmed up.

Repo-Authoritative Mode

By default, HHVM continually checks your PHP and Hack source files to make sure they haven't been modified since it last read them. When your source files are deployed to production this can incur significant costs for no benefit, as the source files are unlikely to be changing frequently.

To fix this, HHVM offers *repo-authoritative mode*. In this mode, you build a byte-code file (the *repo*) from your codebase ahead of time, and deploy that to production, without source files. Then, the HHVM server process reads from the repo and never checks the filesystem for source files—that is, the repo is "authoritative."

As well as reducing the need for filesystem operations, repo-authoritative mode allows HHVM's compiler to make significant optimizations that it otherwise couldn't. Because of the guarantee that the compiler can see all the code that can possibly exist in the process's lifetime, it can do things like function inlining that aren't normally possible.

However, the inability to introduce new code at runtime means that in repo-authoritative mode you can't use `eval()` or `create_function()` (which is actually just a wrapper around `eval()`).

Building the Repo

Before deploying, you have to build the repo. You do so by passing several flags to HHVM. We'll start with the most basic example, building a repo that contains a single file:

```
$ hhvm --hphp -t hhbc -v AllVolatile=true test.php
```

The `--hphp` flag[1] signals that we want to do some offline operation, instead of executing PHP or Hack code. `-t hhbc` means "target HHBC"—that is, we want to output bytecode. `-v AllVolatile=true` turns on an option that disables a rather aggressive optimization that takes some care to use correctly.[2] Finally, we pass filenames to produce bytecode for—in this case, only one.

This results in a file named *hhvm.hhbc* in the current working directory; this is the repo. The repo is actually just a SQLite3 database file, so you can use the `sqlite3` command-line tool to examine it.[3]

In practice, it may be awkward to name all the source files that need to be included on the command line, so HHVM can also accept the name of a file that contains one source file name per line. Let's say we have a file called *files.txt* with the following contents:

```
lib/a.php
lib/b.php
index.php
```

Then we can tell HHVM to use this list as its input:

```
$ hhvm --hphp -t hhbc --input-list files.txt
```

The repo captures the file paths that were passed to HHVM when building the repo, and these paths form a "virtual filesystem," of sorts for the HHVM process that runs from the repo. In concrete terms, when HHVM is running from this repo and the web server gives it a request for some path—say, */some/file.php*—HHVM will look in the repo for a file that was at the path *some/file.php* when the repo was built.

In view of that, things will generally be easiest if you build the repo from the path that will correspond to your web server's document root when deployed. This may vary

---

1 A historical artifact.

2 It's a bit of an oversight that this optimization is enabled by default.

3 There is no human-readable code inside it, but there is human-readable metadata.

depending on how much path rewriting you intend to do at the web server level, though.

Deploying the Repo

Copy the *hhvm.hhbc* file to your production servers. You don't need to copy source files; HHVM will run without them. If you have your web server configured to look in the filesystem to determine what to do with a given request (which is fairly common), you may need to copy your source files for that purpose. However, you could instead just have empty files in a directory structure mirroring your actual codebase, and that would be enough for the web server.

You must use the same HHVM binary to run from the repo as you do to build the repo. Repos are not backward-compatible or forward-compatible. When building a repo, HHVM embeds in it a *repo schema ID*, unique to each HHVM version. When using a repo at runtime, HHVM checks the repo's schema ID against its own, and it won't use the repo if the schema IDs don't match.

It doesn't matter where you put the repo file, as long as the HHVM process can read it. Remember the "virtual filesystem" formulation from before—in repo-authoritative mode, HHVM will never be concerned with the real filesystem, only with the contents of the repo. This also means that the setting of hhvm.server.source_root is irrelevant in repo-authoritative mode.

There are two relevant configuration options: one to tell HHVM to use repo-authoritative mode, and one to tell it where the repo is. This is what you would put in your INI file (substituting the correct pathname):

```
hhvm.repo.authoritative = 1
hhvm.repo.central.path = /path/to/hhvm.hhbc
```

The Admin Server

In server and daemon modes, HHVM provides a mechanism by which you can inspect and control the running server process. The process listens on a separate port, over which you can issue commands with HTTP requests. This functionality is called the *admin server*. It offers a wide range of commands; we'll cover the basics but won't look at all of them in great detail here.

The admin server is turned off by default. You turn it on by specifying a port number for it to listen on—the specific port doesn't matter, as long as it's free and HHVM can bind to it. You should always specify a password as well. You'll give the password along with every request to the admin server:

```
hhvm.admin_server.port = 9001
hhvm.admin_server.password = 9UejLK2jVhy
```

You'll need to set up your web server to listen on a new port and forward requests to the admin server's port as FastCGI requests. In the examples ahead, we'll assume that we picked port number 15213 for the web server to listen on.

 The admin server is potentially very dangerous, which is why it's not enabled by default. Never enable it without a password—a *strong* password, which you rotate regularly—and don't expose its port to the Internet.

Once the HHVM server process is started, you can use the `curl` command-line utility (or a web browser) to send commands to it. In these examples, we'll assume that we're running `curl` on the same machine as the HHVM server process, and that the admin server password is the one configured earlier.

Making a request to / on the admin server will show a help message with a list of possible commands. You don't need to provide the password to get help:

```
$ curl http://localhost:15213/
/stop:              stop the web server
    instance-id     optional, if specified, instance ID has to match
/translate:         translate hex encoded stacktrace in 'stack' param
    stack           required, stack trace to translate
    build-id        optional, if specified, build ID has to match
    bare            optional, whether to display frame ordinates
/build-id:          returns build id that's passed in from command line
/instance-id:       instance id that's passed in from command line
/compiler-id:       returns the compiler id that built this app
/repo-schema:       return the repo schema id used by this app
/check-load:        how many threads are actively handling requests
/check-queued:      how many http requests are queued waiting to be
                    handled
/check-health:      return json containing basic load/usage stats
/check-ev:          how many http requests are active by libevent
/check-pl-load:     how many pagelet threads are actively handling
                    requests
/check-pl-queued:   how many pagelet requests are queued waiting to
                    be handled
/check-mem:         report memory quick statistics in log file
/check-sql:         report SQL table statistics
/check-sat          how many satellite threads are actively handling
                    requests and queued waiting to be handled

... more items omitted ...
```

Each of the commands is a path that you can add to your admin server request. For any of these commands, you have to provide the password that you configured the admin server with, under the GET parameter auth. For example, here's the command `compiler-id`, which shows the Git revision that this HHVM binary was built from:

```
$ curl http://localhost:15213/compiler-id?auth=9UejLK2jVhy
tags/HHVM-3.9.1-0-g0f72cfc2f0a01fdfeb72fbcfeb247b72998a66db
```

Indented items in the help output, like `instance-id` under `/stop`, are the names of GET parameters that you can provide to the command:

```
$ curl http://localhost:15213/stop?auth=9UejLK2jVhy&instance-id=INSTANCEID
```

If you enter the wrong password, the admin server returns the text `Unauthorized`.

hphpd: Interactive Debugging

HHVM comes with an interactive debugger called *hphpd*. In case you're not familiar with the concept, an interactive debugger is a program that lets you control other programs, and inspect their state. You can set it to pause the controlled program at certain points (e.g., when execution enters a specific function, or reaches a specific line of code). You can look at the values of variables during execution and, in some cases, modify them. Interactive debuggers are powerful tools, and they can drastically increase the ease and efficiency of debugging a large, complex program, as compared to the trial-and-error workflow of printf-debugging.

hphpd is also a read-eval-print loop (REPL) for PHP and Hack. You can interactively type in PHP and Hack code, in the context of your codebase (so you can use your library functions and so on), to try out small pieces of code.

If you've used other interactive debuggers like GDB or LLDB, you'll find hphpd quite familiar. In fact, you may not even need to read this chapter; you can probably get started just using hphpd's interactive help command, help.

In this chapter, we'll see how to use hphpd to debug scripts and web apps, how to configure it, and how to get the most out of it.

Getting Started

Start hphpd by typing hhvm -m debug at a shell command line. Instead of executing any code, HHVM will display a welcome message and drop into the *debugger prompt*:

```
$ hhvm -m debug
Welcome to HipHop Debugger!
Type "help" or "?" for a complete list of commands.

Note: no server specified, debugging local scripts only.
```

```
If you want to connect to a server, launch with "-h" or use:
  [m]achine [c]onnect <servername>

hphpd>
```

Whatever you type will appear after the `hphpd>` marker on the last line of output, just like on the shell command line. This is where you type hphpd commands. hphpd's command line uses the GNU Readline library, so it remembers your command history and supports features like Emacs key bindings and navigation of history using the up-arrow and down-arrow keys.

Let's start with the most useful command in hphpd. Simply typing `help` or `?` at the prompt will show a list of commands:

```
hphpd> help


———————————— Session Commands ————————————

    [m]achine                   connects to an HHVM server
    [t]hread                    switches between different threads
    [s]et                       various configuration options for hphpd
    [q]uit                      quits debugger


———————————— Program Flow Control ————————————

    [b]reak                     sets/clears/displays breakpoints
    [e]xception                 catches/clears exceptions
    [r]un                       starts over a program
    <Ctrl-C>                    breaks program execution
    [c]ontinue *                continues program execution
    [s]tep     *                steps into a function call or an expression
    [n]ext     *                steps over a function call or a line
    [o]ut      *                steps out a function call


———————————— Display Commands ————————————

    [p]rint                     prints a variable's value
    [w]here                     displays stacktrace
    [u]p                        goes up by frame(s)
    [d]own                      goes down by frame(s)
    [f]rame                     goes to a frame
    [v]ariable                  lists all local variables
    [g]lobal                    lists all global variables
    [k]onstant                  lists all constants


———————————— Evaluation Commands ————————————

    @                           evaluates one line of PHP code
    =                           prints right-hand-side's value, assigns to $_
    ${name}=                    assigns a value to left-hand-side
    [<?]php                     starts input of a block of PHP code
    ?>                          ends and evaluates a block a PHP code
```

```
[a]bort                        aborts input of a block of PHP code
[z]end                         evaluates the last snippet in PHP5


────────── Documentation and Source Code ──────────

[i]nfo                         displays documentations and other information
[l]ist        *                displays source codes
[h]elp        **               displays this help
?                              displays this help


────────── Shell and Extended Commands ──────────

! {cmd}                        executes a shell command
& {cmd}                        records and replays macros
x {cmd}                        extended commands
y {cmd}                        user extended commands


  * These commands are replayable by just hitting return.
  ** Type "help help" to get more help.
```

The letter enclosed in square brackets at the beginning of some commands means that you can invoke that command just by typing that one letter.

You can type help followed by the name of any other command to get more specific help with that command:

```
hphpd> help variable

─────────────────── Variable Command ───────────────────

[v]ariable            lists all local variables on stack
[v]ariable {text}     full-text search local variables


This will print names and values of all variables that are currently
accessible by simple names. Use '[w]here', '[u]p {num}', '[d]own {num}',
'[f]rame {index}' commands to choose a different frame to view
variables at different level of the stack.

Specify some free text to print local variables that contain the text
either in their names or values. The search is case-insensitive and
string-based.
```

When getting command help, you can use the commands' short names too; help v does the same thing as help variable.

Some commands have *subcommands*, which select between different behaviors the command has. For example, the break command can be used to list breakpoints (break list) or delete them (break clear), among other things. We'll cover each command's subcommands as we go.

Many commands also have arguments, which you pass by typing them at the debugger prompt after the command itself, separated by whitespace, much like passing arguments to a shell command.

You can exit hphpd by either using the quit command or typing Ctrl-C at the debugger prompt. (Typing Ctrl-C while code is executing will pause execution and put you back at the debugger prompt.)

Evaluating Code

You can use the @ command to evaluate Hack code. Everything that you type between the @ and the newline that ends the command will be executed. It can be a single statement or multiple statements (you don't need to add a semicolon at the end):

```
hphpd> @echo "hello\n"
hello

hphpd> @function speak() { echo "speaking\n"; }

hphpd> @speak()
speaking

hphpd> @echo "hello "; echo "world\n"
hello world
```

 hphpd doesn't leave a blank line before each prompt, but they're added here for legibility.

You can use the = command to print the value of an expression:

```
hphpd> = 1 + 2
3

hphpd> = 'hello ' . 'world'
"hello world"
```

After each = command, the value it evaluated to is stored in the variable $_:

```
hphpd> = 'beep'
"beep"

hphpd> @echo $_
beep
```

You can assign a value to a variable just by typing the assignment statement directly as a command. You could do so with @ as well, but it's such a common operation that it's special-cased in the debugger command syntax:

```
hphpd> $hello = 'hello'

hphpd> = $hello
"hello"
```

Finally, there's a command that lets you inspect all local variables at once, much more quickly than by using = repeatedly: the `variable` command. It will print out the names and values of all local variables:

```
hphpd> $nums = array(10, 20, 30)
hphpd> $num = $nums[0]
hphpd> $count = count($nums)
hphpd> variable
$count = 3
$num = 10
$nums = Array
(
    [0] => 10
    [1] => 20
    [2] => 30
)
```

You can pass an argument to the `variable` command, to filter the local variables that will be printed. Any variable whose name contains the command's argument as a substring will be printed. Continuing from the preceding example:

```
hphpd> variable num
$num = 10
$nums = Array
(
    [0] => 10
    [1] => 20
    [2] => 30
)
```

This command will be much more useful once we start executing and debugging real code.

The Execution Environment

The examples we've seen so far were all working in an initially empty execution environment; no source files were loaded.[1] The interesting uses of hphpd happen when working with real codebases.

There are two modes that hphpd can be in: *local* and *remote*. Local mode means that the debugger is working in a PHP/Hack environment within its own process. Remote mode means that it's working in a PHP/Hack environment inside a different process:

---

1 You can use the @ command to evaluate `include` statements and the like, though.

a server-mode or daemon-mode HHVM process. That other process may be on a different machine, but it doesn't have to be; connecting to localhost is the most common way to use remote mode.

You can tell which mode hphpd is in by the debugger prompt. If it just says hphpd>, it's in local mode. If it says something else, it's in remote mode; that something else is the hostname of the machine it's connected to.

You'll use local mode when you're just using hphpd as a REPL, or when debugging a script. Remote mode is for debugging web apps; you'll connect to the HHVM process running your app.

Local Mode

When you start hphpd without arguments, as in simply hhvm -m debug, it will start in local mode, with no program loaded. This is only useful if you want to experiment with individual bits of PHP and Hack code; none of the code in your source files will be available.

You can start hphpd with a filename as an argument, as in hhvm -m debug test.php. This will load that file and prepare to run it. When you issue the run command in hphpd, it will start executing *test.php* from the top, just as if you had typed hhvm test.php at the command line.

Here's *test.php*:

```
<?hh

echo "hello\n";
```

We'll load it up in hphpd and run it:

```
$ hhvm -m debug test.php
Welcome to HipHop Debugger!
Type "help" or "?" for a complete list of commands.

Program test.php loaded. Type '[r]un' or '[c]ontinue' to go.
hphpd> run
hello
Program test.php exited normally.
hphpd>
```

If you type run again, the program will execute again, starting from the top.

After running the program once, any functions, classes, etc. that get defined in the course of running the program will be available; you can call them using @ and = without having the program actually running.

Here's a new *test.php*:

```
<?hh

function func() {
  echo "hello\n";
}
```

Note that there is no top-level code; just running this script won't have any visible effects. We'll just run it once to load the function, and then use it:

```
hphpd> run

hphpd> = func()
hello

hphpd>
```

Now, if you make changes to the file, executing the run command again will reload the file from the filesystem, and you should see your changes reflected.

Remote Mode

To use hphpd's remote mode, you need a server-mode or daemon-mode HHVM process to debug. For details on that, see Chapter 8. The process needs to have its debugger server enabled, so that hphpd can connect to it. It also needs to have *sandbox mode* turned on, which we'll explain later. Here are the configuration options you'll need to set to do all that, in INI format:

```
hhvm.sandbox.sandbox_mode = 1
hhvm.debugger.enable_debugger = 1
hhvm.debugger.enable_debugger_server = 1
```

By default, the process will listen for incoming debugger connections on port 8089; this is configurable with the option hhvm.debugger.port.

Once you have a suitable server process, start hphpd in remote mode by passing the command line argument -h followed by the hostname of the machine to connect to:

```
$ hhvm -m debug -h localhost
Welcome to HipHop Debugger!
Type "help" or "?" for a complete list of commands.

Connecting to localhost:8089...
Attaching to oyamauchi's default sandbox and pre-loading, please wait...

localhost>
```

The command prompt shows that we've successfully connected to the machine. You can get out of remote mode and go back to local mode with the disconnect subcommand of machine.

You can also enter remote mode from local mode, by using the `machine` command with the `connect` subcommand:

```
hphpd> machine connect localhost
Connecting to localhost:8089...
Attaching to oyamauchi's default sandbox and pre-loading, please wait...

localhost>
```

Now we need to take a look at the concept of *sandboxes*, mentioned earlier. In HHVM, a sandbox is a set of configuration options including a document root and a logfile path. HHVM can support multiple sandboxes in a single server-mode process, essentially allowing a single process to serve multiple different web apps.[2] (You may have heard the term "sandbox" in the context of code isolation for security purposes; HHVM's use of the term is unrelated.)

Configuring multiple sandboxes is complex and somewhat beyond our scope here. What's relevant here is that sandbox mode must be turned on for hphpd to be able to debug a server-mode HHVM process, and when you connect to a server-mode HHVM process, you'll have to choose a sandbox to attach to.

When you connect to a server-mode process, you'll attach to a *dummy sandbox*. This is a sandbox created specifically for the debugger; it has no document root and so it has no code loaded. Its only purpose is to provide a PHP/Hack environment to evaluate code in from the debugger prompt. It's analogous to hphpd's local mode with no program loaded.

You can see all the sandboxes on the server with the `list` subcommand of `machine`:

```
localhost> machine list
1       oyamauchi's default sandbox at /oyamauchi/www/
2       __builtin's default sandbox at /home/oyamauchi/test-site/
```

The first entry in the list is the dummy sandbox (note that its path may be nonsense; it's not actually used). The second one is the real one, representing the configuration with which the server is serving web requests.

 The real sandbox won't show up if it hasn't served any requests since the server started up. If you run `machine list` and see only the dummy sandbox, try making a web request to the server.

You need to attach to the real sandbox, which you do with the `attach` subcommand, passing the sandbox number as the argument:

```
localhost> machine attach 2
Attaching to __builtin's default sandbox at /home/oyamauchi/test-site/ and
pre-loading, please wait...

localhost>
```

Now you're in the right context, with that web app's code loaded. You can set breakpoints (see the next section) and view code (see "Viewing Code and Documentation" on page 227), and hphpd will operate on that codebase.

Using Breakpoints

A *breakpoint* is a condition that, when met in the program being debugged, will cause the debugger to stop the program's execution and drop into the debugger prompt. There are several conditions that can be used as breakpoints:

- When execution reaches a certain line in a certain file
- When execution enters a certain function or method
- When a web request at a certain URL begins or ends

Let's start with a simple example. Suppose we have this file, called *test.php*:

```
<?hh

function func(string $first, string $second): void {
  echo $first . "\n";
  echo $second . "\n";
}

func('one', 'two');
```

We'll start up hphpd, and set a breakpoint between the two `echo` statements. To set a breakpoint, you use the hphpd command `break`, followed by the breakpoint's condition.[3] In this case, we'll set one on line 5, the line containing the second `echo` statement—when you set a breakpoint on a line, execution will stop just before any of that line is executed. We specify the location by typing the filename, followed by a colon, followed by the line number (with no whitespace):

```
$ hhvm -m debug test.php
hphpd> break test.php:5
hphpd> run
```

---

[3] For clarity, we'll be using the full commands in this book, but remember that you can shorten them to just the first letter. You can type b `test.php:5` instead of `break test.php:5`, and it will do the same thing.

```
one
Breakpoint 1 reached at func() on line 5 of /home/oyamauchi/test.php
    4    echo $first . "\n";
    5*   echo $second . "\n";
    6 }

hphpd>
```

The script starts executing, echoes one, and then pauses. The debugger prints out the source code surrounding the location where execution is stopped, and marks the relevant line with an asterisk. (If your terminal supports it, the output is colorized as well, highlighting the relevant line.) Note that two has not been echoed yet.

The debugger prompt is visible, meaning the debugger is waiting for a command. From here, you can inspect state with `variable` and evaluation commands, set more breakpoints, continue execution in small increments, or resume normal execution. We'll see how to do all of this in the rest of this section.

Setting Breakpoints

We've seen the syntax for setting a breakpoint at a certain line in a certain file. This is the syntax for setting a breakpoint on a given function:

```
hphpd> break my_function()
Breakpoint 1 set upon entering my_function()
```

Regardless of what parameters the function has, you always put an empty pair of parentheses after the function name.

You may see a message that execution won't break until the function has been loaded. This is generally nothing to worry about; as code executes and files are loaded, the debugger will watch for a function by the given name to be loaded, and when it is, it will ensure the breakpoint gets set.

To set a breakpoint on a method, the argument to the `break` command is the class name, followed by two colons, followed by the method name, followed by an empty pair of parentheses:

```
hphpd> break MyClass::myMethod()
Breakpoint 1 set upon entering MyClass::myMethod()
```

The class-and-method-name pair is resolved lexically; hphpd does not take inheritance or traits into account. In other words, if a method definition with the specified name is written inside the class definition with the provided name, the breakpoint will be set there. If the method is defined in a trait that the class uses, or if it's inherited from an ancestor class, the breakpoint won't be set.

The final form of breakpoint trigger is specific to remote mode, when debugging web requests. You can break at the beginning or end of a web request, as well as at the

beginning of the processing of shutdown functions registered through `regis`
`ter_shutdown_function()`. The syntax for these is `break start`, `break end`, and
`break psp`, respectively.[4]

Each of those three can be modified with a further argument, which is the path part
of a URI.[5] In that case, the breakpoint will only trigger on web requests to that path:

```
hphpd> break start /something/something.php
Breakpoint 1 set start of request when request is /something/something.php
```

Note that the URL that will be checked is the original request URI—the value stored
in `$_SERVER['REQUEST_URI']`. It is not the path of the PHP or Hack file that ends up
getting invoked.

Breakpoint expressions and conditions

Any of the preceding forms of breakpoint can have a Hack expression attached to it,
and hphpd will evaluate the expression every time the breakpoint is hit. The most
common use of this is simply to print out some value at the breakpoint, to avoid having to enter a separate command to do so every time.

The syntax for this is to append `&&` and the Hack expression to a normal breakpoint-
setting command. Suppose we have the following code loaded in hphpd:

```
<?hh

function do_something_expensive(int $level) {
  // ...
}

do_something_expensive(10);
```

We want to break on the call to `do_something_expensive()`, and see what `$level` is.
We can do this as follows:

```
hphpd> break do_something_expensive() && var_dump($level)
Breakpoint 1 set upon entering func() && var_dump($level)

hphpd> run
Breakpoint 1 reached at do_something_expensive() on line 3 of
/home/oyamauchi/test.php
   2
   3*function do_something_expensive(int $level) {}
   4*  // ...
   5*}
```

---

4 "PSP" stands for post-send processing, and is what shutdown functions were originally called in HHVM.

5 For example, in the URI *https://www.example.com/something/something.php?key=val*, the path part is */some-thing/something.php*.

```
int(10)
```

You can also configure a breakpoint with an expression so that the breakpoint will only trigger and stop execution if the expression evaluates to `true`. This is a *conditional breakpoint*. To create one, use the same syntax as for a breakpoint with an expression, but replace the `&&` with `if`.

Here, we'll break on `do_something_expensive()`, but only if its argument is over `9000`. Because the argument passed in this script is `10`, the breakpoint won't trigger:

```
hphpd> break do_something_expensive() if $level > 9000
Breakpoint 1 set upon entering func() if $level > 9000

hphpd> run
Program test.php exited normally.
```

As this example shows, if you set a breakpoint on entering a function, you can use that function's arguments in the breakpoint condition.

Breaking from code

There's one more way to set breakpoints, which is to call the special function `hphpd_break()` in your PHP or Hack code. It can be useful, for example, in situations where the physical layout of the code makes it awkward to set a breakpoint by line number. Here's an example:

```
function f(): void {
  echo "one\n";
  hphpd_break();
  echo "two\n";
}
```

If hphpd is attached when the call to `hphpd_break()` is executed, it will be just as if you had set a breakpoint on that line: execution will pause and you'll be given the debugger prompt. You can step or resume from this breakpoint like any other.

You can also pass a boolean argument to `hphpd_break()`, and it will work as a breakpoint only if the argument is `true`. You can use this as a conditional breakpoint:

```
function f(int $num): void {
  hphpd_break($num < 0);
}

f(1234);  // Will not trigger the breakpoint
f(-123);  // Will trigger the breakpoint
```

In code that is not running under hphpd, `hphpd_break()` does nothing.

Navigating the Call Stack

To orient yourself once stopped at a breakpoint, you can get hphpd to print a stack trace with the `where` command. (GDB users will be happy to learn that `bt` does the same thing.) This fulfills a common purpose of breakpoints, which is simply to find out where some piece of code is being called from.

We'll use this file:

```
<?hh

function one(string $str) {
  echo $str;
}

function two() {
  one("done\n");
}

function three() {
  two();
}

three();
```

We'll set a breakpoint on the `echo` statement and get a stack trace:

```
hphpd> break test.php:4
Breakpoint 1 set on line 4 of test.php

hphpd> r
Breakpoint 1 reached at one() on line 4 of /home/oyamauchi/test.php
   3 function one(string $str) {
   4*  echo $str;
   5 }

hphpd> bt
#0   ()
     at /home/oyamauchi/test.php:4
#1   one ("done\n")
     at /home/oyamauchi/test.php:8
#2   two ()
     at /home/oyamauchi/test.php:12
#3   three ()
     at /home/oyamauchi/test.php:15
```

The stack trace shows the values of arguments to the functions. You can turn this off with a configuration option; see `StackArgs` in Table 9-2 (in "Configuring hphpd" on page 231).

Note that in the stack traces, each frame has a number. The deepest frame (i.e., the one farthest from top-level code) is numbered zero, and the numbers increase as you get closer to top-level code. You can use these to change which frame the debugger is operating on. This affects the evaluation commands @ and = (they operate on the current frame) and the inspection command `variable`. It also affects `list`, which we haven't seen yet but is explained in "Viewing Code and Documentation" on page 227.

Here's an example, where we'll set a breakpoint and want to move to a different frame to see what's going on:

```
<?hh

function do_something_expensive() {
  // ...
}

function do_something() {
  $level = get_level();
  if ($level > 10) {
    do_something_expensive();
  }
}

do_something();

// Define get_level
// ...
```

We'll run this and see what the value of $level was that resulted in do_something_expensive() being called, by moving up to do_something()'s frame and using `variable`:

```
hphpd> break do_something_expensive()
Breakpoint 1 set upon entering do_something_expensive()

hphpd> run
Breakpoint 1 reached at do_something_expensive() on line 4 of
/home/oyamauchi/test.php
    3 function do_something_expensive() {
    4*  // ...
    5 }

hphpd> where
#0  do_something_expensive ()
    at /home/oyamauchi/test.php:10
#1  do_something ()
    at /home/oyamauchi/test.php:14

hphpd> frame 1
#1  do_something ()
    at /home/oyamauchi/test.php:14

hphpd> variable
$level = 9000
```

Navigating Code

Once you're stopped at a breakpoint, there are several commands you can use to move execution forward.

The simplest of these is continue, which will simply resume normal execution. The script or web request will keep running until it terminates or hits another breakpoint. (It may hit the same breakpoint you were stopped at, if execution comes through that code again.) Suppose the following code is loaded hphpd:

```
<?hh

function func() {
  echo "Starting func\n";
  echo "Ending func\n";
}

f();
```

We'll set a breakpoint before the second line of f(), and continue after execution pauses there:

```
hphpd> break test.php:5
Breakpoint 1 set on line 5 of test.php

hphpd> run
Starting func
Breakpoint 1 reached at func() on line 5 of /home/oyamauchi/test.php
  4    echo "Starting func\n";
  5*   echo "Leaving func\n";
  6 }

hphpd> continue
Leaving func
Program test.php exited normally.
```

The more interesting commands are step and next. These will execute the line of code that was about to be executed before the breakpoint was hit, and stop again after it's done. The difference between the two is apparent if the line being executed contains a function or method call. step will enter the function being called, and stop just before executing its first line; next will just go to the next line, without entering the function. In other words, the call stack will never be deeper after doing next.

This is a very powerful way of debugging code. Rather than adding logging code at various places, you can set breakpoints instead and continue execution bit by bit, inspecting state at each step.

Let's look at another example:

```
<?hh

function inner(): void {
  echo "inner\n";
}

function outer(): void {
  echo "outer\n";
  inner();
  echo "done\n";
}


outer();
```

We'll set a breakpoint on outer(), and proceed with next:

```
hphpd> break outer()
Breakpoint 1 set upon entering outer()
But wont break until function outer has been loaded.
hphpd> run
Breakpoint 1 reached at outer() on line 8 of /home/oyamauchi/test.php
    7 function outer(): void {
    8*   echo "outer\n";
    9    inner();

hphpd> next
outer
Break at outer() on line 9 of /home/oyamauchi/test.php
    8    echo "outer\n";
    9*   inner();
   10    echo "done\n";

hphpd> next
inner
Break at outer() on line 10 of /home/oyamauchi/test.php
    9    inner();
   10*   echo "done\n";
   11 }

hphpd> next
done
Break at outer() on line 11 of /home/oyamauchi/test.php
   10    echo "done\n";
   11*}
   12

hphpd> next
Break on line 13 of /home/oyamauchi/test.php
   12
   13*outer();
   14 (END)
```

```
hphpd> next
Program test.php exited normally.
```

Note that execution goes directly from line 9 to line 10: from the call to `inner()`, to the echo of done. The call to `inner()` is being executed—you can see `inner()` being echoed—but the debugger is not stopping inside it.

Now let's do the same thing with **step** instead:

```
hphpd> run
Breakpoint 1 reached at outer() on line 8 of /home/oyamauchi/test.php
    7 function outer(): void {
    8*   echo "outer\n";
    9    inner();

hphpd> step
outer
Break at outer() on line 9 of /home/oyamauchi/test.php
    8    echo "outer\n";
    9*   inner();
   10    echo "done\n";

hphpd> step
Break at inner() on line 4 of /home/oyamauchi/test.php
    3 function inner(): void {
    4*   echo "inner\n";
    5 }

hphpd> step
inner
Break at inner() on line 5 of /home/oyamauchi/test.php
    4    echo "inner\n";
    5*}
    6

hphpd> step
Break at outer() on line 9 of /home/oyamauchi/test.php
    8    echo "outer\n";
    9*   inner();
   10    echo "done\n";

hphpd> step
Break at outer() on line 10 of /home/oyamauchi/test.php
    9    inner();
   10*   echo "done\n";
   11 }

hphpd> step
done
Break at outer() on line 11 of /home/oyamauchi/test.php
   10    echo "done\n";
   11*}
```

```
   12
hphpd> step
Break on line 13 of /home/oyamauchi/test.php
   12
  13*outer();
  14 (END)

hphpd> step
Program test.php exited normally.
```

Now, after we step from line 9, we go to line 4: we're inside inner(). Once we step to the end of inner(), we are back in outer(), on line 10 (the line after the call to inner()).

There is one other command in this category, which is out. It resumes execution until the function you're stopped in has exited, either by returning, by throwing an exception (or by an exception being thrown through it from something deeper in the call stack), or, in the case of a generator, by yielding:

```
hphpd> break outer()
Breakpoint 1 set upon entering outer()
But wont break until function outer has been loaded.
hphpd> run
Breakpoint 1 reached at outer() on line 8 of /home/oyamauchi/test.php
   7 function outer() {
   8*   echo "outer\n";
   9    inner();

hphpd> out
outer
inner
done
Break on line 13 of /home/oyamauchi/test.php
   12
  13*outer();
  14 (END)
```

In this case, we stop at the top of outer(), then do out. hphpd lets the rest of outer() execute, and stops again in the top-level code, resuming just after the call to outer() returns.

You can configure hphpd so that step and next will move forward one *expression* at a time rather than one *line* at a time; see "Configuring hphpd" on page 231, and the SmallSteps option in particular, for details.

To save typing, you can repeat the four flow control commands (continue, next, step, and out) just by hitting Enter at the next debugger prompt. In other words, if you hit Enter at the prompt without typing anything else, and the previous command was one of the four flow control commands, that previous command will be repeated.

 Note that the frame command does *not* change the stack frame that next, step, and out operate in. That is, next will move execution to the next line to be executed anywhere, not the next line to be executed in the stack frame you're looking at; the other two commands are similar. This differs from GDB's behavior, so take note if you're a seasoned GDB user.

Managing Breakpoints

We've seen how to set breakpoints by passing a location to the break command. The same command has several subcommands that you can use to manipulate existing breakpoints.

First, though, let's see how to use the list subcommand to list all existing breakpoints:

```
hphpd> break func()
Breakpoint 1 set upon entering func()

hphpd> break test.php:5
Breakpoint 1 set on line 5 of test.php

hphpd> break list
    1    ALWAYS    upon entering func()
    2    ALWAYS    on line 5 of test.php
```

The first field is the breakpoint number; this is just a unique identifier that you use to refer to that breakpoint in other commands. When hphpd stops at a breakpoint, it will print that breakpoint's number. Breakpoint numbers are monotonically increasing and are not reused, so if you set two breakpoints and then delete breakpoint 1, the remaining breakpoint will still be number 2. If you then set a new one, it will be number 3.

The second field is the breakpoint's state. There are three possible states: ALWAYS, ONCE, and DISABLED. An ALWAYS breakpoint will trigger every time execution reaches it. A ONCE breakpoint will trigger the first time execution reaches it, and then it will become DISABLED. A DISABLED breakpoint does not trigger.

By default, when you create a breakpoint, its state is ALWAYS. You can create a ONCE breakpoint by using the subcommand once, followed by a location:

```
hphpd> break once func()
Breakpoint 1 set upon entering func()

hphpd> break list
  1    ONCE      upon entering func()
```

There are three subcommands to change the state of a breakpoint: enable, disable, and toggle. enable sets a breakpoint's state to ALWAYS, and disable sets it to DISABLED. toggle cycles a breakpoint between the three possible states:

```
hphpd> break func()
Breakpoint 1 set upon entering func()

hphpd> break toggle 1
Breakpoint 1's state is changed to ONCE.

hphpd> break toggle 1
Breakpoint 1's state is changed to DISABLED.

hphpd> break toggle 1
Breakpoint 1's state is changed to ALWAYS.

hphpd> break disable 1
Breakpoint 1's state is changed to DISABLED.

hphpd> break enable 1
Breakpoint 1's state is changed to ALWAYS.
```

To delete a breakpoint altogether, use the subcommand clear, along with the breakpoint number:

```
hphpd> break clear 1
Breakpoint 1 cleared upon entering func()
```

With the subcommands clear, disable, enable, and toggle, you can also use all in place of a breakpoint number, in which case the operation applies to all breakpoints:

```
hphpd> break clear all
All breakpoints are cleared.
```

You can also pass no argument after one of these subcommands, in which case the operation applies to the last breakpoint that was hit:

```
hphpd> break func()
Breakpoint 1 set upon entering func()

hphpd> = func()
Breakpoint 1 reached at func() on line 3 of /home/oyamauchi/test.php

hphpd> break clear
Breakpoint 1 is cleared at func()
```

Viewing Code and Documentation

If code is currently executing—that is, you're stopped at a breakpoint or in the midst of stepping after stopping at a breakpoint—you can use the `list` command to show the surroundings of the code being executed. If you're looking at a different stack frame with the `frame` command, `list` will show the code surrounding the relevant callsite in that frame:

```
hphpd> break func()
Breakpoint 1 set upon entering func()

hphpd> r
Breakpoint 1 reached at func() on line 7 of /home/oyamauchi/test.php
    6 function func(): void {
    7*  echo "Just kidding, it's pretty boring";
    8 }

hphpd> list
list
    1 <?hh
    2
    3 /**
    4  * This is a very interesting function
    5  */
    6 function func(): void {
    7*  echo "Just kidding, it's pretty boring";
    8 }
    9
   10 func();
   (END)
```

After running a `list` command, if you hit Enter at the next debugger prompt without typing anything else, the debugger will show the next few lines of code. You can keep going that way until the end of the file.

There are a wide variety of arguments you can pass to `list`, specifying what code you want to see. Table 9-1 shows all of them.

Table 9-1. Arguments to the list command

To see	Command	Shows
Line ranges	`list 34-45`	Lines 34 through 45 in the current file
	`list 34-`	Line 34 through the end of the current file
	`list -45`	Beginning of the current file up to line 45
	`list 34`	Lines surrounding line 34 in the current file
Line ranges in a file	`list test.php:34-45`	Same as above, but in *test.php*. Paths are relative to sandbox root if attached, or current working directory if not
	`list test.php:34-`	
	`list test.php:-45`	
	`list test.php:34`	
Named entities	`list func`	Source code of the function `func()`
	`list ClassName`	Source code of the class `ClassName` (also works for interfaces and traits)
	`list ClassName::methodName`	Source code of the method `methodName` in the class `ClassName`

You can use the `info` command to look up documentation comments and signatures. Pass the name of a named entity[6] as an argument to the command. To look up a method, use the `ClassName::methodName` notation.

Suppose our *test.php* file has the following contents:

```
<?hh

/**
 * A class
 */
class C {

    /**
```

---

6 A named entity is a function, class, interface, constant, trait, enum, or type alias.

```
   * A method inside the class
   */
  public function method(C $obj): void {
  }
}

/**
 * A function
 */
function f(int $x): void {
}
```

We can get information about the entities defined in the file as follows:

```
$ hhvm -m debug test.php
hphpd> info C
// defined on line 6 to 13 of /home/oyamauchi/test.php
/**
 * A class
 */
class C {
  // methods
  [doc] public function method(C $obj);
}

hphpd> info C::method
// defined on line 11 to 12 of /home/oyamauchi/test.php
  /**
   * A method inside the class
   */
public function C::method(C $obj);

hphpd> info f
// defined on line 18 to 19 of /home/oyamauchi/test.php
/**
 * A function
 */
function f(HH\int $x);
```

This also works for built-in functions, classes, and interfaces:

```
hphpd> info strtoupper
/**
 * Returns string with all alphabetic characters converted to uppercase.  Note
 *   that 'alphabetic' is determined by the current locale. For instance, in the
 *   default "C" locale characters such as umlaut-a will not be converted.
 *
 * @param string $str - The input string.
 *
 * @return string - Returns the uppercased string.
 *
 */
function strtoupper(HH\string $str);
```

Macros

hphpd has a feature for recording and replaying sequences of commands. These sequences are called *macros*. They're automatically saved to a file called *.hphpd.ini* in your home directory, so they persist across hphpd sessions. (That file also holds configuration for hphpd; see "Configuring hphpd" on page 231.)

The command for working with macros is &. To start recording a macro, use it with the subcommand start, then just enter the commands you want to record. When you're finished, use & with the subcommand end:

```
hphpd> & start

hphpd> @echo "hi"
hi

hphpd> & end
```

Now, you can replay that sequence with the subcommand replay. In this example, we don't actually type in the @echo statement; it's executed automatically by hphpd, and we're returned to the debugger prompt after it completes:

```
hphpd> & replay

hphpd> @echo "hi"
hi

hphpd>
```

You can give a macro a name when you start to record it, by passing an argument to the start subcommand. If you don't give it a name, it will have the name default. This means that if you record one macro without a name, then record another without a name, the first one will be overwritten:

```
hphpd> & start some_name

hphpd> @echo "some named macro"
some named macro

hphpd> & end
```

You can pass a name to the replay subcommand to replay the named macro. It replays the default macro by default:

```
hphpd> & replay some_name

hphpd> @echo "some named macro"
some named macro
```

You can see all existing macros with the subcommand list:

```
hphpd> & list
    1  default
      > @echo "hi"
    2  some_name
      > @echo "some named macro"
```

The output shows the number, name, and contents of each macro.

Finally, you can delete a macro with the subcommand clear, but using the macro's number, not its name:

```
hphpd> & clear 1
Are you sure you want to delete the macro? [y/N] y

hphpd> & list
    1  some_name
      > @echo "some named macro\n"
```

Note that, unlike breakpoint numbers, macro numbers are not permanently associated with macros. We deleted macro 1, and the former macro 2 slid up to become the new number 1. This is a quirk of macros' implementation; if you find it strange and inconsistent, you're right.

The macro name startup is treated specially. When hphpd launches and loads settings, it will look for a macro called startup; and if it finds one, it will replay that macro immediately, before taking any input from the debugger prompt.

You may find that there's some collection of utility functions or classes that you often use when debugging. If you put these all in a file, you can include that file from a startup macro, so they're available every time you start hphpd.

Configuring hphpd

The last major command we haven't covered yet is set. This allows you to change some of the configuration options that control hphpd's behavior. Most of them control aspects of hphpd's output. Table 9-2 shows all the available options.

Table 9-2. hphpd configuration

Name	Short name	Possible values	Default value
BypassAccessCheck	bac	on, off	off
LogFile	lf	off or a file path	off
PrintLevel	pl	Integers	5
ShortPrintCharCount	cc	Integers	200

Name	Short name	Possible values	Default value
SmallSteps	ss	on, off	off
StackArgs	sa	on, off	on
MaxCodeLines	mcl	Integers	-1

If you run the set command with no arguments—that is, just type set and nothing else—hphpd will show all the options and their current values. To set an option, pass two arguments to the set command: first, either the name or the short name of the option; and second, the value to set it to (e.g., set bac on or set LogFile off). Let's take a closer look at the options:

BypassAccessCheck

Turning this on will make hphpd ignore the protected and private access modifiers in code that is invoked from the debugger prompt. Code running in web requests won't be affected.

LogFile

If the value of this option is anything other than off, it will be interpreted as a file path, and hphpd will transcribe all of its output to that file. It doesn't capture your input.

PrintLevel

This controls the maximum amount of object and array nesting that the print command will print. If it's zero or negative, there is no maximum; objects and arrays will be printed in full, unless there's recursive nesting. If there is recursive nesting, printing will still be truncated when the recursion starts, regardless of this option's value.

ShortPrintCharCount

This controls the maximum number of characters that will be printed in a single = command. If it's zero or negative, there is no maximum. If an = command would result in more characters than the maximum, hphpd will ask if you want to see the rest; you answer, as is usual with interactive command lines, by typing either y or n.

SmallSteps

This controls the behavior of the step and next commands. If it's turned off (as it is by default), those commands will take you to (approximately) the next line, whereas if the option is turned on, they will take you to (approximately) the next *expression* that gets evaluated.

StackArgs

> If this option is turned on, the backtraces printed by the `where` command will show the arguments that were passed to the functions in the backtrace.

MaxCodeLines

> When hphpd stops at a breakpoint, or after a `step` or `next` command, it will print out the source code where it's stopped, with the relevant part highlighted. In some cases, this can be a lot of code that spans a lot of lines—a large array expression with each element on its own line, for example. This option can be used to limit the number of lines that get printed in these situations, to avoid overwhelming your terminal.
>
> If this option is set to `0`, no code will be printed when stopping at a breakpoint. If it's negative (as it is by default), there is no limit.

hphpd saves your settings in a file in your home directory called *.hphpd.ini*, and will reload them the next time you run hphpd. You can edit this file manually to change your saved settings.

Hack Tools

A programming language's features are only part of what makes it good. To be useful, a language needs to have a good tooling ecosystem around it: editor and IDE support, debuggers, analysis and linting tools, etc. The Hack typechecker is built on a powerful static analysis platform that can support many of these uses.

The standard HHVM/Hack installation ships with several tools for inspecting code, as well as for migrating code from PHP to Hack and transpiling Hack code to PHP. This chapter is about those tools.

Inspecting the Codebase

The core of the Hack typechecker's infrastructure is a server that remembers a set of facts about the codebase. Checking for type errors with hh_client is but one way of querying this set of facts. This section describes other options available to hh_client to query data:

--search

Use this flag to perform a fuzzy search for a given symbol name. Pass a single argument after the flag as the string to search for. Note that this will search built-in symbols as well:

```
$ hh_client --search wrap
File "/home/oyamauchi/hack/test.php", line 58, characters 7-13: Wrapper,
class
```

The search is very responsive: the typechecker server indexes the codebase and doesn't need to read any source files to do the search.

There are several related flags that can be used to restrict the kinds of symbols that will be returned: --search-class, --search-function, --search-constant, and `--search-typedef` (which searches type aliases). Each of these is used the same way as plain `--search` and returns output in the same format.

`--type-at-pos`

Use this flag to ask the typechecker what it thinks the type of an expression is. Pass a filename, line number, and column number on the command line, separated by colons, to inspect the expression at that position:

```
$ cat test.php
<?hh // strict

function reversed_digits(int $x): string {
  return strrev((string)$x);
}

function main(): void {
  $f = fun('reversed_digits');
  echo $f(123);
}
# Get type of $x within reversed_digits
$ hh_client --type-at-pos test.php:4:25
int

# Get type of result of string cast
$ hh_client --type-at-pos test.php:4:17
string

# Get type of $f in main()
$ hh_client --type-at-pos test.php:8:3
(function(int $x): string)
```

The type given is for the *innermost* expression at the given position. For example, if you query at the character a in the expression $a + $b, the result will be the type of $a, not of $a + $b. In this case, if you want the type of the whole expression, you have to query at the character +.

Note that the output of `--type-at-pos` may not be a valid type annotation; it's purely for informational purposes. Most notably, for values of the special "unannotated" type (see "Code Without Annotations" on page 18), `--type-at-pos` outputs _ (a single underscore).

`--find-refs` *and* `--find-class-refs`

Use `--find-refs` to search for references to a given function or method, and `--find-class-refs` to search for references to a given class. Pass the name of the class, function, or method to search for as the single argument after the flag:

```
$ cat test.php
<?hh // strict
```

```
class C {}

class D extends C {}

function main(): void {
  $c = new C();
}

$ hh_client --find-class-refs C
File "/home/oyamauchi/hack/test.php", line 8, characters 12-12:
    C::__construct
File "/home/oyamauchi/hack/test.php", line 5, characters 17-17: C
2 total results
```

--inheritance-ancestors *and* --inheritance-children

Use these flags to print all the ancestors or descendants of a given class, respectively. Despite the name, --inheritance-children really does print all descendants, not just direct children:

```
$ cat test.php
&#x3c;?hh // strict

class GrandparentClass {}

class ParentClass extends GrandparentClass {}

class ChildOne extends ParentClass {}

class ChildTwo extends ParentClass {}

$ hh_client --inheritance-ancestors ChildOne
File "/home/oyamauchi/hack/test.php", line 7, characters 7-14: ChildOne
    inherited from File "/home/oyamauchi/hack/test.php", line 5,
    characters
    7-17: ParentClass
File "/home/oyamauchi/hack/test.php", line 7, characters 7-14: ChildOne
    inherited from File "/home/oyamauchi/hack/test.php", line 3,
    characters
    7-22: GrandparentClass

$ hh_client --inheritance-children
GrandparentClass
File "/home/oyamauchi/hack/test.php", line 3, characters 7-22:
GrandparentClass
    inherited by File "/home/oyamauchi/hack/test.php", line 9,
    characters 7-14:
    ChildTwo
File "/home/oyamauchi/hack/test.php", line 3, characters 7-22:
GrandparentClass
```

```
            inherited by File "/home/oyamauchi/hack/test.php", line 7,
            characters 7-14:
            ChildOne
    File "/home/oyamauchi/hack/test.php", line 3, characters 7-22:
    GrandparentClass
            inherited by File "/home/oyamauchi/hack/test.php", line 5,
            characters 7-17:
            ParentClass
```

Scripting Support

The typechecker client can produce the output for any of its commands in JSON,
which lets you easily integrate it with other tools: editors, IDEs, code linters, refactoring tools, etc. Just add the flag `--json` to any `hh_client` command line, before all
other arguments:

```
$ cat test.php
<?hh // strict

function main(): void {
  $var = 1 + "3";
}

$ hh_client --json
{
  "passed": false,
  "errors": [
    {
      "message": [
        {
          "descr": "Typing error",
          "path": "/home/oyamauchi/hack/test.php",
          "line": 4,
          "start": 14,
          "end": 16,
          "code": 4110
        },
        {
          "descr": "This is a num (int/float) because this is used in an
          arithmetic operation",
          "path": "/home/oyamauchi/hack/test.php",
          "line": 4,
          "start": 14,
          "end": 16,
          "code": 4110
        },
        {
          "descr": "It is incompatible with a string",
          "path": "/home/oyamauchi/hack/test.php",
          "line": 4,
          "start": 14,
```

```
        "end": 16,
        "code": 4110
      }
    ]
  }
],
"version": "0939324e1252832cf6f65c51ff2cb811dad307ba Mar  8 2015 23:44:12"
}
```

The output shown here has been formatted for legibility; hh_client's JSON output
has no extraneous whitespace.

Migrating PHP to Hack

Hack's creators know better than most how difficult it is to do an en-masse conversion of a large codebase. When Hack was first conceived, Facebook had a PHP codebase of tens of millions of lines, being worked on simultaneously by hundreds of
engineers.

The benefits of Hack are compounded when most of a codebase is in Hack. For Facebook, this meant that some way to automatically migrate large swaths of code was
essentially a hard requirement for Hack to gain any traction. The codebase was too
large, and changed too quickly, for a manual approach to be workable.

As a result, the standard HHVM/Hack installation includes several tools for automated migration of PHP code to Hack.

The Hackificator

The first measure to take in converting a PHP codebase to Hack is to use the Hackificator, which performs an initial broad-strokes conversion. It scans a directory for
PHP files, and performs two steps in those files:

1. It makes some simple, mechanical changes to preempt Hack errors. For example,
   typehinted parameters with null default values are changed to make the typehints nullable. That is, function f(int $x = null)—valid in PHP, a type error
   in Hack—would be changed to function f(?int $x = null).

2. It changes the opening <?php tag to <?hh, with the strictest mode that doesn't
   introduce any typechecker errors. This will usually be partial or decl mode.

The Hackificator doesn't touch anything else. Its purpose is to do the minimum possible to make code visible to the Hack typechecker.

Before running the Hackificator, there must be no typechecker errors in any files that
are already Hack. That is, running hh_client must output No errors!. The Hackificator will refuse to run if there are errors.

Top-down or bottom-up migration

An important point to note is that the Hackificator processes files one at a time, in undefined order. The result of the run can therefore be different depending on the order in which it ends up processing files.

To illustrate this, let's take a reduced version of a fairly common situation. In one PHP file, we have an abstract superclass. Scattered across many other PHP files are concrete subclasses—tens or even hundreds of them. In this example, we'll just look at one.

Suppose we have files *WorkItem.php*:

```php
<?php

abstract class WorkItem {
  abstract public function doWork();
}
```

and *AckermannWorkItem.php*:

```php
<?php

class AckermannWorkItem extends WorkItem {
  public function doWork() {
    $this->running = true;
    // ...
  }
}
```

The first thing to note is that if we turn both files into partial-mode Hack files, there will be errors: the concrete subclass is using a property that isn't declared. Therefore, the best we can do is to have one file in partial mode, with the other either in decl mode or in PHP.

If `hackificator` processes *WorkItem.php* first, it will put that file in partial mode. Because the subclass is still in PHP, it's invisible to the typechecker, and *WorkItem.php* by itself has no errors in partial mode.[1] Then, when it processes *AckermannWorkItem.php*, it can only put the file in decl mode: because the superclass is in Hack, it can analyze the whole hierarchy and determine that the property `running` isn't declared, which is an error in anything other than decl mode.

If `hackificator` processes *AckermannWorkItem.php* first, it will put that file in partial mode. Its superclass is still in PHP so it's invisible to the typechecker. The typechecker assumes that the property `running` is declared in the superclass, and doesn't report an error. Then, when it tries converting *WorkItem.php* to Hack, undeclared

---

1 In strict mode, of course, there is an error: doWork() has no return type annotation.

property errors pop up in *AckermannWorkItem.php*, because its superclass is now visible to the typechecker. Then `hackificator` has to revert *WorkItem.php* back to PHP; it can't go back to *AckermannWorkItem.php* to back off to decl mode (which would silence the error) after processing it.

The first pattern, migrating the superclass first, is a *top-down* migration to Hack. The advantage of this is that any new subclasses can start off in Hack and get the benefit of thorough typechecking with knowledge of their superclass, even while other subclasses have yet to be migrated. The fully typechecked portion of the hierarchy steadily, linearly increases from 0% to 100% as the migration proceeds.

The second pattern, migrating the superclass after all of its subclasses are in Hack, is a *bottom-up* migration. The advantage of this is that it gets more code into Hack sooner. However, the typechecker is handicapped in the subclasses, because it has no knowledge of their superclass. Much of the hierarchy is checked with this handicap from the beginning of the migration, with almost none of it checked without handicap until the very end.

Because of the way the Hackificator works, it's far more likely to produce bottom-up conversions, simply because there are many subclasses and one superclass, so it's more likely to encounter a subclass first. If you want to ensure a top-down conversion, convert the superclass manually before running the Hackificator.

Neither pattern is strictly better than the other, and you can use both within the same codebase, on different class hierarchies. We're discussing them here mostly so that you know what to expect when using the Hackificator, and to help you make a considered choice.

Facebook's Migration to Hack

When Facebook migrated its codebase to Hack, it was done bottom-up. It didn't come to be that way as part of some master plan; it was an emergent phenomenon. The thinking about top-down versus bottom-up was an output of this experience, not an input.

Facebook's bottom-up migration had some pitfalls. The codebase had a core `WorkItem`-like class with over 25,000 descendants. Even when most of the descendants had been successfully migrated, putting the superclass of the whole hierarchy into Hack was still a large undertaking, because a lot of typechecker errors were exposed by finally making the entire hierarchy fully checkable.

To get around this, we ended up defining a trait called `CrippleHackTypechecking` in a PHP file and using that trait from `WorkItem` descendants that started showing errors when `WorkItem` itself was put in Hack. The trait had no functionality; its purpose was to selectively handicap the typechecker in some descendants.

From there, the rest of the migration was essentially a second, top-down pass: gradually fixing descendants and removing `CrippleHackTypechecking` from them.

Facebook has never done a large-scale, fully top-down PHP-to-Hack migration, so it remains unknown whether that approach would have revealed pitfalls.

Upgrading typechecker modes

There's another conversion the Hackificator can do, which is to inspect Hack files (but not PHP files) and upgrade them to the strictest mode that doesn't cause typechecker errors. Activate this with the command-line flag `-upgrade` (single hyphen).

This will often come in useful because the Hackificator's default behavior will almost never produce a strict-mode file. This is because strict mode requires all return types to be annotated, but Hack's return type annotation syntax is illegal in PHP (in all 5.x versions and earlier).

It can be useful to combine `hackificator -upgrade` with `hh_server --convert`, described in the next section. That tool adds annotations, which may get a partial-mode file into a state where it can be upgraded to strict mode cleanly.

Inferring and Adding Type Annotations

Adding type annotations is trickier, and requires a fair bit more manual work. The typechecker includes a mode in which it tries to infer the types of unannotated values, by working backward from annotated and known types, and annotates the inferred types in the code.

It's important to note that this process isn't perfect. The inferred type annotations are guaranteed not to cause typechecker errors, but they may turn out to be wrong at runtime. Because of that, all of the added type annotations are soft, so that they'll cause warnings instead of fatal errors at runtime.

To deal with the resulting proliferation of soft typehints, there are two other tools that complement this one: one that reads a logfile and removes soft typehints that have produced warnings in the log, and another which that all soft typehints in a file.

Adding annotations

The tool to add annotations only works on Hack files (any mode). It's part of the typechecker server, and you invoke it as follows:

```
$ hh_server --convert my_project my_project
```

After the `--convert` flag, there are two arguments: first, the directory in which to actually make modifications; and second, the top-level directory of the project. The separation of the two allows you to restrict the modifications to a subset of the project, which helps keep the work in manageably sized chunks when dealing with a large codebase. The two arguments are allowed to be the same, and it's best if they are: the more code the tool can work with at once, the more effective it can be.

This inference process is considerably slower than the one the typechecker uses for Hack files, because it's not function-local. For example, when processing a function with unannotated parameters, it will find that function's callsites to see what arguments are passed. If it finds consistent argument types, it will add the appropriate annotations.

Removing incorrect annotations

Once these annotations are added, try them out. Running tests is the best starting point. The added annotations don't change any behavior except for warnings, so they shouldn't cause tests to fail, but running tests is a convenient way to run the code. In addition, run any command-line scripts you can; if your project is a web app, start up a web server and visit some pages. The aim here is to exercise as much of your code as possible.

While doing this, you have to capture error messages. If you're running scripts or tests from the command line, the error messages go to standard out. You can just redirect standard out to a file:

```
$ hhvm testfile.php > errors.log
```

This will capture everything from standard out, including output from the script, but that's not a problem. The annotation-removal tool uses regular expressions to search for very specific error messages, so the script's output shouldn't interfere.

If you're running HHVM as a server, error messages again go to standard out by default. You can use a configuration option to have error messages written to a file instead:

```
$ hhvm -m server -d hhvm.log.file=errors.log
```

After running your code, if any soft type annotations failed, you'll see error messages in the log that look like the following example—these are what the annotation-removal tool looks for:

```
Warning: Argument 1 to f() must be of type @int, string given in
/home/oyamauchi/hack/testfile.php on line 5
Warning: Value returned from function f() must be of type @int, string given in
/home/oyamauchi/hack/testfile.php on line 6
```

It's important to note that the annotation-removal tool extracts the file path from the error message and looks for the file at exactly that path. If the file path in the logs is relative, the tool will resolve it relative to its current working directory.

HHVM outputs absolute file paths in error logs by default. This can be a problem if, for example, you gather logs from one machine and do the annotation removal on another machine with your project's source at a different path. To deal with this, you can strip the path to the project root from the log messages using a tool like `sed` (the full usage of which is beyond the scope of this book):

```
$ sed -e 's!/home/oyamauchi/hack/!!g' < errors.log > errors-relative-paths.log
```

Finally, with a suitable log file, removing the incorrect annotations is very simple. If the error log has relative paths, make sure you're in the right working directory. Then, use the command `hack_remove_soft_types`:

```
$ hack_remove_soft_types --delete-from-log errors.log
```

Hardening annotations

When you're confident that the remaining annotations are correct, you can make all the remaining annotations hard. This is also done with `hack_remove_soft_types`:

```
$ hack_remove_soft_types --harden lib/core.hh
```

The tool only accepts a single file as an argument for now. If you want to apply the operation to all the files in a directory, you can use the `find` utility. This example applies it to every file whose name ends with *.hh* in the directory *lib* and all of its sub-directories, recursively:

```
$ find lib -type f -name '*.hh' -exec hack_remove_soft_types --harden '{}' ';'
```

Transpiling Hack to PHP

HHVM is currently the only execution engine that supports Hack. This means that anyone who can't make the switch to HHVM can't run Hack code. If you're the author of a PHP library, this probably seems like a good reason not to migrate your code to Hack—there would be no sense in migrating when doing so would shut out many of your potential users.

The Hack transpiler was developed by the Hack team to assuage these concerns. The transpiler is a tool that automatically converts the codebase into PHP. The purpose isn't to convert a Hack codebase to PHP so that you can develop it in PHP. Rather, the transpiler is meant to be used as a build step: you develop in Hack, and transpile to PHP as the final step before packaging. You ship two versions of your code: the original Hack version, for people who use HHVM and Hack; and the transpiled PHP version, for people who don't.

The transpiler ships with HHVM, and you run it with the command `h2tp`. Give it the path to your Hack codebase, and a path where it can put the resulting PHP code. It will inspect any file with the extension *.php* or *.hh*. Any other files will be copied to the destination directory unmodified:

```
$ ls -a my_project
.  ..  .hhconfig  main.hh

$ h2tp my_project my_project_transpiled
The Conversion was successful

$ ls -a my_project_transpiled
.  ..  .hhconfig  main.php
```

The output PHP code is not meant to be edited. All comments are stripped, and formatting isn't guaranteed to be preserved. The code isn't needlessly obfuscated, though, so it shouldn't be hard to understand a stack trace from the PHP code.

Once the PHP code has been generated, there is one more setup step. The generated code will make use of Hacklib, a collection of support functions and classes that are used by the transpiled code. Hacklib comes as part of the Hack/HHVM installation and is installed, by default, at path */usr/share/hhvm/hack/hacklib*.

First, copy Hacklib into the directory containing your project's transpiled PHP code:

```
$ cd my_project_transpiled

$ cp -r /usr/share/hhvm/hack/hacklib .
```

Second, add a line of code that will be executed before any of the generated files are loaded (via `include`, `require`, etc.). Put the path to Hacklib's main file in the global variable `HACKLIB_ROOT`. For example, if the Hacklib code was copied to the top-level directory of the project:

```
$GLOBALS['HACKLIB_ROOT'] = __DIR__ . '/hacklib/hacklib.php';
```

Conversions

This section won't go into full detail about all of the conversions that the transpiler does, but will explain enough to give you an idea of what to expect in the generated PHP code.

It's important to note that the transpiled PHP code will run less efficiently than the original Hack code, even on the same execution engine. As we'll see in this section, some common Hack constructs have to be replaced with less efficient PHP constructs —for example, some equality comparisons have to be replaced with function calls.

The transpiler will try to convert all Hack files, and won't touch PHP files. It determines what language a file is in by its opening tag—<?hh or <?php—not by its file extension.

Here are the most important things the transpiler does:

- All type annotations are removed. This also means that type aliases can simply be deleted, as type annotations are the only place where they're used.

- Collection literals (see "Literal Syntax" on page 104) are replaced with new expressions, where supported. The collection classes can still be used in PHP.

- Lambda syntax (see "Lambda Expressions" on page 74) is replaced with regular closure syntax. The typechecker finds which variables need to be captured from the enclosing scope and generates the appropriate use list.

- Enums (see "Enums" on page 59) are converted into classes, with the enum members as class constants. The special enum functions are provided by a trait from Hacklib.

- Shapes (see "Array Shapes" on page 71) and tuples are replaced with arrays.

- Attributes (see "Attributes" on page 77) are removed, except __Memoize, which is not supported; see the next section.

- Trait requirements (see "Trait and Interface Requirements" on page 86) are removed.

- Constructors with promoted arguments (see "Constructor Parameter Promotion" on page 76) are unfolded to declare the necessary properties and assign to them in the constructor's body.

- The nullsafe method call operator (see "Nullsafe Method Call and Property Access" on page 85) is simulated using a Hacklib class with the magic method __call().

- Because the collection classes' behavior in casting and equality comparisons isn't special-cased in PHP like it is in Hack, some instances of those constructs have to be modified. For example, here is Hack code that relies on empty collections evaluating to false when cast to booleans:

```
function average(Vector<num> $nums): num {
  if (!$nums) {
    throw new InvalidArgumentException(
      "Can't average an empty vector"
    );
  }

  // ...
}
```

To get equivalent behavior in PHP, the transpiler will use a helper function from Hacklib:

```
function average($nums) {
  if (!\hacklib_cast_as_boolean($nums)) {
    throw new InvalidArgumentException(
      "Can't average an empty vector"
```

```
        );
    }

    // ...
}
```

Unsupported Features

There are several Hack features that the transpiler can't convert to PHP. If it encounters any of these, the transpiler will give up on the entire file. It will never partially convert a file, or produce PHP code that doesn't behave the same as the original Hack code.

The PHP code that the transpiler generates to simulate Hack features is compatible with PHP versions 5.4 and later. However, if you use features from a later version of PHP, such as generators (introduced in PHP 5.5), the transpiler will not touch those, and the output will only run on PHP 5.5 and later.

Here are the features that the transpiler doesn't support:

- Async functions (see Chapter 6). Running async functions requires extensive support from the runtime, and it's not possible to simulate this in pure PHP in a reasonable way. It's possible to convert async functions by simply removing the `async` and `await` keywords; this would produce correct results, but with no parallelism. The transpiler may start doing that in the future.

- The `__Memoize` special attribute (see "Special Attributes" on page 79). Unlike other attributes, which are simply removed, `__Memoize` will cause a conversion failure. This attribute requires runtime support, and is tricky to simulate in pure PHP. The memoization pattern is easy to implement manually, though, as a workaround.

- Traits that implement interfaces (see "Trait and Interface Requirements" on page 86).

- Collection literals as initial values for non-static properties (see "Literal Syntax" on page 104). This is because a collection literal has to be converted to a `new` expression in PHP, and those aren't allowed as property initializers. The restriction only applies to non-static properties because the initializers for static properties can simply be moved outside the class.

Index

Symbols

" " (quotes, double), enclosing apostrophe in
    text in XHP, 176
& command, working with macros in hphpd,
    230
    & list, 230
    & replay, 230
    & start and & end, 230
&& operator, 98
&&, appending to breakpoint-setting com-
    mand, 217
' (apostrophe) in text in XHP, 176
* (repetition) operator (XHP), 180
+ (repetition) operator (XHP), 180
-> method call syntax, 96
: (colon) in XHP class names, 176
:: method call syntax, 96
= command in hphpd, 210, 212
== (equality) operator, use with collections, 108
=== (identity) operator, use with collections,
    109
==> operator, 75
? (repetition) operator (XHP), 181
?-> (nullsafe method call and property access)
    operator, 85
@ command in hphpd, 210, 212
@required attributes, 175, 177
[] (square brackets)
    appending values to Vectors, Sets, and
        Maps, 107
    use with collections, 105
__ (double underscore) in special attribute
    names, 79
| (alternation) operator (XHP), 181

|| operator, 98
∧ (caret), bitwise xor operator, 98

A

admin server, 204
    security practices with, 205
    sending commands via curl utility, 205
Alternative PHP Cache (APC), 122
and operator, 98
any attribute specifier (XHP), 180
any pseudotype, 18
arguments
    parameters versus, 5
    typed variadic arguments, typechecker rules
        for, 25
array shapes, 71-74
array type, 6
    in PHP, 99
arraykey type, 7
arrays
    collections interoperating with, 120
        converting collections to arrays, 120
        use with built-in and user functions, 120
    copy-on-write in PHP, 102
    generic, syntax of, 15
    implementing Traversable in PHP, 111
    keys containing string representations of
        integers, 105
    subtypes and generics, 52
    tuples as, 7
    using collections instead of, 101
    value semantics, 102
array_diff() function, 122
array_filter() function, 137

C

call stack, navigating from hphpd breakpoint, 219

callable types, 12

  async and, 131

case-insensitive name lookup, 94

categories

  in custom XHP classes, 181

  in XHP children declarations, 181

  parser transformation of declarations, 193

chained method calls, 8

chains of dependencies, 141

character references (HTML), 171

child objects (XHP), 169

  distinguishing attributes from, 189

  passing context to, 182

  XHPAlwaysValidChild interface, 192

children declarations, XHP classes, 179

  parser transfomation of, 193

class attribute, managing with XHPHelpers, 186

classes

  collection, 118

  enums as pseudoclasses, 61

  looking up documentation in hphpd, 229

  using traits, restrictions on, 86

  XHP, 169

    core classes, hierarchy of, 194

    creating your own, 176-186

    distinguishing attributes from children, 189

    no additional public API, 187

classname type, 10

closing tags (XHP), 169

closures

  as callable type, 13

  async, 127

  return type annotations, 4

  simplification with lambda expressions, 74

  type inference on functions containing, 31

Collection interface, 115

collection literals, 104, 247

collections, 99-123

  adding values to, 107

  advantages of using, 101

  await-a-collection helpers, 145

  classes in Hack, 99

  concrete classes, 118

  deleting values from, 107

equality comparisons with == operator, 108

general collection interfaces, 114

identity comparisons with === operator, 109

immutable, 110

interoperating with arrays, 120

  conversion to arrays, 120

  use with built-in and user functions, 120

iterating over with foreach, 106

reading and writing, 105

reference semantics, 102

specific collection interfaces, 115

subtypes and generics, 52

type annotations for, 110

  core interfaces, 110

command-line interface (HHVM), wrapper script for, 201

command-line mode, 200

comments

  documentation comments versus attributes, 77

  HH_FIXME, syntax of, 89

Composer package manager, 129, 169

conditional breakpoints, 218

configuring HHVM, 197

  admin server, 204

  repo-authoritative mode, 202

    building the repo, 203

    deploying the repo, 204

  server mode, 200

  specifying configuration options, 197

    important options, 198

  warming up the JIT, 201

configuring hphpd, 231

connection pools (MySQL async extension), 157

connections, database (MySQL async extension), 155

__ConsistentConstruct attribute, 79

ConstCollection interface, 115

ConstMap interface, 117

constraint type, adding to opaque type alias, 65

constraints on generic type parameters, 47-49

constructor parameter promotion, 76

constructors, old-style, 93

ConstSet interface, 116

ConstVector interface, 103, 116

Container interface, 111

contains() method, 106

About the Author

Owen Yamauchi is a software engineer at Facebook, where he works on the HHVM team. Before joining Facebook in 2009, he interned at VMware and Apple. Owen grew up in Belgium and earned his BS in computer science at Carnegie Mellon.

Colophon

The animal on the cover of *Hack and HHVM* is a *gray fox* (*Urocyon cinereoargenteus*), which is one of the two only living species of the genus *Urocyon*, considered to be among the most primitive canids. The other is the Channel Island fox. The gray fox is an omnivore found from southern Canada to the northern part of South America. It feeds on the eastern cottontail, shrews, birds, rodents, and jackrabbits, depending on where it lives. In some areas in the western United States, the gray fox eats primarily insects and vegetation; all gray foxes eat a diet rich in fruits.

The gray fox is known for having grizzled upper parts, a black tip on its tail, and a strong neck. Males and females are very similar, save for the female's slightly smaller size. The gray fox typically measures from 76 to 112.5 cm (29.9 to 44.3 in) in length including its tail, which takes up about 27.5 to 44.3 cm (108 to 17.4 in) of that length; this species weighs between 3.6 to 7 kg (7.9 to 15.4 lb).

The gray fox has the exceptional ability to climb trees, which it shares with the Asian raccoon dog, also a canid. This is its tactic for escaping many predators—domestic dogs or coyotes—or reaching tree-bound food sources. It ascends using its strong, hooked claws to scramble up trees, and can climb vertical trunks without branches up to 18 meters. It descends trees by jumping from branch to branch or by climbing slowly backwards. The gray fox is nocturnal and nests in hollow trees or stumps, sometimes up to 30 feet off the ground.

The gray fox is monogamous, mating in early March in the north and in February in the south. Gestation lasts up to 53 days, and litter sizes range from 1 to 7 kits. At three months old, offspring begin hunting with their parents, and at four months, kits can forage on their own. In the autumn, the young leave the family group, having reached sexual maturity.

Many of the animals on O'Reilly covers are endangered; all of them are important to the world. To learn more about how you can help, go to *animals.oreilly.com*.

The cover image is from Wood's *Animate Creation*. The cover fonts are URW Typewriter and Guardian Sans. The text font is Adobe Minion Pro; the heading font is Adobe Myriad Condensed; and the code font is Dalton Maag's Ubuntu Mono.

Have it your way.

Get even more for your money.

Join the O'Reilly Community, and register the O'Reilly books you own. It's free, and you'll get:

- $4.99 ebook upgrade offer
- 40% upgrade offer on O'Reilly print books
- Membership discounts on books and events
- Free lifetime updates to ebooks and videos
- Multiple ebook formats, DRM FREE
- Participation in the O'Reilly community
- Newsletters
- Account management
- 100% Satisfaction Guarantee

Signing up is easy:

1. Go to: oreilly.com/go/register
2. Create an O'Reilly login.
3. Provide your address.
4. Register your books.

Note: English-language books only

To order books online:
oreilly.com/store

For questions about products or an order:
orders@oreilly.com

To sign up to get topic-specific email announcements and/or news about upcoming books, conferences, special offers, and new technologies:
elists@oreilly.com

For technical questions about book content:
booktech@oreilly.com

To submit new book proposals to our editors:
proposals@oreilly.com

O'Reilly books are available in multiple DRM-free ebook formats. For more information:
oreilly.com/ebooks